PENGUIN SHAKESPEARE

Founding Editor: T. J. B. Spencer
General Editor: Stanley Wells
Supervisory Editors: Paul Edmondson, Stanley Wells

T. J. B. SPENCER, sometime Director of the Shakespeare Institute of the University of Birmingham, was the founding editor of the New Penguin Shakespeare, for which he edited both *Romeo and Juliet* and *Hamlet*.

STANLEY WELLS is Emeritus Professor of the University of Birmingham and Chairman of the Shakespeare Birthplace Trust. He is general editor of the Oxford Shakespeare and his books include *Shakespeare: The Poet and His Plays*, *Shakespeare: For All Time*, *Looking for Sex in Shakespeare*, *Shakespeare's Sonnets* (with Paul Edmondson) and *Shakespeare and Co.*

A. R. HUMPHREYS was Professor of English at the University of Leicester. He edited *Julius Caesar* for the Oxford Shakespeare, *Much Ado About Nothing* and *King Henry IV: Parts 1* and *2* for the Arden edition, and *Henry V* for Penguin.

CATHERINE ALEXANDER, formerly a lecturer at the Shakespeare Centre, Stratford, is a Fellow of the Shakespeare Institute, University of Birmingham. Her research interests are in Shakespeare in performance and eighteenth-century Shakespeare. She is co-editor, with Stanley Wells, of *Shakespeare and Race* and *Shakespeare and Sexuality*, and editor of *Shakespeare and Language* and *Shakespeare and Politics* (all for Cambridge University Press).

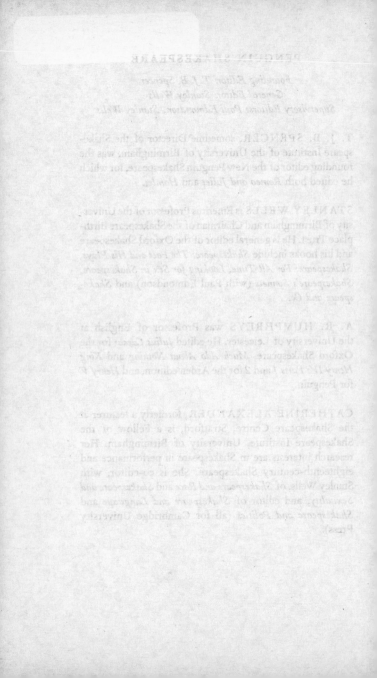

PENGUIN SHAKESPEARE

Founding Editor: T. J. B. Spencer
General Editor: Stanley Wells
Supervisory Editors: Paul Edmondson, Stanley Wells

T. J. B. SPENCER, sometime Director of the Shakespeare Institute of the University of Birmingham, was the founding editor of the New Penguin Shakespeare, for which he edited both Romeo and Juliet and Hamlet.

STANLEY WELLS is Emeritus Professor of the University of Birmingham and Chairman of the Shakespeare Birthplace Trust. He is general editor of the Oxford Shakespeare and his books include Shakespeare: The Poet and His Plays, Shakespeare: For All Time, Looking for Sex in Shakespeare and (with Paul Edmondson) Shakespeare's Sonnets.

A. R. HUMPHREYS was Professor of English at the University of Leicester. He edited 1 and 2 Henry IV for the Arden Shakespeare, Much Ado About Nothing and Henry IV Parts 1 and 2 for the New Penguin Shakespeare, and Henry V for the Penguin.

CATHERINE ALEXANDER, formerly a lecturer at the Shakespeare Centre, Stratford, is a fellow of the Shakespeare Institute, University of Birmingham. Her research interests are in Shakespeare in performance and eighteenth-century Shakespeare. She is co-editor, with Stanley Wells, of Shakespeare and Race and Shakespeare and Sexuality, and editor of Shakespeare and Language and Shakespeare and Politics (all for Cambridge University Press).

William Shakespeare

HENRY VIII

Edited with a Commentary by A. R. Humphreys
Introduced by Catherine M. S. Alexander

PENGUIN BOOKS

Published by the Penguin Group
Penguin Books Ltd, 80 Strand, London WC2R 0RL, England
Penguin Group (USA) Inc., 375 Hudson Street, New York, New York 10014, USA
Penguin Group (Canada), 90 Eglinton Avenue East, Suite 700, Toronto, Ontario, Canada M4P 2Y3
(a division of Pearson Penguin Canada Inc.)
Penguin Ireland, 25 St Stephen's Green, Dublin 2, Ireland (a division of Penguin Books Ltd)
Penguin Group (Australia), 250 Camberwell Road, Camberwell, Victoria 3124, Australia
(a division of Pearson Australia Group Pty Ltd)
Penguin Books India Pvt Ltd, 11 Community Centre, Panchsheel Park, New Delhi – 110 017, India
Penguin Group (NZ), cnr Airborne and Rosedale Roads, Albany, Auckland 1310, New Zealand
(a division of Pearson New Zealand Ltd)
Penguin Books (South Africa) (Pty) Ltd, 24 Sturdee Avenue, Rosebank, Johannesburg 2196, South Africa

Penguin Books Ltd, Registered Offices: 80 Strand, London WC2R 0RL, England

www.penguin.com

This edition first published in Penguin Books 1971
Reissued in the Penguin Shakespeare series 2006

2

This edition copyright © Penguin Books, 1971
Further Reading, Account of the Text and Commentary copyright © A. R. Humphreys, 1971
General Introduction and Chronology copyright © Stanley Wells, 2004
Introduction, The Play in Performance and Revised Further Reading copyright
© Catherine M. S. Alexander, 2006

All rights reserved

The moral right of the editors has been asserted

Designed by Boag Associates
Set in 11.5/12.5 PostScript Monotype Fournier
Typeset by Palimpsest Book Production Limited, Polmont, Stirlingshire
Printed in England by Clays Ltd, St Ives plc

ISBN-13: 978-0-141-01740-2
ISBN-10: 0-141-01740-6

www.greenpenguin.co.uk

Penguin Books is committed to a sustainable future
for our business, our readers and our planet.
The book in your hands is made from paper
certified by the Forest Stewardship Council.

Contents

Contents

General Introduction

Every play by Shakespeare is unique. This is part of his greatness. A restless and indefatigable experimenter, he moved with a rare amalgamation of artistic integrity and dedicated professionalism from one kind of drama to another. Never shackled by convention, he offered his actors the alternation between serious and comic modes from play to play, and often also within the plays themselves, that the repertory system within which he worked demanded, and which provided an invaluable stimulus to his imagination. Introductions to individual works in this series attempt to define their individuality. But there are common factors that underpin Shakespeare's career.

Nothing in his heredity offers clues to the origins of his genius. His upbringing in Stratford-upon-Avon, where he was born in 1564, was unexceptional. His mother, born Mary Arden, came from a prosperous farming family. Her father chose her as his executor over her eight sisters and his four stepchildren when she was only in her late teens, which suggests that she was of more than average practical ability. Her husband John, a glover, apparently unable to write, was nevertheless a capable businessman and loyal townsfellow, who seems to have fallen on relatively hard times in later life. He would have been brought up as a Catholic, and may have retained

Catholic sympathies, but his son subscribed publicly to Anglicanism throughout his life.

The most important formative influence on Shakespeare was his school. As the son of an alderman who became bailiff (or mayor) in 1568, he had the right to attend the town's grammar school. Here he would have received an education grounded in classical rhetoric and oratory, studying authors such as Ovid, Cicero and Quintilian, and would have been required to read, speak, write and even think in Latin from his early years. This classical education permeates Shakespeare's work from the beginning to the end of his career. It is apparent in the self-conscious classicism of plays of the early 1590s such as the tragedy of *Titus Andronicus*, *The Comedy of Errors*, and the narrative poems *Venus and Adonis* (1592–3) and *The Rape of Lucrece* (1593–4), and is still evident in his latest plays, informing the dream visions of *Pericles* and *Cymbeline* and the masque in *The Tempest*, written between 1607 and 1611. It inflects his literary style throughout his career. In his earliest writings the verse, based on the ten-syllabled, five-beat iambic pentameter, is highly patterned. Rhetorical devices deriving from classical literature, such as alliteration and antithesis, extended similes and elaborate wordplay, abound. Often, as in *Love's Labour's Lost* and *A Midsummer Night's Dream*, he uses rhyming patterns associated with lyric poetry, each line self-contained in sense, the prose as well as the verse employing elaborate figures of speech. Writing at a time of linguistic ferment, Shakespeare frequently imports Latinisms into English, coining words such as abstemious, addiction, incarnadine and adjunct. He was also heavily influenced by the eloquent translations of the Bible in both the Bishops' and the Geneva versions. As his experience grows, his verse and prose become more supple,

the patterning less apparent, more ready to accommo-
date the rhythms of ordinary speech, more colloquial in
diction, as in the speeches of the Nurse in *Romeo and
Juliet*, the characterful prose of Falstaff and Hamlet's
soliloquies. The effect is of increasing psychological
realism, reaching its greatest heights in *Hamlet*, *Othello*,
King Lear, *Macbeth* and *Antony and Cleopatra*. Gradually
he discovered ways of adapting the regular beat of the
pentameter to make it an infinitely flexible instrument for
matching thought with feeling. Towards the end of his
career, in plays such as *The Winter's Tale*, *Cymbeline* and
The Tempest, he adopts a more highly mannered style,
in keeping with the more overtly symbolical and emblem-
atical mode in which he is writing.

So far as we know, Shakespeare lived in Stratford till
after his marriage to Anne Hathaway, eight years his
senior, in 1582. They had three children: a daughter,
Susanna, born in 1583 within six months of their marriage,
and twins, Hamnet and Judith, born in 1585. The next
seven years of Shakespeare's life are virtually a blank.
Theories that he may have been, for instance, a school-
master, or a lawyer, or a soldier, or a sailor, lack evidence
to support them. The first reference to him in print, in
Robert Greene's pamphlet *Greene's Groatsworth of Wit*
of 1592, parodies a line from *Henry VI, Part III*, implying
that Shakespeare was already an established playwright.
It seems likely that at some unknown point after the birth
of his twins he joined a theatre company and gained
experience as both actor and writer in the provinces and
London. The London theatres closed because of plague
in 1593 and 1594; and during these years, perhaps recog-
nizing the need for an alternative career, he wrote and
published the narrative poems *Venus and Adonis* and *The
Rape of Lucrece*. These are the only works we can be

certain that Shakespeare himself was responsible for
putting into print. Each bears the author's dedication to
Henry Wriothesley, Earl of Southampton (1573–1624),
the second in warmer terms than the first. Southampton,
younger than Shakespeare by ten years, is the only person
to whom he personally dedicated works. The Earl may
have been a close friend, perhaps even the beautiful and
adored young man whom Shakespeare celebrates in his
Sonnets.

The resumption of playing after the plague years saw
the founding of the Lord Chamberlain's Men, a company
to which Shakespeare was to belong for the rest of his
career, as actor, shareholder and playwright. No other
dramatist of the period had so stable a relationship with a
single company. Shakespeare knew the actors for whom
he was writing and the conditions in which they performed.
The permanent company was made up of around twelve
to fourteen players, but one actor often played more than
one role in a play and additional actors were hired as
needed. Led by the tragedian Richard Burbage (1568–1619)
and, initially, the comic actor Will Kemp (d. 1603), they
rapidly achieved a high reputation, and when King James
I succeeded Queen Elizabeth I in 1603 they were renamed
as the King's Men. All the women's parts were played by
boys; there is no evidence that any female role was ever
played by a male actor over the age of about eighteen.
Shakespeare had enough confidence in his boys to write
for them long and demanding roles such as Rosalind (who,
like other heroines of the romantic comedies, is disguised
as a boy for much of the action) in *As You Like It*, Lady
Macbeth and Cleopatra. But there are far more fathers
than mothers, sons than daughters, in his plays, few if any
of which require more than the company's normal comple-
ment of three or four boys.

The company played primarily in London's public playhouses – there were almost none that we know of in the rest of the country – initially in the Theatre, built in Shoreditch in 1576, and from 1599 in the Globe, on Bankside. These were wooden, more or less circular structures, open to the air, with a thrust stage surmounted by a canopy and jutting into the area where spectators who paid one penny stood, and surrounded by galleries where it was possible to be seated on payment of an additional penny. Though properties such as cauldrons, stocks, artificial trees or beds could indicate locality, there was no representational scenery. Sound effects such as flourishes of trumpets, music both martial and amorous, and accompaniments to songs were provided by the company's musicians. Actors entered through doors in the back wall of the stage. Above it was a balconied area that could represent the walls of a town (as in *King John*), or a castle (as in *Richard II*), and indeed a balcony (as in *Romeo and Juliet*). In 1609 the company also acquired the use of the Blackfriars, a smaller, indoor theatre to which admission was more expensive, and which permitted the use of more spectacular stage effects such as the descent of Jupiter on an eagle in *Cymbeline* and of goddesses in *The Tempest*. And they would frequently perform before the court in royal residences and, on their regular tours into the provinces, in non-theatrical spaces such as inns, guildhalls and the great halls of country houses.

Early in his career Shakespeare may have worked in collaboration, perhaps with Thomas Nashe (1567–c. 1601) in *Henry VI, Part I* and with George Peele (1556–96) in *Titus Andronicus*. And towards the end he collaborated with George Wilkins (*fl.* 1604–8) in *Pericles*, and with his younger colleagues Thomas Middleton (1580–1627), in *Timon of Athens*, and John Fletcher (1579–1625), in *Henry*

VIII, *The Two Noble Kinsmen* and the lost play *Cardenio*. Shakespeare's output dwindled in his last years, and he died in 1616 in Stratford, where he owned a fine house, New Place, and much land. His only son had died at the age of eleven, in 1596, and his last descendant died in 1670. New Place was destroyed in the eighteenth century but the other Stratford houses associated with his life are maintained and displayed to the public by the Shakespeare Birthplace Trust.

One of the most remarkable features of Shakespeare's plays is their intellectual and emotional scope. They span a great range from the lightest of comedies, such as *The Two Gentlemen of Verona* and *The Comedy of Errors*, to the profoundest of tragedies, such as *King Lear* and *Macbeth*. He maintained an output of around two plays a year, ringing the changes between comic and serious. All his comedies have serious elements: Shylock, in *The Merchant of Venice*, almost reaches tragic dimensions, and *Measure for Measure* is profoundly serious in its examination of moral problems. Equally, none of his tragedies is without humour: Hamlet is as witty as any of his comic heroes, *Macbeth* has its Porter, and *King Lear* its Fool. His greatest comic character, Falstaff, inhabits the history plays and *Henry V* ends with a marriage, while *Henry VI, Part III*, *Richard II* and *Richard III* culminate in the tragic deaths of their protagonists.

Although in performance Shakespeare's characters can give the impression of a superabundant reality, he is not a naturalistic dramatist. None of his plays is explicitly set in his own time. The action of few of them (except for the English histories) is set even partly in England (exceptions are *The Merry Wives of Windsor* and the Induction to *The Taming of the Shrew*). Italy is his favoured location. Most of his principal story-lines derive from printed writings; but the structuring and translation of these narratives into dramatic terms is Shakespeare's own, and he invents much additional material. Most of the plays contain elements of myth and legend, and many derive from ancient or more recent history or from romantic tales of ancient times and faraway places. All reflect his reading, often in close detail. Holinshed's *Chronicles* (1577, revised 1587), a great compendium of English, Scottish and Irish history, provided material for his English history plays. The *Lives of the Noble Grecians and Romans* by the Greek writer Plutarch, finely translated into English from the French by Sir Thomas North in 1579, provided much of the narrative material, and also a mass of verbal detail, for his plays about Roman history. Some plays are closely based on shorter individual works: *As You Like It*, for instance, on the novel *Rosalynde* (1590) by his near-contemporary Thomas Lodge (1558–1625), *The Winter's Tale* on *Pandosto* (1588) by his old rival Robert Greene (1558–92) and *Othello* on a story by the Italian Giraldi Cinthio (1504–73). And the language of his plays is permeated by the Bible, the Book of Common Prayer and the proverbial sayings of his day.

Shakespeare was popular with his contemporaries, but his commitment to the theatre and to the plays in performance is demonstrated by the fact that only about half of his plays appeared in print in his lifetime, in slim paperback volumes known as quartos, so called because they were made from printers' sheets folded twice to form four leaves (eight pages). None of them shows any sign that he was involved in their publication. For him, performance was the primary means of publication. The most frequently reprinted of his works were the non-dramatic poems – the erotic *Venus and Adonis* and the more moralistic *The Rape of Lucrece*. The *Sonnets*, which appeared in 1609, under his name but possibly without his consent, were less successful, perhaps because the vogue for sonnet sequences, which peaked in the 1590s, had passed by then. They were not reprinted until 1640, and then only in garbled form along with poems by other writers. Happily, in 1623, seven years after he died, his colleagues John Heminges (1556–1630) and Henry Condell (d. 1627) published his collected plays, including eighteen that had not previously appeared in print, in the first Folio, whose name derives from the fact that the printers' sheets were folded only once to produce two leaves (four pages). Some of the quarto editions are badly printed, and the fact that some plays exist in two, or even three, early versions creates problems for editors. These are discussed in the Account of the Text in each volume of this series.

Shakespeare's plays continued in the repertoire until the Puritans closed the theatres in 1642. When performances resumed after the Restoration of the monarchy in 1660 many of the plays were not to the taste of the times, especially because their mingling of genres and failure to meet the requirements of poetic justice offended against the dictates of neoclassicism. Some, such as *The Tempest* (changed by John Dryden and William Davenant in 1667 to suit contemporary taste), *King Lear* (to which Nahum Tate gave a happy ending in 1681) and *Richard III* (heavily adapted by Colley Cibber in 1700 as a vehicle for his own talents), were extensively rewritten; others fell into neglect. Slowly they regained their place in the repertoire, and they continued to be reprinted, but it was not until the great actor David Garrick (1717–79) organized a spectacular jubilee in Stratford in 1769 that Shakespeare began to be regarded as a transcendental genius. Garrick's idolatry prefigured the enthusiasm of critics such as Samuel Taylor Coleridge (1772–1834) and William Hazlitt (1778–1830). Gradually Shakespeare's reputation spread abroad, to Germany, America, France and to other European countries.

During the nineteenth century, though the plays were generally still performed in heavily adapted or abbreviated versions, a large body of scholarship and criticism began to amass. Partly as a result of a general swing in education away from the teaching of Greek and Roman texts and towards literature written in English, Shakespeare became the object of intensive study in schools and universities. In the theatre, important turning points were the work in England of two theatre directors, William Poel (1852–1934) and his disciple Harley Granville-Barker (1877–1946), who showed that the application of knowledge, some of it newly acquired, of early staging conditions to performance of the plays could render the original texts viable in terms of the modern theatre. During the twentieth century appreciation of Shakespeare's work, encouraged by the availability of audio, film and video versions of the plays, spread around the world to such an extent that he can now be claimed as a global author.

The influence of Shakespeare's works permeates the English language. Phrases from his plays and poems – 'a tower of strength', 'green-eyed jealousy', 'a foregone conclusion' – are on the lips of people who may never have read him. They have inspired composers of songs, orchestral music and operas; painters and sculptors; poets, novelists and film-makers. Allusions to him appear in pop songs, in advertisements and in television shows. Some of his characters – Romeo and Juliet, Falstaff, Shylock and Hamlet – have acquired mythic status. He is valued for his humanity, his psychological insight, his wit and humour, his lyricism, his mastery of language, his ability to excite, surprise, move and, in the widest sense of the word, entertain audiences. He is the greatest of poets, but he is essentially a dramatic poet. Though his plays have much to offer to readers, they exist fully only in performance. In these volumes we offer individual introductions, notes on language and on specific points of the text, suggestions for further reading and information about how each work has been edited. In addition we include accounts of the ways in which successive generations of interpreters and audiences have responded to challenges and rewards offered by the plays. The Penguin Shakespeare series aspires to remove obstacles to understanding and to make pleasurable the reading of the work of the man who has done more than most to make us understand what it is to be human.

                                                    Stanley Wells

The Chronology of Shakespeare's Works

A few of Shakespeare's writings can be fairly precisely dated. An allusion to the Earl of Essex in the chorus to Act V of *Henry V*, for instance, could only have been written in 1599. But for many of the plays we have only vague information, such as the date of publication, which may have occurred long after composition, the date of a performance, which may not have been the first, or a list in Francis Meres's book *Palladis Tamia*, published in 1598, which tells us only that the plays listed there must have been written by that year. The chronology of the early plays is particularly difficult to establish. Not everyone would agree that the first part of *Henry VI* was written after the third, for instance, or *Romeo and Juliet* before *A Midsummer Night's Dream*. The following table is based on the 'Canon and Chronology' section in *William Shakespeare: A Textual Companion*, by Stanley Wells and Gary Taylor, with John Jowett and William Montgomery (1987), where more detailed information and discussion may be found.

The Two Gentlemen of Verona	1590–91
The Taming of the Shrew	1590–91
Henry VI, Part II	1591
Henry VI, Part III	1591

Introduction

Shakespeare is undoubtedly responsible for the place and
perception of some monarchs in popular culture. It is
difficult to imagine representations of Richard III,
Macbeth, Henry V or Cleopatra that don't owe something, and in many cases a great deal, to the reading,
staging or filming of Shakespeare's telling of English,
Scottish or Roman history. Perceptions and representations of King Henry VIII, on the other hand, have little
or nothing to do with Shakespeare, and it is telling that
there is only one filmed version of the play (BBC, 1979).
The King's prominent place in the popular English historical imagination has been determined for our time by film
(*The Private Life of Henry VIII*, 1933, with Charles
Laughton as Henry), music hall song ('I'm 'Enery the
Eighth I am . . . I got married to the widow next door, |
She's been married seven times before . . .'), portraits
(particularly the enduring Holbein feet-apart, full-frontal
pose), the rhyme used to remember the fates of Henry's
wives ('Divorced, beheaded, died, | Divorced, beheaded,
survived'), television series and the enduring nonsense
of cod history such as Sellar's and Yeatman's *1066 and
All That* of 1930 ('Henry VIII was a strong King with a
very strong sense of humour and VIII wives, memorable
amongst whom were Katherine the Arrogant, Anne of

Cloves, Lady Jane Austen, and Anne Hathaway ...')
rather than Shakespeare.

Something of a Henry stereotype, with the much-
married image replaced by that of the religious leader
and innovator and certainly possessed of the solid physical presence, was already firmly rooted by the early
1600s, when Shakespeare wrote his play, and familiarity
with the monarch is clearly indicated by the title of the
work when it was first printed in the 1623 Folio: *The
Famous History of the Life of King Henry the Eighth*. He
was the subject of folk songs, and his physical image was
familiar, for example, from the illustration on the title
page of the 1535 Coverdale Bible and more distinc-
tively in the Great Bible, *The Bible in English* of 1539,
which contained a prologue by Thomas Cranmer, the
Archbishop of Canterbury. Henry is depicted as the
Supreme Head of the Church of England passing bibles
to Cranmer (representing the church) and Thomas
Cromwell (the Lord Chamberlain from 1539, here representing the state), who hand them on to the bishops and
the lords. Crowds below, carefully ranked, listen to the
Bible and proclaim the King, the educated speaking in
Latin – 'Vivat Rex' – and the humble, at the very bottom
of the page, in English. The 1570 and 1610 editions of
John Foxe's *Acts and Monuments* (better known as the
Book of Martyrs and one of the sources for Shakespeare's
play) reinforced the royal image and the religious message
with a print of the enthroned Henry, his foot on
Pope Clement VII indicating the break with Roman
Catholicism, and Cranmer handing the king a copy of
the Great Bible. The 1613 quarto edition of Samuel
Rowley's play about Henry VIII, *When You See Me, You
Know Me*, first published in 1605, has a woodcut of the
king on its title page that is instantly recognizable as the

image of Henry from Holbein's Whitehall mural of 1537 (the huge preliminary sketch for this work can be seen in the Tudor Gallery of the National Portrait Gallery in London). Rowley's was hardly a historical record – it featured much clowning by the court jesters and a disguised king walking the streets at night and being imprisoned for fighting – and nor was it the only play of the period to feature Henry: two (with a main focus on Cardinal Wolsey) were written for the Admiral's Men in 1601; and a chap-book (a small pamphlet of popular tales), *The King and the Cobbler*, and a jest-book were common reading.

So the Henry known both to the Jacobean and the modern age owes little or nothing to Shakespeare and, indeed, the dramatist – or dramatists, since (as is discussed below and in Further Reading) the consensus is that John Fletcher co-authored the play – added little to what was already known. In fact the title character of the play appears in only nine of the seventeen scenes, is entirely absent from the fourth act and has just eighty-two speeches, many of them very short. Shakespeare's Henry is at times a neutral and unchanging cipher and at other times so ambiguous as to be inaccessible. This is not to suggest that his play is not about the king or history, popular or otherwise, but to point to its limited impact as a representation of the monarch and to suggest that the King, in terms of the dramatic action, occupies a place that is peripheral to events and frequently appears to function as a passive agent in their progression. But a character as well known as Henry was to the original audience did not necessarily require exploration or explication: part of the pleasure for the audience and part of its compact with the dramatist was surely the knowledge of 'real' events and persons that it took to the theatre and which, it discovered, Shakespeare chose to omit – the execution of Anne Bullen (Boleyn), for example, or Henry's subsequent wives; the reigns of Edward (1547–53) and Mary (1553–8). This has led some commentators, perhaps with expectations of a royal title character imaginatively drawn and with singular prominence who will be presented onstage with the subtlety or vividness of an earlier Henry or a Richard, to suggest that when Shakespeare returned to the writing of English history plays in 1613 having not tackled the subject since *Henry V* in 1599 (an interval probably not unconnected with restrictions placed on the publication of English history in June 1599 and the subsequent relaxation of censorship in the early Jacobean period), he produced a play that was bland and sycophantic and apparently uncritical of its eponymous monarch. Such a response does the play a major disservice.

Henry VIII is undoubtedly different from the earlier chronicle history plays: it is less concerned with the construction of a narrative; it is static, episodic (not dissimilar to the co-authored *Sir Thomas More*, which is also concerned with the reign of Henry VIII); it has no subplots and a narrower range of rhetorical strategies. Much critical writing about the play has concentrated on this difference and has often equated it with inadequacy. Such a view is likely to reflect the expectations and Shakespearian experiences of a commentator who is anticipating a history play closer to the earlier models, which are so frequently read, and increasingly performed, as a series of action narratives rather than independent dramas. Detractors may also misread the subject(s) of the play, ignoring the generic slipperiness that it shares with the other 'late' plays, taking little notice of its unique stagecraft, sliding over the ambivalence of the presentation of key events of the Reformation and overlooking the alternative title – the challenging *All is True*. For while this play may add little or nothing to a knowledge or understanding of the King, this is less Henry's play than that of the ambitious Wolsey, the spurned Queen Katherine (and as she is the character with the greatest 'fictional' additions she becomes, in part, the most satisfyingly dramatic creation for many modern audiences), the silent infant Elizabeth, celebrated in the post-christening final scene, and even King James, alluded to, presciently, in Cranmer's penultimate speech. *Henry VIII* makes explicit the bias of history and politics in the way they re-present events – which is such a prominent feature of our own times as well as Shakespeare's own – while exploiting the theatrical nature of history and politics. Shakespeare manipulates his medium and his material so that the stage informs the reading of history, and history provides the opportunity for ostentatious stagecraft.

One of the challenges for a dramatist when writing about history, particularly when dealing with recent events – and *Henry VIII* is the closest Shakespeare comes to writing about his own period – is that many in his audience know the plot and the outcome and have a clear image of the monarch(s) in question. So less interest may reside in what happens in narrative or event, although there may be interest in the political or religious stance or the direction of sympathy, than in the specifically dramatic – the visual effects, the use of space, the effects created through device of report and representation, the stagecraft that enables the dramatist to hold attention and sympathy while juggling with moral, historical and political ambiguity. And it is the difference from Shakespeare's earlier history plays and its distinctive style that make *Henry VIII* a rewarding drama to study and to stage.

On 31 May 1520, King Henry VIII set sail from Dover with a retinue that included the Lord Chancellor of England (Cardinal Wolsey, the Archbishop of York), the Archbishop of Canterbury, the Archbishop of Armagh and four bishops, the Dukes of Buckingham and Suffolk, the Marquis of Dorset, nine earls, twenty-one barons, three Knights of the Garter and eighty-seven other knights. Henry's queen, Katherine, was accompanied by, amongst others, the Earl of Derby, three bishops, four barons, thirty-three knights, the Duchess of Buckingham, six countesses and sixteen baronesses. These companions had their own retinues and, using the list in the Bodleian Library (Bod. Ms Ashmole 1116, ff. 955–99v), it is possible to calculate that the total party heading for France was made up of 5,832 people and 3,217 horses. The occasion prompting such ostentation was the most extravagant summit conference of the sixteenth century, the meeting between Henry VIII and Francis I of France in the neutral territory between the villages of Guines, part of English-owned Calais, and Ardres, part of France. The English, technically the hosts and engaged in cosmetic diplomacy with the French while pursuing an alliance with the Holy Roman Emperor, Charles V (Queen Katherine's nephew and a much stronger potential ally than Francis), erected an enormous, theatrical palace of wood and glass that included state apartments and galleries, while the French gathered in gloriously accoutred pavilions. The Tudor chronicler Edward Hall devotes almost 1,500 words to a description of Henry's palace alone in his 1550 account of the king's life:

Also at the foot of the same palace was another crest all of fine set gold whereon hanged rich and marvellous cloths of Arras wrought of gold and silk, compassed of many ancient stories, with which cloths of Arras, every wall and chamber were hanged, and all windows so richly covered, that it passed [surpassed] all other sights before seen. In every chamber in place convenient were cloths of estate, great and large of cloth of gold, of tissue, and rich embroidery, with chairs covered with like cloth, with pommels of fine gold: and great cushions of rich work of the Turkey making, nothing lacked of honourable furnishment. (Hall, *Henry VIII*, pp. 191–2)

Although the meeting place had been known for years as the *val doré* (golden valley) it was the dominant gold cloth, so evident as decoration in this passage from Hall, and prominently displayed in the lavish costumes worn by participants, that led to the occasion being named 'The Field of Cloth of Gold'. What followed the initial encounter between the kings were competing national displays of sport, drama, music, architecture, costume, food and drink that are thought to have cost a seventh of Henry's annual income. While it entered the popular Tudor imagination and reinforced Henry's image, at home and abroad, as a widely accomplished monarch, the meeting achieved little on the international political front.

Shakespeare uses a report of The Field of Cloth of Gold for the opening scene of *Henry VIII*, grounding the play with a recognized historical event, and employing the dramatically convenient inconvenience of the Duke of Buckingham's 'untimely ague' (I.1.4), which has confined him to his chamber, to necessitate the Duke of Norfolk's detailed description of 'the view of earthly

glory' (I.1.14) and allowing for discussion of the chore-
ographer of the event, Wolsey, and the animosity that
the Cardinal inspires. At the end of the scene Shakespeare
is able to employ 'gold' as shorthand for Wolsey's mal-
practice when Buckingham presciently announces, 'My
surveyor is false. The o'er-great Cardinal | Hath showed
him gold. My life is spanned already' (I.1. 222–3). None
of this was news to the first audiences. Wolsey's shortcomings were well recorded by his contemporaries and
subsequently became legendary. From the year following
The Field of Cloth of Gold the alliterative verse of John
Skelton (1460?–1529 and tutor to Henry before he became
king) demonstrates the resentment of political abuses,
personal excesses and the over-ambition for which Wolsey
had become reviled by all sections of society:

> So much ragged right of a ram's horn;
> So rigorous revelling, in a prelate specially;
> So bold and so bragging, and was so basely born;
> So lordly of his looks, and so disdainly;
> So fat a maggot, bred of flesh-fly;
> Was never such a filthy gorgon, nor such an epicure,
> Since Deucalion's flood, I make the fast and sure.
>
> ('Speke Parott', ll. 505–11,
> *The Complete English Poems*)

It is not always possible to determine which of the
available sources Shakespeare drew on for his version of
history and character: accounts by Edward Hall, Raphael
Holinshed, John Stow, John Speed, George Cavendish
and John Foxe are all employed, and the problem lies, in
part, in determining the extent to which they themselves
borrowed from each other. In the case of much of his
representation of Wolsey, however, the attribution is

clear. The sick Queen Katherine, having learned of Wolsey's death from Griffith, describes him thus:

> He was a man
> Of an unbounded stomach, ever ranking
> Himself with princes; one that by suggestion
> Tied all the kingdom. Simony was fair play;
> His own opinion was his law. I'th'presence
> He would say untruths, and be ever double
> Both in his words and meaning. He was never,
> But where he meant to ruin, pitiful.
> His promises were as he then was, mighty,
> But his performance as he is now, nothing.
> Of his own body he was ill, and gave
> The clergy ill example. (IV.2.33–44)

In this passage Shakespeare has followed Holinshed almost verbatim:

This Cardinal was of great stomach, for he counted himself equal with princes, and by crafty suggestion got into his hands innumerable treasure: he forced little on simony, and was not pitiful, and stood affectionate in his own opinion: in open presence he would lie and say untruth, and was double both in speech and meaning: he would promise much and perform little: he was vicious of his body, and gave the clergy evil example. (Holinshed, *Chronicles*, p. 992)

However, Shakespeare is doing more here than reusing a convenient source. In determining who will provide the description and the circumstances of its delivery he is directing the audience's response. The Holinshed source passage is part of an extended biography (with authorial acknowledgements to Stow) that is presented to the reader following an account of Wolsey's death. The views expressed are not attributed to any speaker: there is no 'voice' at this moment – it is an anonymous account. In selecting Katherine, a character who has by this stage in the play elicited audience sympathy through circumstance and personal qualities, to voice the criticism, it may be argued that Shakespeare is endorsing the derogatory view of Wolsey. This is a very different effect from Buckingham's criticism delivered at the start of the play before an audience has had a chance to assess his veracity.

The strained relationship between the key players in Henry's court, evidenced in the opening scene, is given a visual as well as a rhetorical emphasis, made overtly theatrical, as one of the detailed stage directions, which are characteristic of this play, makes explicit:

Enter Cardinal Wolsey, the purse borne before him, certain of the guard, and two Secretaries with papers. The Cardinal in his passage fixeth his eye on Buckingham, and Buckingham on him, both full of disdain. (I.1.114)

Buckingham's excessive reaction to this silent confrontation and his desire to 'outstare' his adversary, despite Norfolk's suggestion of temperance and restraint, make his arrest at the end of the scene inevitable, but the function of this moment is more than to raise the tension of the storytelling: the episode signals the flamboyantly theatrical nature of the play to come (as in the emphasis on 'eye', or seeing, that is repeated throughout this scene), the narrative patterning of a highly structured drama: report alternating with display, and the manipulation of history that will culminate in the final tableau of the presentation of the infant Elizabeth.

Henry's and Anne Bullen's daughter Elizabeth was born on 8 September 1533 and christened three days later, and the staging of this event is Shakespeare's final *coup de théâtre* and distortion of history. The extended stage direction that opens the last scene of the play provides an accurate, if slightly abbreviated, account of the processions that framed the ceremony that took place in the Church of the Observant Friars close to Greenwich Palace, where Elizabeth was born:

Enter trumpets, sounding; then two Aldermen, Lord Mayor, Garter, Cranmer, Duke of Norfolk with his marshal's staff, Duke of Suffolk, two noblemen bearing great standing bowls for the christening gifts; then four noblemen bearing a canopy, under which the Duchess of Norfolk, godmother, bearing the child richly habited in a mantle, etc., train borne by a lady ... (V.5.1)

But the certainty of Garter's proclamation, after '*the troop pass once about the stage*,' 'Heaven, from thy endless goodness, send prosperous life, long, and ever happy, to the high and mighty Princess of England, Elizabeth!', immediately echoed by Cranmer, disguises the alarm and uncertainty that clouded the real occasion. The birth of a boy had been widely predicted, and the parents desired and had planned for such an event. Henry, who had engaged in high personal, political and religious risks to obtain a male heir, had been considering whether to call the child Edward or Henry, and Anne's pre-prepared letter announcing the birth had to be amended hastily so that the appropriate thanks to God for the deliverance of a 'prince' were redirected to cover the birth of a 'princes' (*sic*). None of this is evident in Shakespeare's final triumphant scene which revels in prescient certainties: 'What is her name?' 'Elizabeth.'

In part it is the tone and action of the final scene that distinguish *Henry VIII* from Shakespeare's earlier history plays and lead some critics to seek connections with other plays in the canon. Thus it has been identified, generically, with the other plays that he wrote towards the end of his career and has been subject to the same reassessment and new readings that they have attracted. It has long been suggested that *Pericles* (1607), *The Winter's Tale* (1609), *Cymbeline* (1610), *The Tempest* (1611) and *Henry VIII* have a number of unusual features in common that distinguish them from the rest of the canon and make John Heminges' and Henry Condell's first Folio labelling and attribution inappropriate (*The Winter's Tale* and *The Tempest* in the 'Comedy' section, *Cymbeline* a 'Tragedy', *Henry VIII* a 'History', and the co-authored *Pericles* missing from the Folio altogether). They have been dubbed Romance, Tragicomedy, Last Plays, Late Plays, Masque and Myth. They contain elements that distance them from dramatic realism – aspects of hymeneal celebration, fairytale, fantasy, the morality play, the masque – as well as topical responses to political and cultural events. It has been pointed out that each play features a powerful father figure and a daughter, in this case Henry and Elizabeth – his first daughter, the unpopular Catholic Queen Mary, is effectively missing from the play other than as a commendation in a letter written by her dying mother (IV.2.131–8) – and in each case the father has a flaw, although Henry's failings in the course of the narrative are less exposed than Leontes', Cymbeline's or Prospero's. Paul Jesson played Henry in Stratford in 1996–7 (see Play in Performance section) having previously performed as Prospero and saw great similarities between the roles: their power and confidence, their influence but also their great failings and, unusually perhaps, their vulnerability. In each play the

daughter is transparently an innocent: Cranmer stresses
the point in his claim that the infant Elizabeth is a 'pure
soul' and he enumerates the unsullied attributes that she
will maintain through life:

> All princely graces
> That mould up such a mighty piece as this is,
> With all the virtues that attend the good,
> Shall still be doubled on her. Truth shall nurse her,
> Holy and heavenly thoughts still counsel her;
> She shall be loved and feared. (V.5.25–30)

It is this feature that led to a biographical reading of
the group of plays in the early twentieth century: the
suggestion that Shakespeare doted on one of his daughters and wished to commend her or that there was something in a troubled relationship between them that he
desired to put right. Yet while the virtuous and pure representation of the daughter Elizabeth may be compared to
Perdita in *The Winter's Tale*, Miranda in *The Tempest* or
Imogen in *Cymbeline*, there is another royal, redemptive
presence in *Henry VIII* that subverts such neat comparisons: Elizabeth's mother, Anne Bullen, perceived by the
gentlemen who are witnesses to the coronation as:

> the goodliest woman
> That ever lay by man; which when the people
> Had the full view of, such a noise arose
> As the shrouds make at sea in a stiff tempest
> ...
> At length her grace rose, and with modest paces
> Came to the altar, where she kneeled, and saint-like
> Cast her fair eyes to heaven, and prayed devoutly.
> (IV.1.69–72; 82–4)

While it may be possible to read in the language that describes the popular response to these events (the noise, the reaction of the 'great-bellied women', the crowd in the Abbey, so packed that 'a finger | Could not be wedged in more' and whose 'rankness of . . . joy' was stifling) something potentially anarchic or sexually unsettling, nevertheless, in a passage apparently free of irony, the effect is of restoration or reconciliation. Even if Shakespeare's audience was aware – as the original coronation audience was certainly aware – that Anne, in Cranmer's recorded words, was 'somewhat big with child', the knowledge that the child is Elizabeth reinforces the redemptive effect. It is only in the positioning of this scene that the moment acquires ambiguity, and the audience is reminded of the third 'innocent' woman in this play, for the coronation procession and its report is followed immediately by the moving scene of Katherine's vision and imminent death. This moment, too, ties *Henry VIII*, generically, with the late plays: they are all concerned with power, authority and succession, and in each of them women are the moral surrogates and suffer for the men. In Katherine's dying moments the king's power is confirmed, and the succession, in this skilful editing of the historical record, is assured, and yet Shakespeare carefully retains sympathy for both protagonists. The former queen is palpably suffering, yet she respects Griffith's generous description of Wolsey (and the audience learns of Wolsey's repentance, which ties up another loose end and confirms the redemptive nature of the play), she wishes the king well, blesses him, requests good treatment for her daughter and, in a moment that is surely a crowd-pleaser as well as confirming her own virtue, petitions the king to make very specific arrangements for the well-being of her faithful servants. Her goodness is further reinforced by the vision that she, and the off- but not the onstage audience, share. Drawing in its detail on the Book of Revelation, and subsequently described by Katherine in biblical terms, it is a clear signal that her destiny is assured: white-robed and golden-masked figures repeatedly hold a garland above her head, '*At which, as it were by inspiration, she makes in her sleep signs of rejoicing, and holdeth up her hands to heaven*' (IV.2.82). While music replaces speech at this moment the audience may be moderately certain that this is a Protestant rather than a Catholic vision, having seen Katherine insist on the use of English instead of Latin in her discussion with the Cardinals Wolsey and Campeius earlier in the play (III.1.41ff.).

The redemptive and mythical qualities of the late plays as a group are achieved in *Henry VIII* not only through Katherine's generosity towards Wolsey, but also by the power of his own final speeches that acknowledge error, the penitence exhibited by and through all the major characters, Henry's intervention to save Cranmer in the fourth trial scene and, of course, the celebratory 'happy ending'. This tone and narrative manipulation have led some scholars to sense in the plays more than a whiff of immortality and spirituality, but *Henry VIII* has fewer overt magical or supernatural moments than the others, and this feature is as likely to be read by modern scholars as Shakespeare's response to history rather than to the serenity or reassurances of religion. While it may be argued that Shakespeare distorts the record to impose a providential pattern on events it is equally true that the patterning of the narrative reflects humanism as much as theology: it is history and politics here, rather than religion, that can be observed and learned from.

*

The development of historically focused cultural criticisms (particularly the movements that have emerged since the 1980s known in the United States as New Historicism and in Britain as Cultural Materialism), which study a wide range of discursive practices and look outside the texts, has seen a growth of scholarly interest in Shakespeare's history: the period that he dramatizes, the period in which he wrote and the historical style and method of his period, particularly what 'history' meant and the ways in which it was recorded. This has led to a closer, politicized examination of Shakespeare's employment of history – his omissions, additions and amendments to the historical record(s) – that looks beyond the immediate needs of dramaturgy and questions, for example, whether the playwright was endorsing or subverting his historical past and present. The answers to such a question tend to reflect a critical split: those who prior to 1980 read *Henry VIII*, whether as history, romance or late play, generically or chronologically, saw Shakespeare endorsing orthodoxy and tradition in religion and politics – uncritical of the king and, indeed, subsequent monarchs, laying national and international problems at Wolsey's door and reticent about religious change. Those who read the play post-1980, whether as history or politicized late play, found it much more ambiguous and suggested that in the unusual combination of a providential and/or teleological view of history (the confidence of the ending of the play) and the antiquarian approach (the careful yet selective use of sources) there is clear evidence of the influence of humanism and an intentional appropriation and manipulation of different ways of reading the past.

So what did Shakespeare do with the historical record? Between the fixed historical points of The Field of

Cloth of Gold (June 1520) and the christening of Elizabeth (September 1533) he contracts, transposes and manipulates events. Some of his minor changes may reflect no more than the pragmatic needs of his theatre that require the reattribution of speech or action to reflect the number of available actors, or the demands of creating a coherent, compelling narrative from thirteen busy years. Historically, The Field of Cloth of Gold and Buckingham's execution are a year apart, and six years separate Henry's first encounter with Anne Bullen and the trial and death of Buckingham, incidents that in the play occur in consecutive scenes. Some changes are more significant and imply a connection, a cause-and-effect relationship, between persons and events – Shakespeare places Henry's marriage to Anne (1536) before the fall of Wolsey (1529), for example – while other transpositions create a disconnection that may be read as dramatic or political: the death of Katherine (1536) occurs before the birth of Elizabeth (1533). This transposition allows the play to conclude with a celebration of future monarchy (the audience's immediate past and present) rather than with the closure of a death that took place seventy years before.

Shakespeare's manipulation of Thomas More is particularly ambiguous. He leads Anne's coronation procession, although it was common knowledge that, while friends had sent him money to purchase a new gown for the occasion, he was ostentatiously absent, and indeed it is not easy to spot him in the play. Cromwell reports his appointment, 'Sir Thomas More is chosen | Lord Chancellor' (III.2.393–4), and in the following scene the extended stage direction that lists the Order of the Coronation procession has, as the third item on the list, '*Lord Chancellor, with purse and mace before him*' (IV.1.36).

Although More had been executed in 1535, Shakespeare has him presiding over the trial of Thomas Cranmer (1543), an elision and repositioning that also wipes from the play Anne Bullen's trial and execution (1536), Cromwell's trial and execution (1540) and Henry's third divorce (1540). These are significant anachronisms that many have argued throw light on the importance of trials and justice in the play and draw attention to More's own, subsequent trial – not part of the play – and give a specific focus to the issue of malice versus integrity. In comparing More's published statements that placed parliament, not the king, as the highest authority in the land with the opposite case that he made at Cranmer's trial, Gerard B. Wegemer posits that the play 'Leads us to consider what would have been unspeakable in Tudor times: Could the king be guilty of the same charge he brought against Buckingham, Wolsey, More, Anne Boleyn, and Cromwell – i.e., the charge of malice?' ('Henry VIII on Trial', p. 86). Such readings, of course, assume both an authorial intent and an historically knowledgeable and aware audience – in either Stuart or modern times – intelligence that is hard to measure.

But whatever critical approach is employed with the play there is no doubt that *Henry VIII* draws attention to the historical record and, from the Prologue on, to history itself. A 'history play' is ostensibly a contradiction in terms, an apparent attempt to combine the 'fact' of record with the 'fiction' of play, whether the fiction is the conflations required by the constraints of performance length and playhouse conditions, the demands of creation of dramatic effect and the need to engage a paying audience, or whether fiction is something imaginatively original, the artistic act. A history play, then, invites an audience to consider the 'truth' or invention

of its presence, and *Henry VIII* makes the invitation
particularly explicit:

> Such as give
> Their money out of hope they may believe
> May here find truth too. Those that come to see
> Only a show or two, and so agree
> The play may pass, if they be still, and willing,
> I'll undertake may see away their shilling
> Richly in two short hours. (Prologue 7–13)

And the Prologue continues, almost teasingly, to draw
attention to the relationship between artifice (fiction),
selectivity and reality. It speaks of dramatic deception,
of 'chosen truth' and, in a phrase reminiscent of the
Chorus in *Henry V*, invites the audience to collude and
contribute to the illusion: 'Think ye see | The very
persons of our noble story | As they were living.'

As the play progresses the interplay between fact and
fiction is further exploited and explored through two
dominant devices. First is Shakespeare's ostentatious use
of written and spoken records and the language that has
accrued to both. He distinguishes clearly between eyewitness accounts and reports of various sorts and makes
explicit the status of the information or evidence that is
conveyed. The Surveyor in Act I, scene 2, for example,
is bidden to 'recount' and 'relate' his intelligence about
the Duke of Buckingham and duly reports his 'speech',
'words', 'oath' and 'what he spoke'. Yet such apparently
formal witness is less reliable than the 'buzzing' that is
encountered in the second act of a 'separation | Between
the King and Katherine' (II.1.148–9) that causes Henry
to command the Lord Mayor 'To stop the rumour and
allay those tongues | That durst disperse it' (II.1.152–3).

Clearly the injunction fails, as the Lord Chamberlain subsequently reports, 'These news are everywhere, every tongue speaks 'em' (II.2.37). At the same time that the audience questions the veracity of the information it receives and learns to place more reliance on opinion (II.2.123), rumour and 'secret' (V.1.17) than on witness statements, it is being presented with written records and the formal annals of statecraft: warrants, commissions, schedules, inventories, lists, papers of state and religion, publications of marriage and coronation and letters. Throughout the play Shakespeare is very specific about the routes and relay of information, and, indeed, the plot and the dramatic effects hinge upon the use and abuse of such records and evidence culminating in the collision of true and false communication (and true and false religion in this Reformation context) of Cranmer's trial in V.3 and the accusations that he has 'misdemeaned' himself,

> Toward the King first, then his laws, in filling
> The whole realm, by your teaching and your chaplains' –
> For so we are informed – with new opinions,
> Diverse and dangerous, which are heresies,
> And, not reformed, may prove pernicious. (V.3.15–19)

It is in the focus on information – from a variety of sources and reliable and unreliable – that can be seen the wisdom of Judith Anderson's comment: 'The distinction between *Henry VIII* and Shakespeare's more universally admired history plays is, perhaps, not that it is more historical but that it is less fictional' (Anderson, *Biographical Truth*, p. 131).

It is also this emphasis on reported event rather than action that makes *Henry VIII* a remarkably *un*theatrical play while at the same time being, in a visual sense, amongst Shakespeare's most theatrical dramas. For if 'telling', through a variety of means, is one device, the other is ostentatious 'showing' or, as the Prologue invites the audience, to 'see . . . richly', anticipating the 'shows, | Pageants, and sights' that the Second Gentleman identifies to his companion in Act IV (1.10–11). 'Show' is evident in the detailed formality of the entrances of Wolsey (I.1.114), the King (start of I.2), Queen Katherine (I.2.8), or Buckingham after his arraignment (II.1.54), for example, where order, costume, properties and gesture indicate status and relationship and suggest that audience observation is important. The stage directions at these moments are as close to sources – historical records – as any speech in the play. The masque at Wolsey's palace (Act I, scene 4) is a more complex show requiring music and disguise and the careful choreography of its preliminaries by the Lord Chamberlain. The account, again, is very close to sources (in this case, Holinshed) apart from two important details: Anne Bullen was absent and Wolsey failed to recognize the King. Shakespeare's dramatic licence at this moment serves two purposes – it gives a shape, focus and prominence to the scene and it raises questions about Henry's veracity when he subsequently asserts that it is only his conscience about the legitimacy of his marriage that prompts his separation from Katherine.

The combination of 'show' and 'tell' provides a uniquely patterned play that subverts expectations of dramatic convention and climax and at the same time draws attention to structure and, indeed, to the play as theatre. In plot terms it is the four 'falls' of Buckingham, Katherine, Wolsey and – almost – Cranmer that shape the play, but style is as significant. The Porter's account of the crowd massed for the christening of Elizabeth is both a clear instance of 'tell' and the most overt example of theatrical self-referencing: 'These are the youths that thunder at a playhouse, and fight for bitten apples' (V.4.59–60); but the unsubtle discussion between the two Gentlemen at the start of Act IV is surely a knowing device, an open acknowledgement of their dramatic function as 'tellers': 'At our last encounter | The Duke of Buckingham came from his trial' and 'May I be so bold to ask what that contains, | That paper in your hand?' (IV.1.4–5; 13–14). For the original audiences, too, Henry's choice of venue for Katherine's trial – 'The most convenient place that I can think of | For such receipt of learning is Blackfriars' (II.2.136–7) – serves as a further knowing and possibly ironic reference to theatre and its function. Blackfriars, on the north bank of the Thames, was the indoor playing space of Shakespeare's company, the King's Men. *Henry VIII* may well have been performed there.

The confines of the stage are able to make explicit a court world that on the one hand has great public magnificence but on the other affords little personal space. Shakespeare exploits and dramatizes the lack of privacy of the Tudor court: there is never a moment when a character is alone on stage and, unusually, there are no soliloquies. The effect is reinforced by the presence of the King as a hidden onstage audience watching much of Cranmer's trial (Act V, scenes 2 and 3) as perhaps he has watched earlier in Act II, scene 2. Some distinct places may be deduced from the action that occurs in them or from the signalling of forthcoming events while other scenes are less clearly set and, to a modern audience at least, have less obvious implications. Yet the lack of specificity of Act II, scene 2, for example,

allied to the presence on stage of specific characters, acts
as a visual demonstration of the developing and shifting
shape of the political structure of the period and the
establishment of two distinct authorities: the Privy
Chamber (the power of the household and court) and
the Council (the power of the administration). An uneasy
and competitive relationship developed between
members of each group and, indeed, their ownership of
space. It may be assumed from the stage direction at
II.2.60 – '*The King draws the curtain* ...' – that the
setting is his most private apartments, the Privy Chamber
and the Lord Chamberlain's domain, and yet Wolsey, in
whom the power of the Council is embodied, is
welcomed into this sanctum by the King. Here the
confines of the stage serve to demonstrate shifts of
power, influence and favouritism and highlight, perhaps,
the King's failure to govern wisely. Further evidence
of the King's lax hold on administrative effectiveness
may be seen in the details of the stage directions accompanying Wolsey's entrances: his first appearance at
I.1.114, '*the purse borne before him*', suggests that he holds
the power of the Exchequer; his arrival at Katherine's
trial (Act II, scene 4) when the purse is accompanied
by '*the great seal, and a cardinal's hat*' indicates the exten-
sion of his executive and religious power, and functions
as visual shorthand for an inappropriate accumulation
of office, a blurring of responsibilities, and, by implication, a failure of Henry's statecraft.

Probably the best-known historical 'fact' about *Henry
VIII* is that the first Globe theatre burned down during
a performance of the play on 29 June 1613. Sir Henry
Wotton's letter to Sir Edmund Bacon is the most
commonly quoted account:

The King's players had a new play, called *All is True*, representing some principal pieces of the reign of Henry VIII, which was set forth with many extraordinary circumstances of pomp and majesty, even to the matting of the stage; the Knights of the Order, with their Georges and garters, the Guards with their embroidered coats, and the like: sufficient in truth within a while to make greatness very familiar, if not ridiculous. Now, King Henry making a masque at the Cardinal Wolsey's house, and certain chambers being shot off at his entry, some of the paper, or other stuff, wherewith one of them was stopped, did light on the thatch, where being thought at first but an idle smoke, and their eyes being more attentive to the show, it kindled inwardly, and ran round like a train, consuming within less than an hour the whole house to the very grounds.

The interest here, apart from the information that helps to date the play and the details of its staging, is the title that Wotton uses to identify the play he saw – *All is True* – a title that was used by another eyewitness to the fire, Henry Bluett:

On Tuesday last there was acted at the Globe a new play called *All is True*, which had been acted not passing 2 or 3 times before. There came many people to see it insomuch that the house was very full, and as the play was almost ended the house was fired with shooting off a chamber which was stopped with tow which was blown up into the thatch of the house and so burned down to the ground.

If indeed the play as first performed had the title *All is True* (and the General Editors of the 1986 Oxford Complete Works are sufficiently convinced of the case to use it in their edition), then it may be seen as a commen-

tary on Shakespeare's use of history. While it is always
difficult to recognize, in print, the inflections of irony,
nevertheless the alternative title coupled with eighteen
uses of the word 'true' and twenty deployments of 'truth'
(or 'untruth') would seem an invitation to consider critically the veracity of what is presented and, in the play's
use of historical records, its presentation of monarchs
and politicians, its manipulation of time, even to question the nature of truth itself.

In addition to considering how Shakespeare represents
or misrepresents the past it is valuable to look at what he
does with his present and, indeed, the nature of that
present. The play concludes with the baptism of
Elizabeth, but none of the first audiences in the Globe
had memories long enough to recall that event. However,
many would remember her funeral and may well (as,
perhaps, did Shakespeare himself) have formed part of
the crowd that mourned on that occasion. Elizabeth died
on 24 March 1603 at Richmond Palace, and two days later
her coffin was moved down the Thames, by night, and
with a torchlight procession, to lie in state at Whitehall
Palace. The state funeral took place on 28 April –
Shakespeare was just thirty-seven – a remarkable and
carefully managed occasion that included a formal procession which contemporary estimates number between
1,000 and 1,500 strong. The British Library has the
coloured ink drawings that are the first ever illustrations
of the funeral of an English monarch and show the
plumed horses accoutred in black drawing the coffin-
bearing chariot surmounted with a lifelike effigy of the
queen, in scarlet robes and with a characteristic red wig.
The occasion may be described as theatrical, with
costumes, representation, evident choreography and
design, and attracted a very large audience of Londoners.

The drawings do not show the crowds, but John Stow describes the packed streets and the emotional response 'as the like hath not been seen or known in the memory of man' (*Annals* (1631), p. 815). Shakespeare himself may have witnessed the scene that he describes at the end of the play:

> But she must die –
> She must, the saints must have her – yet a virgin;
> A most unspotted lily shall she pass
> To th'ground, and all the world shall mourn her.
> (V.5.59–62)

The mourners were responding to a carefully created image that had been developed during the Queen's life, and is most evident in the visual symbolism of portraits of the period, to reinforce her reputation and capacity to govern wisely, to stress her personal qualities of mercy, fairness, wisdom and toughness on the domestic front and in her dealings with Europe, and to turn her much vaunted virginity into a political strength. Roy Strong (in, for example, *The Cult of Elizabeth: Elizabethan Portraiture and Pageantry* (1977)) has argued that the visual representations of the image in particular were intentionally developed, post-Reformation, to replace Catholic ritual, and so images of the Virgin Queen replaced those, now removed from the churches, of the Blessed Virgin Mary just as religious festivals were replaced by secular celebrations of monarchy – pageants, tilts, tournaments and processions. So symbolism that had formerly represented and accrued to one virgin became attached to the other with both political and religious intent. But this movement, usually known as the Cult of Elizabeth or the Cult of Gloriana, was not confined to the visual. The Queen was known as Cynthia or Diana, Astraea, Belphoebe, or was named after heroines of the Old Testament, and was equated nominally and in print as well as in paint with the phoenix, the pelican and the ermine: 'by many names most dear to us', as John Hayward put it, preaching at Paul's Cross three days after Elizabeth's death. The image proliferated and gathered momentum during the reign of James as the initial enthusiasm for the Stuarts diminished and Elizabeth was transformed, memorially, into the perfect Protestant ruler of a vanished golden age. It is evident in the resurgence of interest in Edmund Spenser's *Faerie Queene* (1590, 1596) during the early Stuart period and in popular ballads too:

> She never did any wicked act
> To make her conscience prick her
> Nor ever would submit to him
> That calld himself Christs Vicar.
> . . .
> A Sleep she lyes, and so shee must lye
> Untill the day of Doom
> But then shee'l arise & pisse out the Eyes
> Of the proud Pope of Rome. (Quoted in
> Watson, *England's Elizabeth*, pp. 48–9)

It is illuminating to read *Henry VIII* in this context and to note the use that Shakespeare makes of the established Protestant Elizabeth iconography in the final scene of the play. Cranmer describes her as 'The bird of wonder . . . the maiden phoenix' (V.5.40), a symbol first employed by Nicholas Hilliard in his portrait of the 1570s. It was used by Elizabeth's brother, Edward VI, and suggests the endurance of a hereditary monarchy as well as conveying

a sense of the unique and of chastity. The image proliferated, post-Armada (1588), and was a common device
in medals and jewelled pendants. Cranmer draws on
further popular imagery when he describes Elizabeth as
'yet a virgin; | A most unspotted lily' (V.5.60–61); in
addition to the obvious pure, white lily reference here,
the association is with the ermine as a symbol of chastity,
employed by William Segar in his portrait of 1585. The
Queen has a crowned ermine, a creature whose white fur
was frequently used as a metaphor for chastity, on her
left arm – 'rather dead than spotted' as Sir Philip Sidney's
Arcadia (1590) has it. Elizabeth's christening is a clear
reminder in language as well as staged event of the qualities that had accrued to a Protestant monarch, but *Henry
VIII* was not alone in such an emphasis.

It is significant to note the number of plays from the
Jacobean period that had an Elizabethan focus. This is
not to argue that Shakespeare was a Protestant propa-
gandist but to suggest that it is helpful to be mindful of
the competitive, commercial theatre world of the period:
Henry VIII is as likely to be cashing in on popular religious and political trends as reflecting the religious disposition of its author. Contemporary plays celebrated
Elizabeth's triumph over her persecution by her Catholic
half-sister Queen Mary (the daughter of Henry and
Katherine) and promoted her not only in their texts.
Thomas Heywood's immensely popular *If You Know not
Me, You Know Nobody: or, The Troubles of Queen Elizabeth*
of 1605 has a woodcut of Elizabeth on its title page,
showing a throned monarch with an orb and sceptre and
identifiable particularly through the elaborate jewelled
headdress as a version of the popular posthumous
engraving by Crispin van de Passe from a portrait by
Isaac Oliver. The play concludes with Elizabeth kissing

an explicitly English bible and encouraging the popula-
tion to read it too:

> Who builds on this, dwells in a happy state.
> This is the fountain clear immaculate,
> That happy issue that shall us succeed,
> And in our populous kingdom this book read:
> For them as for our own selves we humbly pray,
> They may live long and blessed; so lead the way.

The second part of Heywood's play (1606) has a number
of subtitles including 'and the famous Victory in 1588',
alluding to the defeat of the Spanish Armada, the event
that concludes the drama, and the title page features a
woodcut, sometimes attributed to Nicholas Hilliard. The
pose is not dissimilar to the famous Armada portraits of
the period, although in this study the seated Queen is
framed by roses, rather than imperial emblems, which
may be read as symbols of her charity, Christian love
and virginity. While the Queen is present – as an onstage
character and an illustration in the printed text – in both
of Heywood's plays, she remains invisible and offstage
in Samuel Rowley's *When You See Me You Know Me* of
1605. She has an important role, however, in an episto-
lary contest with her sister. Mary writes to encourage her
brother, Prince Edward, to pursue Roman Catholicism
while Elizabeth's letter encourages his Protestantism:

> Sweet Prince I salute thee with a sister's love,
> Be steadfast in thy faith, and let thy prayers
> Be dedicate to God only, for 'tis he alone
> Can strengthen thee, and confound thine enemies,
> Give a settled assurance of thy hopes in heaven,
> God strengthen thee in all temptations,

And give thee grace to shun idolatry,
Heaven send thee life to inherit thy election,
To God I commend thee, who still I pray preserve thee.

And Elizabeth's letter works: 'This I embrace,' declares Edward, 'away idolatry.'

Thomas Dekker's *Whore of Babylon*, printed in 1607, is the most explicit expression of Elizabeth as a Protestant heroine, as is immediately evident from the authorial prefixed address: 'The general scope of this dramatical poem is to set forth, in tropical and shadowed colours, the greatness, magnanimity, constancy, clemency, and other the incomparable heroical virtues of our late Queen, and on the contrary part the inveterate malice, treasons, machinations, underminings, and continual bloody stratagems of that purple whore of Rome . . .' Following a prologue, the play, a mix of history, allegory and religion, proceeds with a dumbshow that is an explicit reminder of Elizabeth's coronation. As she processed from the Tower of London to Westminster on 14 January 1559 she encountered five formal pageants – dumbshows with accompanying written or spoken texts. At the fourth pageant on Cheapside she was approached by

one personage whose name was Time, appareled as an old man with a scythe in his hand, having wings artificially made, leading a personage of lesser stature than himself, which was finely and well appareled, all clad in white silk, and directly over her head was set her name and title in Latin and English.

(Kinney, *Elizabethan Backgrounds*, p. 28)

This person of lesser stature, Truth, handed the Queen the Bible in English, prominently labelled 'The Word of Truth'. She kissed it, held it up to the crowd, laid it to her breast and thanked the city. Dekker's dumbshow presents a sad, dishevelled and sleeping Truth, impervious to Time's efforts to wake her until, following the funeral procession of Roman Catholic Mary and the start of Elizabeth's reign, she suddenly revives. Throughout this early Jacobean period, then, Elizabeth is explicitly presented as the embodiment of Protestant Truth, and at the end of *Henry VIII*, after Elizabeth's christening, Cranmer tells the King that 'Truth shall nurse her, | Holy and heavenly thoughts still counsel her' (V.5.28–9). Perhaps it is at this moment that the alternative title, *All is True*, has a very specific contemporary resonance. Shakespeare is not just drawing attention to historical veracity or the nature of truth but making a claim about the status of Protestantism.

In addition, however, to the concluding focus on the infant Elizabeth *Henry VIII* also includes a passage of praise to her heir King James:

> Who from the sacred ashes of her honour
> Shall star-like rise, as great in fame as she was,
> And so stand fixed
> . . .
> Wherever the bright sun of heaven shall shine,
> His honour and the greatness of his name
> Shall be, and make new nations. He shall flourish,
> And like a mountain cedar reach his branches
> To all the plains about him. (V.5.45–7; 50–54)

This may be read as expediency or courtesy (James was, after all, the patron of Shakespeare's theatre company, the King's Men) but it is worth considering the other Stuart who lurks if not as a textual then as a contextual presence in this play. At least two of the Jacobean 'Elizabeth' plays

(*When You See Me You Know Me* and *Whore of Babylon*)
were performed by 'The high and mighty Prince of Wales
his servants', that is, the playing company whose patron
was King James's son, Henry. The Prince, born in 1594,
was the godson of Queen Elizabeth, and his personal qualities, his firm Protestantism and his aggressive attitude to
Europe made him an increasingly popular figure, particularly after the Catholic Gunpowder Plot of 1605 and as
his father's reputation diminished. As Elizabeth was transformed into the perfect Protestant ruler of a vanished
golden age, so Henry was seen as her natural successor,
and his early death in 1612 caused much religious, political and popular consternation. If Henry Wotton and
Henry Bluett were indeed viewing a 'new' play when the
Globe burned in 1613 then the alternative *All is True* title
has a particular Protestant resonance here that extends
beyond its specific associations with Elizabeth and incor-
porates her anticipated heir. Yet many scholars have also
linked the play to the celebrations for the marriage in 1613
between James's daughter, Elizabeth, and Prince Frederick,
the Elector Palatine and leader of the Calvinist (Protestant)
faction in Germany, which went some way to overcoming
the distress at Prince Henry's death. While *Henry VIII*
was not one of the six King's Men plays that were requi-
sitioned for court entertainments at this period, that does
not preclude it being a public response to the pleasure with
which the marriage was greeted. So in writing a play about
the past that has clear textual and contextual links with his
present, and implying a continuity of governance and religious observance, Shakespeare may well be expressing the
hopes of his audience for a future that has equal stability.

Early accounts of the reception of the play show a limited
interest in its representation of history, religion and

politics although one record, a letter from Robert Gell to Sir Martyn Stuteville of 29 July 1626, describes a visit to the theatre of an audience member, George Villiers, the then Duke of Buckingham and an unpopular court favourite, with a keener awareness of history than most. The visit took place shortly before his assassination:

On Tuesday his Grace [the Duke of Buckingham] was present at the acting of K. Hen. the 8 at the Globe, a play bespoken of purpose by himself; whereat he stayed till the Duke of Buckingham was beheaded, & then departed. Some say, he should rather have seen the fall of Cardinal Wolsey, who was a more lively type of himself, having governed this kingdom 18 years, as he hath done 14.

When the London theatres reopened after the Restoration of the monarchy new audiences encountered the play for the first time, and Samuel Pepys wrote in his *Diary* of the initial excitement provoked by William Davenant's revival of 'a rare play . . . the story of Henry the 8th with all his wives' (10 December 1663) for the Duke's Company. The King and court planned to attend what was said to be 'an Admirable play' (22 December 1663) and Pepys' friend Captain Ferrers reported 'the goodness of the new play' (24 December 1663) but his own reaction was different. He wrote of a 'much cried up play . . . which though I went with resolution to like it, is so simple a thing, made up of a great many patches, that, besides the shows and processions in it, there is nothing in the world good or well done' (1 January 1664). It is not clear whether it was the production, his assessment of the play or the taste of the age that had changed and enabled him to respond more positively in 1668: he 'was mightily pleased, better than ever I expected, with the history and shows of it'.

An anonymous pamphlet of 1698, written in response to Jeremy Collier's criticism of the stage, challenged the play less for its style or historical accuracy than its failure to employ the classical unities:

the audience shall be almost quite shocked at such a play as *Henry VIII* or the *Duchess of Malfi*. And why, because here's a marriage and the birth of a child, possibly in two Acts, which points so directly to ten months length of time that the play has very little air of reality, and appears too much unnatural.

When in 1709 Nicholas Rowe edited the first multi-volume Collected Works of Shakespeare he accounted for its acknowledged historical shortcomings by speculating, without evidence, on the nature of the relationship between the playwright and his monarch:

In his *Henry VIII* that Prince is drawn with that greatness of mind, and all those good qualities which are attributed to him in any account of his reign. If his faults are not shewn in an equal degree, and the shades in this picture do not bear a just proportion to the lights, it is not that the artist wanted either colours or skill in his disposition of 'em; but the truth, I believe, might be, that he forbore doing it out of regard to Queen Elizabeth, since it could have been no very great respect to the memory of his mistress, to have expos'd some certain parts of her father's life upon the stage.

Lewis Theobald, a subsequent editor of Shakespeare, wrote to William Warburton in 1730 when part way through his task and seemingly little concerned with history or history plays:

And now, dear Sir, I have done with this Play and Volume I wish we were as well over the historical sett. The two *Henry IVs*, *Henry V*, and *Henry VIII* are full of entertainment and fine things. *John*, *Richard II* and *Richard III* are of the middling stamp: but the three parts of *Henry VI* scarce come up to that character.

Warburton himself, not the most sensitive editor of the period but an influential one, extended the categorization and ranking evident in Theobald's response and chose in his edition of 1747 to comment on the quality of the works by 'dividing them into four Classes, and so giving an estimate of each Play reduced to its proper Class'. He dispensed with History as a category, simply allocating each play to 'Comedies' or 'Tragedies' and listed *Henry VIII* fourth in class II of Tragedies, thus giving it a higher estimate than eleven other plays including *Antony and Cleopatra*, *Richard II*, *Coriolanus* and *Romeo and Juliet*. Warburton concludes his rankings with a note: 'It may just be worth while to observe, in this place, that the whole first Act of *Fletcher's Two Noble Kinsmen* was wrote by *Shakespear*, but in his worst manner.'

While it is evident that the eighteenth century had a higher estimation of the play than the twentieth, there was a growing dissatisfaction with its structure and style, although at the same time there was a reluctance to attribute its perceived weaknesses to Shakespeare. John Upton, objecting in *Critical Observations on Shakespeare* (1748) that the play should have ended with the marriage of Henry to Anne Bullen, suggested 'and what is still worse, when the play was some time after acted before K. James, another prophetical patch of flattery was tacked to it'. In the same year Peter Whalley, in *An Enquiry into the Learning of Shakespeare*, like Rowe before him, engaged in special pleading:

You must have remarked, I think, that the Poet himself was sensible of the Imperfections of his Plots ... for he attempts in many Places to apologize for his Weakness, and reflects severely upon the Judgment of his Audience (particularly in the Prologue ... to *Henry the 8th*).

In his 1765 edition of Shakespeare, Samuel Johnson is blunter than most:

The play of *Henry the Eighth* is one of those which still keeps possession of the stage, by the splendour of its pageantry ... Yet pomp is not the only merit of this play. The meek sorrows and virtuous distress of *Catherine* have furnished some scenes which may be justly numbered among the greatest efforts of tragedy. But the genius of *Shakespeare* comes in and goes out with *Catherine*. Every other part may be easily conceived, and easily written.

While there was growing critical dissatisfaction with the play throughout this period and into the nineteenth century there was little questioning of authorship, other than of the Prologue and Epilogue, until James Spedding, influenced by Alfred Tennyson, asked 'Who wrote Shakespeare's *Henry VIII*?' in the *Gentleman's Magazine* of August 1850. He identified many imperfections:

The effect of the play as a whole is weak and disappointing. The truth is that the interest instead of rising towards the end, falls away utterly, and leaves us in the last act among persons whom we scarcely know and events for which we do not care.

The strongest sympathies which have been awakened in us run
opposite to the course of the action.

He accounted for what he perceived as the imperfections
by suggesting that the play was a collaboration and named
John Fletcher, Shakespeare's known collaborator on *The
Two Noble Kinsmen* and *Cardenio* and his successor as
chief dramatist of The King's Men, as the co-author,
attributing specific scenes and roughly two-thirds of the
play to him. The most recent edition of the play, the
Arden Shakespeare, Third Series, edited by Gordon
McMullan and published in 2000, gives the authors on
the title page as 'William Shakespeare and John Fletcher'
as had the Oxford edition. In 150 years a speculation has
become an orthodoxy, a surprising development given
the apparent lack of evidence to support the claim. What
happened to cause the shift? Those who believe that
Shakespeare is the sole author usually begin their case
with the assumption that when Shakespeare's co-actors
and business colleagues John Heminges and Henry
Condell listed *The Life of King Henry the Eight* in chrono-
logical sequence as the last play in the 'Histories' section
of the Catalogue (that is, the Contents list) of *Mr William
Shakespeares Comedies, Histories, & Tragedies. Published
according to the True Originall Copies* (the first Folio) and
thus became responsible for its first appearance in print
in 1623, they were confident of its authorship. It is possible
to conjecture that, as they excluded other clearly co-
authored plays (*Pericles*, *The Two Noble Kinsmen*, *Sir
Thomas More* and *Edward III*) they can have had no
doubts about *Henry VIII*. The fourth and fifth stanzas of
a contemporary, anonymous manuscript ballad, 'A Sonnet
upon the pitiful burning of the Globe playhouse in
London', refer quite explicitly to the presence of

Heminges and Condell at the memorable performance of the play when the Globe burned down and may provide further evidence of their first-hand knowledge:

> Out run the Knights: out run the Lords
> And there was great ado
> Some lost their hats & some their swords
> Then out run Burbage too
> The reprobates though drunk on Monday
> Prayed for the fool and Henry Condye.
> Oh sorrow pitiful sorrow and yet all this is true.
>
> The periwigs & drum-heads fry
> Like to a butter firkin
> A woeful burning did betide
> To many a good buff jerkin;
> Then with swollen eyes like drunken Flemings
> Distressed stood old stuttering Heminges.
> Oh sorrow pitiful sorrow and yet all this is true.

On the other hand it is perfectly possible for Heminges and Condell to have known that *Henry VIII* was collaborative and to have included it to round off the historical sequence.

Those who argue for joint authorship frequently begin, as did Spedding, with doubts about the quality of the play (usually concerned with its structure, the treatment of the central character and its difference from the other histories) and with a reluctance, therefore, to assign a deficient drama solely to Shakespeare. Fletcher is suggested as co-author and, in the absence of external evidence, metrical, stylistic and linguistic analyses have been employed to find internal support for collaboration and to identify the authorship of individual passages, assuming a clear division of labour. Sole authorship proposers have countered this position by arguing that *Henry VIII* is remarkably coherent, and variations in style within the play or generic difference from the rest of the canon may be accounted for as imaginative or experimental authorial intent. Furthermore the closeness to and consistency of the play with its source material has suggested to some that there must have been a degree of planning and consultation between putative co-authors that is at odds with what is known of theatre working practice. For others the enduring difficulty remained that, despite the attempt to find objective evidence for collaboration, the premise remained a subjective one – that *Henry VIII* was a flawed play, Fletcher a lesser playwright than Shakespeare, so Shakespeare wrote the best bits and Fletcher was responsible for the less effective passages, the flaws. However, in addition to the unfounded criticism of Fletcher's skill, there is something implicitly and conservatively bardolatrous in this position, and Brian Vickers's intensive examination, *Shakespeare Co-Author: A Historical Study of Five Collaborative Plays*, identifies an intriguing pattern in the investigation of Shakespeare's collaborations with Fletcher: a mid-nineteenth-century attribution of scenes written by each dramatist; the findings subsequently consolidated using different methods; conservators denying the findings and asserting sole authorship; and recent scholars with more powerful analytical tools validating the original division of scenes between the two authors. Vickers is the most comprehensive source for details of the analyses of linguistic difference (the work of David Lake, Macdonald Jackson and Jonathan Hope, for example), phrase length, syntactical features (including W. M. Baillie's use of computer programmes) and contractions (J. L. Halio in the Oxford edition) that enable him to conclude, 'All of the scholars who have performed objective tests on the play agree with the authorship division proposed by James Spedding in 1850.' While consensus, broadly, has been achieved, it should be noted that an adjunct to the debate has been the suggestion that questions of authorship matter little to audiences and are an obscure and less important area of critical studies. It is certainly true that much of the late nineteenth-century and twentieth-century work on the play has been concerned with authorship (and thus authority), and it is the major focus of most editions, but the result has been a detailed consideration of the text, an internal examination and a comparison with other texts that ultimately illuminates its merits. Late twentieth-century and twenty-first-century criticism has turned to genre, to political readings of the play, and to its dramatic vitality. A concern with the effect and effectiveness of the totality of the play in performance is coming to the fore. R. A. Foakes, for example, in the 1957 Arden edition of the play, was one of the first to recognize its *dramatic* strengths and to write of its unique structure determined by the four trials. Subsequently others have seen force of purpose and intent rather than weakness in Shakespeare and Fletcher's different use of history and in *Henry VIII*'s closeness in design and style to the other late plays.

The Epilogue, usually attributed to Fletcher because of its colloquialism and simple rhyme scheme, presciently identifies a critical split in the response to the play, perhaps, in itself, an authorial acknowledgement of difference:

'Tis ten to one this play can never please
All that are here.

It is not evident who boldly speaks these lines: it does not appear to be a character from the play and the tone and substance is so very different from the opening Prologue (which makes explicit connections to the drama it precedes) that it may well be a different actor. The Epilogue is formulaic in its appeal for audience approval yet nevertheless, in its negative as well as its positive assertions, serves as a shorthand account for the mixed reception of this challenging play.

Catherine M. S. Alexander

The Play in Performance

The staging of *Henry VIII* presents a series of unique challenges, some generated by the demands of the text but others, rather like the critical reception of the play, generated by the gap between audience expectation and staged actuality. These two difficulties are responsible for what must be the patchiest stage history of any Shakespeare play, for while performances were frequent and popular up to and including the Edwardian period, many are best described as heavily cut adaptations, and professional productions in the UK in the last twenty years can be counted on the fingers of one hand.

Many have found an integral imbalance in the play's structure and shape that has contributed further to its limited performance history. August Wilhelm von Schlegel identified the difficulties in 1808:

Catharine is, properly speaking, the heroine of the piece; she excites the warmest sympathy by her virtues, her defenceless misery, her mild but firm opposition, and her dignified resignation. After her, the fall of Cardinal Wolsey constitutes the principal part of the business. Henry's whole reign was not adapted for dramatic poetry. It would have merely been a repetition of the same scenes: the repudiation, or the execution of his wives, and the disgrace of his most estimable ministers,

which was usually soon followed by death. Of all that distinguished Henry's life Shakespeare has given us sufficient spec-
imens. But as, properly speaking, there is no division in the
history where he breaks off, we must excuse him if he gives
us a flattering compliment of the great Elizabeth for a fortu-
nate catastrophe. The piece ends with the general joy at the
birth of that princess, and with prophecies of the happiness
which she was afterwards to enjoy or to diffuse. It was only
by such a turn that the hazardous freedom of thought in the
rest of the composition could have passed with impunity:
Shakespeare was not certainly himself deceived respecting this
theatrical delusion. The true conclusion is the death of
Catharine, which under a feeling of this kind, he has placed
earlier than was conformable to history. (*The Romantics on
Shakespeare* (1992), pp. 370–71)

His observations are worth extended quotation because
his assumptions are still so widely shared: that the central
character (the hero or, in Schlegel's reading, the heroine)
is identified by virtue and the degree of *suffering* he
experiences; that style ('dramatic poetry') must exclude
repetition; that the conventions of dramatic shape require
death to conclude or provide the climax of the plot; and
that Shakespeare needs excusing for his manipulation of
history.

There is a further difficulty: many Shakespeare plays
remain popular on stage because of their ambiguities,
because they can be reworked and reset for new ages and
places and can, in the post-modern sense, have meanings
imposed upon them. *Henry VIII* and its audiences, however, have been very resistant to such manipulation. It
has proved difficult to present the play and its issues
out of period and create the contemporary relevance
that, for some, is Shakespeare's appeal. The title character

is a case in point: the historical figure is familiar and inhabits a world that is one of the best known in English history. His reign is singularly different from any other. In the play he engages in some of the activities for which he is best remembered – he divorces, remarries once and fathers a child – but while these moments (unique and defining but still potentially transferable to new ages) are an implicit part of the drama they are never, quite, the major focus of the action. The divorce from Katherine is peripheral to her trial, the marriage to Anne peripheral to her coronation, the paternity of Elizabeth peripheral to her christening. Where, exactly, are Henry's great scenes? There is an expectation that his will be the greatest part, but it makes fewer demands on an actor, has a narrower range, than the roles of Wolsey and Katherine. Henry's scenes are a series of snapshots of moments in a life rather than part of a continuous narrative that audiences might expect, and the only moment that has the potential to come near to the 'Bluff King Hal' image of popular imagination is the masque scene, when he encounters Anne Bullen for the first time.

An even stronger preconception and expectation is of Henry's appearance: few, surely, who see Shakespeare's earlier history plays do so with such fixed ideas about the physique and costume of their central characters. Yet the enduring influence of the Holbein representation of King Henry makes an imaginative, non-conventional representation – a slim King, say, or one costumed out of period – almost impossible. The engraving that accompanies the play in the first illustrated edition of Shakespeare (and, indeed, the first *edited* Collected Works after the seventeenth-century folios), by Nicholas Rowe in 1709, features three elegant courtiers in the contemporary court dress of Queen Anne – frock coat and breeches – but historicizes, to the Holbein model, the figure of the King. The tradition for all but the most daring of directors is to limit the potential of performance.

A common response has been to exploit the broad general awareness of the appearance of the King, his contemporaries and the period they inhabited and exaggerate the visual elements of the play to create, in a literal sense, 'a show'. From the Restoration on, when William Davenant first employed scene painters and restaged the play at Lincoln's Inn Fields theatre in December 1663, attempts at presenting a visual historical realism have dominated productions. His 'show' was largely created through new costume and pageantry, 'all new Cloath'd in proper Habits', as John Downes described it, and through the appearance and disposition of actors rather than manipulation of set, and established new standards of display. The prevailing non-naturalistic acting style characterized by static posture and a codified use of gesture lent itself to performance that was less continuous action than a punctuated narrative. Davenant's production, however, may have had some claim to Shakespearian authenticity. John Downes, Davenant's book-keeper, suggests an intriguing line of descent:

The part of the King was so rightly and justly done by Mr Betterton, he being instructed in it by Sir William [Davenant], who had it from old Mr Lowen [an actor with the King's Men], that had his instructions from Mr Shakespeare himself, that I dare and will aver, none can, or will come near him in this age, in the performance of that part. (*Roscius Anglicanus* (1708))

It is sometimes suggested that it is Thomas Betterton, playing opposite John Verbruggen as Wolsey, who is the Henry in the illustration in Nicholas Rowe's edition.

The play remained immensely popular throughout the eighteenth and nineteenth centuries, with all the major actor-managers mounting increasingly spectacular productions. David Garrick, while credited with a much more naturalistic playing style and less operatic use of voice than Betterton, nevertheless opted for spectacle and in 1762 employed over 150 performers for the coronation procession. Kemble, who created his reputation for a visual playing style with the production of *Henry VIII* with which he began his management of Drury Lane in 1788, and which is also remembered for the performance of his sister, Sarah Siddons, as Queen Katherine, subsequently introduced a lavish banquet (1811) that was commented on for its historical realism. Charles Kean, at the Princess's theatre from 1855, was able to exploit advances in stage technology: he took Buckingham to execution in a barge with four oarsmen; he employed 'The Grand Moving Panorama Representing London', and is credited with the first use of a 'follow-spot', a beam of light that focused on the host of angels during Katherine's vision. All of these early effects took time to stage and could only be achieved at the expense of savage textual cuts. Garrick left out the Gentlemen, most of Act III, scene 1 (the Cardinals' visit to Katherine) and cut much of the Porter and longer speeches; the cuts made by Kemble, who published his own revised version of the play, included all Act III, scene 1, the part of Dr Butts and the coronation. Henry Irving's production, from 1892, excised much of the fourth and fifth acts and created a remarkable three-level set for the crowds at the coronation.

The concern with spectacle and the effect of cuts, which extended into the twentieth century with Beerbohm Tree's production of 1910 (which deleted 47 per cent of the text), can disturb the balance of the play, throwing attention on occasion – staged moments and tableaux – rather than on individuals and their dialogue, with the result that the play becomes depoliticized or, at least, that the focus is on the uninterrogated trappings of state. For this reason, perhaps, the performance history of *Henry VIII* became associated with the celebration of national events and performances were confined to the United Kingdom: the play was not performed in Japan, for example, until 1980. The 1727 production by Colley Cibber at Drury Lane introduced an elaborate coronation procession for Anne Bullen to coincide with the coronation of George II. It was the choice for a Royal Command Performance before Queen Victoria and Prince Albert in 1848, with Charlotte Cushman as Katherine and Samuel Phelps as Henry. Tree revived his production in 1911 for the coronation of George V and then took the play to New York in 1916 to mark the tercentenary of Shakespeare's death, while in Stratford and at the Old Vic, in London, Ellen Terry marked the occasion with a performance of a Queen Katherine scene. Tyrone Guthrie's 1949 Stratford-upon-Avon production was revived for the coronation of Queen Elizabeth II in 1953 and when, after World War II, the Old Vic was able to return to the Waterloo Road it celebrated by presenting the entire Shakespearian canon, an ambitious project that was finally completed in 1958 with *Henry VIII*. The crowd scenes, and particularly Elizabeth's christening, are easily manipulated for extravagant displays of nationalism and royalist devotion. John Gielgud, playing Wolsey and best remembered for shedding real tears at his downfall, has a salutary anecdote about the practical difficulties of performing in elaborate costumes: 'The stage at the Vic is not very wide, and in the trial scene both Katherine

[Edith Evans] and Wolsey were encumbered by enormously long trains, and we spent the whole scene moving past each other warily to avoid them getting entangled' (*Shakespeare – Hit or Miss*, p. 85).

Spectacle and pageantry have frequently been achieved through large casts of extras but the play presents casting challenges that are less concerned with numbers than decisions about the central characters. Records suggest that in the early years it was Henry himself who was regarded as the star role, a decision in keeping with a playing style that was characterized by 'exteriority', but with the growth of expectation that stage characters would possess palpable inner lives and could be approached by both actors and audiences through 'interiority' then the favoured parts became Katherine and Wolsey. This was undoubtedly reinforced by the cultural assumption (and theatre company practice) that a play would have a male and female lead. Thus the 'star pairings' shifted from King and Queen (Betterton and his wife Mary Saunderson; James Quin and Mary Porter in the eighteenth century; Kemble and Sarah Siddons), and accounts of the performance history of the play frequently record the emotional displays of Katherine and Wolsey and explore the psychological interest they engender – Gielgud's tears and Katherine, as performed by Siddons, Terry or Ashcroft, fighting then dying – while references to Henries become confined to Holbeinesque comparisons.

Perhaps what both Schlegel and productions with an emphasis on pictorial realism have failed to recognize is the potential in performance for an extended display of dramatic irony: a staging that exploits both the audience's knowledge of 'real' events and the discrepancy between what is flamboyantly displayed and what is

known. This approach was evident in the Royal
Shakespeare Company's production of the play on the
thrust stage of the Swan Theatre in Stratford-upon-Avon
in 1996–7 (and subsequently at the Young Vic Theatre
in London and on tour in the United States), directed by
Gregory Doran. Immediately after the Prologue massive
metal doors opened to allow for the forward propulsion
of a golden, three-tiered block mounted by Henry (Paul
Jesson) on a golden horse, flanked by Katherine (Jane
Lapotaire) and Wolsey (Ian Hogg), a tableau that was a
clear allusion to The Field of Cloth of Gold. Yet any
suggestion that Doran and his designer, Robert Jones,
were opting for uninterrogated pictorial realism was
undercut by the speedy removal of the wordless display
and by the permanent presence of the large letters cut
into the architrave at the rear of the stage proclaiming
'ALL IS TRUE'. Even without a question mark this use
of the play's alternative title was enough to imply cyni-
cism and make the audience alert to the ambiguities of
the subsequent representation of history. And the
simplicity of the production that followed, on a stage that
was, for the most part, bare, showed how effective the
play can be when stripped of visual splendour and the
text is allowed to do the work.

'The text' in this case should extend to the stage directions. It was long argued that stage directions of this
period were playhouse additions, perhaps added by the
book-keeper, but there is a growing view that they may
be authorial and, in *Henry VIII* at least, they offer stim-
ulating opportunities and guidance for actors and directors, reveal aspects of original staging, and allow for
visual nuances to grow from the text rather than be
imposed upon it. The second stage direction of the first
scene, for example ('*Enter Cardinal Wolsey . . .*'), which

can be adhered to without extravagant display, estab-
lishes status, relationship and, through stage properties,
two of the driving strands of the play: Wolsey's greed
and the importance of evidence and the written word —
papers. In addition to choreographing an entrance, the
direction that then describes Henry's first appearance at
the start of the second scene, '*leaning on the Cardinal's
shoulder*', allows an actor exploration of character and
relationship that is not conveyed in the spoken text. The
specificity of the instructions eight lines later, at the
Queen's entrance, that stipulate the movement of both
Henry and Katherine and their kiss, requires the sort of
exploration in rehearsal that is normally generated by
spoken lines not stage directions. The most ambiguous
direction — and the one therefore that affords the greatest
scope in performance — occurs part way through Act II,
scene 2: '*The King draws the curtain and sits reading
pensively*'. Where, on either a modern stage or originally,
at the Globe, has Henry been concealed? Has the audience, in this mini-metatheatrical moment, known that he
was there? Have the other characters on stage? Has the
King been listening to the conversations about his
marriage and divorce and the role of Wolsey? And what
is he reading? It may be a religious work; an illustration
in his Psalter (now in the British Library) shows him
reading in his bedchamber; it may be a legal or financial
document; it may be no more than a cover for his over-
hearing. Answers to such questions will influence the audience's response to the King at this moment and, more
importantly, colour its reception of his subsequent behaviour. William Hazlitt, in his *Characters of Shakespeare's
Plays* (1817), asserts: 'We have often wondered that Henry
VIII as he is drawn by Shakespeare, and as we have seen
him represented in all the bloated deformity of mind and

person, is not hooted from the English stage.' A careful exploration of stage directions gives this play greater subtlety and allows for a more sophisticated representation of character, history and politics than performances – and Hazlitt – have generally allowed.

Catherine M. S. Alexander

subtlety and all...   ...ted representation of character, history and politics than performances

Further Reading

SOURCES AND HISTORICAL
BACKGROUND

Henry VIII is so faithful to its sources that editions often
include long extracts from Holinshed's *Chronicles* (second
edition, 1587) and Foxe's *Acts and Monuments*; see the
editions by W. A. Wright (1895 – including material from
George Cavendish's *Negotiations of Thomas Wolsey*
(1641)), D. Nichol Smith (1899), C. K. Pooler (1915), and
S. Schoenbaum (1967). Particularly valuable are the
extracts given in R. A. Foakes's revised Arden edition
(1957), which clearly relates source-episodes to the play's
scenes, and in J. C. Maxwell's New Cambridge edition
(1962), which presents the relevant chronicle material
before the annotations of each scene.

Sources are fully reprinted and analysed in G. Bullough's *Narrative and Dramatic Sources of Shakespeare*,
Volume 4 (1962) – this includes extracts from Samuel
Rowley's *When You See Me You Know Me* (1605) as well
as Holinshed and Foxe. W. G. Boswell-Stone's *Shakespeare's Holinshed* (1896), and *Holinshed's Chronicle as
Used in Shakespeare's Plays* (1927), as edited by A. and
J. Nicoll in Everyman's Library, are handy sources for
the historical material; both italicize the words most

closely reproduced, but the most satisfactory modern edition for following Holinshed's narrative is *Shakespeare's Holinshed: An Edition of Holinshed's Chronicles (1587)*, selected, edited and annotated by Richard Hosley (New York, 1968). There are editions of Rowley's *When You See Me You Know Me* by Karl Elze (1874), with a list of features common to it and *Henry VIII*, and in the Malone Society Reprints by F. P. Wilson and J. Crow (1952). John Skelton's verses, critical of Wolsey, can be found in Penguin's edition of Skelton, *The Complete English Poems* (1983).

Peter Saccio compares the reality of Henry's reign with Shakespeare's dramatized version in *Shakespeare's English Kings: History, Chronicle, and Drama* (1977), and reliable and readable historical accounts of the period can be found in Eric Ives's *The Life and Death of Anne Boleyn* (2004) and David Starkey's *The Reign of Henry VIII: Personalities and Politics* (1985) and *Six Wives: The Queens of Henry VIII* (2003). The intellectual life of the period is revealed in James P. Carley's *The Books of Henry VIII and His Wives* (2005). Joyceline G. Russell's immensely detailed *The Field of Cloth of Gold: Men and Manners in 1520* (1969) is the best source of background information for the opening scene of the play, and contemporary details of the occasion can be found in Edward Hall's sixteenth-century *Henry VIII* in the 1904 edition with an introduction by Charles Whibley. Gerard B. Wegemer discusses the relationship between the play and Thomas More's trial in 'Henry VIII on Trial: Confronting Malice and Conscience in Shakespeare's *All is True*' in *Shakespeare's Last Plays: Essays in Literature and Politics*, edited by Stephen W. Smith and Travis Curtwright (2002).

For the historical context of the period of the play's

composition David Bergeron's *Shakespeare's Romances and the Royal Family* (1985) and Michael Dobson and Nicola J. Watson's *England's Elizabeth: An Afterlife in Fame and Fantasy* (2002) are helpful. Judith H. Anderson's *Biographical Truth: the Representations of Historical Persons in Tudor-Stuart Writing* (1984) compares Shakespeare's use of history in *Henry VIII* with others in the canon, and in '*Art Made Tongue-tied by Authority*': *Elizabethan and Jacobean Dramatic Censorship* (1990) Janet Clare considers the formal constraints on writing history. Andrew Gurr's *The Shakespeare Company 1594–1642* (2004) is an indispensable guide to contemporary playing conditions, staging and theatre organization and is a useful source for original documentation concerning *Henry VIII*. Further sources can be located in Arthur Kinney's *Elizabethan Backgrounds: Historical Documents of the Age of Elizabeth I* (1975), and Henry Bluett's description of the Globe fire is discussed by M. J. Cole in 'A New Account of the Burning of the Globe', *Shakespeare Quarterly* 32 (1981).

For contemporary understanding and readings of history see Dominique Goy-Blanquet's 'Elizabethan Historiography and Shakespeare's Sources' in *The Cambridge Companion to Shakespeare's History Plays*, edited by Michael Hattaway (2002), and Ivo Kamps's *Historiography and Ideology in Stuart Drama* (1996).

TEXTS

The earliest edition is that in the First Folio (1623), of which there are modern facsimiles edited by Sidney Lee (1902), H. Kökeritz and C. T. Prouty (1955), and Charlton Hinman (1969). C. K. Pooler's original Arden edition of *Henry VIII* (1915) abounds in illustrative material; R. A. Foakes's revised Arden (1957) and J. C. Maxwell's New Cambridge (1962) editions are outstanding, with excellent introductions and annotations. Other good modern editions are those by John Munro (London Shakespeare, Volume 4, 1958) and F. D. Hoeniger (*The Complete Pelican Shakespeare*, 1969). The Signet edition by S. Schoenbaum (1967) has a useful introduction, source material, and extracts from critical commentaries. John Margeson's summary of the authorship debate in the New Cambridge edition (1990) is clear and concise and the third appendix of Gordon McMullan's edition (Arden Third Series, 2000) provides a useful diagram of the range of authorial attribution. Jay L. Halio's edition (Oxford, 1999) includes new stylistic measurements of authorship and is perhaps the most even-handed account of the issue.

Analyses of textual matters are to be found in E. K. Chambers, *William Shakespeare*, Vol. 1 (1930), W. W. Greg, *The Shakespeare First Folio* (1955), R. A. Foakes, in *Studies in Bibliography*, Vol. 2 (1958), and J. C. Maxwell's edition. The unusually elaborate stage directions are discussed by W. J. Lawrence, in 'The Stage Directions in *King Henry VIII*', *Times Literary Supplement* (18 December 1930), and P. Alexander (*Times Literary Supplement*, 1 January 1931).

AUTHORSHIP

A balanced and fair account of the arguments for and against dual authorship is given in R. A. Foakes's Arden edition; the conclusion is that Shakespeare was sole author. Equally skilful, but concluding in the opposite

sense, is J. C. Maxwell's discussion in the New Cambridge edition. The editions by John Munro and F. D.
Hoeniger (see above) have briefer but clear and inform-
ative examinations of the problem. For a clear assessment of the range of tests that have been applied to the
text, including Jonathan Hope's important *The
Authorship of Shakespeare's Plays: A Socio-linguistic Study*
(1994), see Brian Vickers's *Shakespeare, Co-Author: A
Historical Study of Five Collaborative Plays* (2002). In
'"To Reform and Make Fitt": *Henry VIII* and the Making
of "Bad" Shakespeare' Iska Alter argues that the authorship debate has diverted attention from the dramatic
strengths of the play (in Maurice Charney's *"Bad"
Shakespeare: Revaluations of the Shakespeare Canon*
(1988)).

Against collaboration: the following are the more note-
worthy arguments against collaboration, set out chronologically.

A. C. Swinburne, *A Study of Shakespeare* (1880), recog-
nizes Fletcherian qualities yet judges the play to be all
Shakespeare's, being marked by 'pathos and concentra-
tion' beyond Fletcher's powers and by a 'unity or concord
of inner tone' which is Shakespeare's. The essay is readable, but its criticism is not sharp enough to validate its
stylistic judgements.

Baldwin Maxwell, 'Fletcher and Shakespeare' (*Manly
Anniversary Studies* (1923); revised in *Studies in Beaumont, Fletcher, and Massinger* (1939)), rejects Fletcher as
participant on the grounds that his manner elsewhere
shows differences of syntax, metre, and style from his
supposed share in *Henry VIII*, and a much looser use of
sources.

Peter Alexander, 'Conjectural History, or Shakespeare's *Henry VIII*' (*Essays and Studies of the English Association*, edited by H. J. C. Grierson, Volume 16, 1930), rejects arguments based on the imprecisions of line-counts and similar statistics, and the guesswork of some of Spedding's speculations, and finds throughout the play the 'compassionate spirit of the Fourth Period'. But the argument, briefly resumed in *Shakespeare's Life and Art* (1939), is critically disappointing, and many of the contentions are little more than debating points.

G. Wilson Knight, '*Henry VIII* and the Poetry of Conversion' (*The Crown of Life*, 1947), comes out whole-heartedly against collaboration, asserting that those elements which look Fletcherian are fundamentally related to Shakespeare's poetic, moral, and symbolical procedures throughout his writing life.

Hardin Craig, *An Interpretation of Shakespeare* (1948): the play is 'written throughout ... in the latest variety of Shakespeare's last style', 'consistently well-planned', and 'from the point of view of form ... one of his greatest achievements', and so not collaborative. These contentions are unconvincing, but the account of the play is pleasant and balanced though without special insights; a useful point is made (as against Hazlitt's anti-Henry diatribe) that the Elizabethans viewed Henry, on the whole, favourably.

R. A. Foakes, in a well-conducted argument (Arden edition, 1957), admits the force of claims for collaboration, but concludes that the play shows wide-ranging and single-minded scholarship in its use of source material and that it is allied in spirit and imaginative processes to Shakespeare's other late plays.

G. Bullough, *Narrative and Dramatic Sources of Shakespeare*, Volume 4 (1962): a single directing mind is indicated by the evidence of coherent controlling intentions, integration of plot, and well-dovetailed use of sources.

Paul Bertram, '*Henry VIII*: the Conscience of the King' (*In Defense of Reading*, edited by R. A. Brower and R. Poirier (1962)), defends the play's unity in terms of the main characters' relations with the King – 'The action . . . shows us a King who reigns becoming a King who rules' – and this unity, as well as the deliberate interconnecting of events, suggests single authorship. In *Shakespeare and 'The Two Noble Kinsmen'* (New Brunswick, 1965), Bertram restates the argument for unity of themes, and includes a long survey of the authorship controversy.

A. C. Sprague, *Shakespeare's Histories: Plays for the Stage* (1964), considers metrical counts unreliable, and collaboration which left the major scenes to the junior partner unlikely. Divided authorship would hardly produce such unifying themes of greatness spiritually redeemed, expressed with integrity of feeling.

For collaboration: the fundamental essay is that of James Spedding, whose 'Who Wrote Shakespere's *Henry VIII*?' appeared in the *Gentleman's Magazine* for August 1850 and was reprinted as 'On the Several Shares of Shakspere and Fletcher in the Play of *Henry VIII*' in *Transactions of the New Shakspere Society* for 1874. Many later commentators either accept Spedding's case as proven or add to it minor (though often useful) corroborative evidence. Independently of Spedding, Ralph Waldo Emerson in a lecture published in *Representative Men* (1850) had announced two styles in the play, the earlier by a thoughtful writer marked by a conscious and artificial eloquence, the later by Shakespeare, spontaneous and original. The following are the more note-

worthy later arguments for collaboration, set out
chronologically.

Ashley H. Thorndike, *The Influence of Beaumont and
Fletcher on Shakespeare* (1901), detects a marked prepon-
derance of 'them' in the 'Shakespeare' scenes and of
"em' in the 'Fletcher'.

Marjorie Nicolson, 'The Authorship of *Henry VIII*'
(*Publications of the Modern Language Association of
America*, Volume 37, 1922), speculates that Shakespeare
established the themes (mainly the precariousness of high
place) and that Fletcher amplified them, worked them
through, and provided pathos and social entertainment.
The argument is not convincing.

A. C. Partridge, *The Problem of 'Henry VIII' Reopened*
(1949), supports Spedding on grounds of stylistic and
syntactical differences, and the differing distributions
of the expletive 'do', 'hath'/'has', 'them'/"em', and
'ye'/'you', suggesting also that Shakespeare may have
written part of IV.2 (before Katherine's vision) and of
Cranmer's eulogy in V.5.

E. M. Waith, *The Pattern of Tragi-Comedy in Beaumont
and Fletcher* (1952): *Henry VIII* is accepted as collaborative; the eloquence of the major speeches in Fletcher's
share is the kind he uses for his 'biggest effects', and the
pageantry is congenial to his procedures.

Ants Oras, '"Extra Monosyllables" in *Henry VIII* and
the Problem of Authorship' (*Journal of English and
Germanic Philology*, Volume 52, 1953), analyses the
different rhythms produced by such extra monosyllables
in the 'Shakespeare' and 'Fletcher' scenes. A useful essay,
though the sense of rhythm is not impeccable.

W. W. Greg, *The Shakespeare First Folio* (Oxford,
1955): textual matters are the main concern, but joint
authorship is accepted as proven.

John Munro, London Shakespeare edition, Volume 4 (1958): the various arguments are defined with care; the conclusion is that Spedding was 'generally right'.

R. A. Law, 'The Double Authorship of *Henry VIII*' (*Studies in Philology*, Volume 56, 1959): this thorough and convincing survey of evidence presents a firm conclusion for joint authorship from the distribution of light/weak endings, endings consisting of verbs and unstressed pronouns, sentence- and syntax-forms, and the dramatic characteristics of the two shares.

Kenneth Muir, *Shakespeare as Collaborator* (1960), does not deal specifically with *Henry VIII* but shares *The Two Noble Kinsmen* between Shakespeare and Fletcher, on grounds of rhythmical habits, style, and image-associations, in a way which throws an interesting light on procedures for studying *Henry VIII*.

Marco Mincoff, '*Henry VIII* and Fletcher' (*Shakespeare Quarterly*, 1961): this admirable analysis subjects the evidence to a most scholarly and critical scrutiny, resulting in the conclusion that 'every single test applied leads to the same clear division into two separate styles, and one of these styles always points to Fletcher ... It is not a question of slight, or even of marked, fluctuations with regard to one or two indicators alone, but of two fundamentally different styles.'

J. C. Maxwell, New Cambridge edition (1962), argues cogently against single authorship, taking metrical, prosodic, and grammatical peculiarities to corroborate a division made out clearly on stylistic grounds.

Clifford Leech, *Shakespeare: the Chronicles* (1962): no decisive solution is thought likely, but the play's lack of true structure and development 'reminds us of Fletcher. Here we do not have the sense that as the play proceeds we are approaching an increasingly complex view of the characters and situation.' In *The John Fletcher Plays* (1962) the idea is further discussed that 'at different moments we are offered differing views of the play's events and characters'. This inconsistency is like Fletcher's practice.

M. P. Jackson, 'Affirmative Particles in *Henry VIII*' (*Notes and Queries*, Volume 207, October 1962): the varying uses of 'ay', 'yea', and 'yes' in the two shares of the play correspond to the contrasted practices of Shakespeare and Fletcher elsewhere.

GENERAL CRITICISM

The best criticism is to be found in the introductions to the revised Arden and New Cambridge editions; briefer but very effective commentary is offered by John Munro in the London Shakespeare edition, Volume 4, by F. D. Hoeniger in *The Complete Pelican Shakespeare*, and by G. Bullough in *Narrative and Dramatic Sources of Shakespeare*, Volume 4.

William Hazlitt, in *Characters of Shakespeare's Plays* (1817), offers little of critical significance, but expresses a characteristically strong objection to the King, as gross, blustering, vulgar, and hypocritical; this may provoke one to a more judicious assessment, prompted less by anti-monarchical fervour and more by recognition of Henry's care for just government and his kingdom's welfare, which the play makes clear. The ambiguity about Henry's 'conscience' is discussed in the Commentary on I.4.75.

G. Wilson Knight's essay '*Henry VIII* and the Poetry of Conversion' (*The Crown of Life*, 1947) is insufficiently discriminating in collecting and 'comparing' features from the whole body of Shakespeare's work. The analysis of style it offers to prove Shakespeare's sole authorship is too subjectively biased to carry conviction.

J. F. Kermode's 'What is Shakespeare's *Henry VIII* about?' (*Durham University Journal*, N.S. Volume 9, 1948; reprinted in *Shakespeare: the Histories*, edited by E. M. Waith (1965) and in *Shakespeare's Histories: An Anthology of Modern Criticism*, edited by William A. Armstrong, (1972)) is a shrewd, interesting essay, arguing that Henry is the play's centre, essential to England's welfare, 'exercising certain God-like functions'; the structure is that of a new kind of *Mirror for Magistrates*, a 'late morality, showing the state from which great ones fall'.

In 'The Structure of the Last Plays' (*Shakespeare Survey 11*, 1958) Clifford Leech suggests that the last plays (*Henry VIII* most evidently) imply cycles of action larger than the plays' own compass.

J. R. Sutherland's 'The Language of the Last Plays' (*More Talking of Shakespeare*, edited by John Garrett (1959)) comments interestingly on the late plays' supercharged writing and daring stylistic procedures, which threaten to become too complex for drama.

E. M. W. Tillyard, in 'Why Did Shakespeare Write *Henry VIII*?' (*Critical Quarterly*, Volume 3, 1961), judges it to be written with professional competence but without consistent vitality – a play of 'the Master in his old age' (Shakespeare was forty-nine) – much below *The Winter's Tale* and *Cymbeline* in quality, but revealing 'prodigious skill and experience' in making a well-constructed play from Holinshed's heterogeneous material.

John Wasson's essay 'In Defense of *Henry VIII*' (*Research Studies of Washington University*, Volume 32, Number 3, September 1964) argues that, judged in the terms of a history play – a sequence of events, rather

than analysis of character – it is well constructed, with
a coherent design, and that 'the theme is the significance
of the age of Henry VIII and the relationships among
the events of that age'. The succession of falls from high
place is not a dramatic weakness but a true account of
the course of history, accompanied by the approved moral
of noble acquiescence.

Reassessments of the play, largely driven by new
generic readings, are significant elements of Howard
Felperin's *Shakespearean Romance* (1972), Jennifer
Richards's and James Knowles's *Shakespeare's Late
Plays: New Readings* (1999) and Peter L. Rudnytsky's
essay '*Henry VIII* and the Deconstruction of History'
(*Shakespeare Survey* 43, 1991). Political readings of the
play are integral to Leonard Tennenhouse's 'Strategies
of State and Political Plays . . .' in *Political Shakespeare:
New Essays in Cultural Materialism*, edited by Jonathan
Dollimore and Alan Sinfield (1985) and *Power on Display:
The Politics of Shakespeare's Genres* (1986), and form part
of Simon Palfrey's *Late Shakespeare: A New World of
Words* (1997). Phyllis Rackin's *Stages of History:
Shakespeare's English Chronicles* (1990) has a focus on class
and gender and the subversive potential of the repre-
sentation of history.

STAGE HISTORY

The introductions of John Margeson's edition (New
Cambridge, 1990) and Gordon McMullan's edition
(Arden, 2000) include illustrated performance histories
covering a range of playing spaces, with the latter
providing perceptive commentary on 'authenticity'.
Pepys's visits to *Henry VIII* are recorded in his *Diary*,

edited by R. C. Latham and W. Matthews (1970–83), and eighteenth-century comments on performance (and criticism) are most easily located in Brian Vickers's *Shakespeare: The Critical Heritage* (1974–81). Jonathan Bate's collection *The Romantics on Shakespeare* (1992) includes Schlegel's and Hazlitt's comments on *Henry VIII*. The stage history is well related by G. C. D. Odell in *Shakespeare – From Betterton to Irving* (two volumes, 1920; reprinted 1966), and C. B. Young in the New Cambridge edition. C. B. Hogan's *Shakespeare in the Theatre, 1701–1800* (two volumes, 1952, 1957) enumerates performances and cast lists. There are shorter but useful discussions by A. C. Sprague in *Shakespeare's Histories: Plays for the Stage* (1964) and R. A. Foakes in the new Arden edition. W. Moelwyn Merchant's *Shakespeare and the Artist* (1959) has interesting pages on some of the scenic effects, and particularly on Queen Katherine's trial scene as presented by J. P. Kemble and some later producers. Muriel St Clare Byrne, writing on 'A Stratford Production: *Henry VIII*' (*Shakespeare Survey* 3, 1950), gives a finely observant account of Tyrone Guthrie's distinguished revival of 1949, stressing the character balances – 'a play for genuine team-work ... not rival stars ... a play about the Tudor succession by an Elizabethan'. G. Wilson Knight's description, in his *Principles of Shakespearean Production* (1936; revised as *Shakespearian Production*, 1964), of this play as he staged it in 1934 at the Hart House Theatre, Toronto, is a document of truly sympathetic insight. Hugh M. Richmond gives a detailed account of six productions, including the BBC version, in *Shakespeare in Performance: King Henry VIII* (1994). John Gielgud writes of playing Wolsey in *Shakespeare – Hit or Miss* (1991) and Paul Jesson and Jane Lapotaire give revealing accounts of performing as Henry and Katherine in Stratford in 1996 in Robert Smallwood's *Players of Shakespeare 4: Further Essays in Shakespearian Performances by Players with the Royal Shakespeare Company* (1998).

A. R. Humphreys,
revised by Michael Taylor
and Catherine M. S. Alexander

KING HENRY THE EIGHTH

The Characters in the Play

KING HENRY THE EIGHTH

DUKE OF BUCKINGHAM
DUKE OF NORFOLK
DUKE OF SUFFOLK
EARL OF SURREY
LORD ABERGAVENNY
LORD SANDS (Sir Walter Sands)
LORD CHAMBERLAIN
LORD CHANCELLOR
SIR HENRY GUILFORD
SIR THOMAS LOVELL
SIR NICHOLAS VAUX
SIR ANTHONY DENNY

CARDINAL WOLSEY
THOMAS CROMWELL, in Wolsey's service, afterwards
   in the King's
SECRETARY to Wolsey
SERVANT to Wolsey
CARDINAL CAMPEIUS
CAPUCHIUS, ambassador from the Emperor Charles
   the Fifth
GARDINER, Secretary to the King, afterwards Bishop
   of Winchester

PAGE to Gardiner
BISHOP OF LINCOLN
THOMAS CRANMER, Archbishop of Canterbury
BRANDON
SERGEANT-AT-ARMS
SURVEYOR to the Duke of Buckingham
Three GENTLEMEN
SCRIBE
CRIER
MESSENGER to Queen Katherine
KEEPER of the Council Chamber
DOCTOR BUTTS
PORTER
Porter's MAN
GARTER KING-OF-ARMS

QUEEN KATHERINE, wife of King Henry, afterwards
    divorced
GRIFFITH, gentleman usher to Queen Katherine
PATIENCE, Queen Katherine's woman
GENTLEWOMAN ⎫
                      ⎬ attending upon Queen Katherine
GENTLEMAN   ⎭

ANNE BULLEN
OLD LADY, friend of Anne Bullen

Speaker of the PROLOGUE and EPILOGUE

Lords, Ladies, Gentlemen; Bishops, Priests, Vergers;
Judges; Lord Mayor of London, Aldermen, Citizens;
Guards, Tipstaves, Halberdiers; Scribes, Secretaries;
Attendants, Pursuivants, Pages, Choristers, Musicians,
Dancers as spirits appearing to Queen Katherine

The Prologue

I come no more to make you laugh. Things now
That bear a weighty and a serious brow,
Sad, high, and working, full of state and woe,
Such noble scenes as draw the eye to flow,
We now present. Those that can pity here
May, if they think it well, let fall a tear;
The subject will deserve it. Such as give
Their money out of hope they may believe
May here find truth too. Those that come to see
Only a show or two, and so agree   10
The play may pass, if they be still, and willing,
I'll undertake may see away their shilling
Richly in two short hours. Only they
That come to hear a merry, bawdy play,
A noise of targets, or to see a fellow
In a long motley coat guarded with yellow,
Will be deceived; for, gentle hearers, know
To rank our chosen truth with such a show
As fool and fight is, beside forfeiting
Our own brains, and the opinion that we bring   20
To make that only true we now intend,
Will leave us never an understanding friend.
Therefore, for goodness' sake, and as you are known
The first and happiest hearers of the town,

Be sad, as we would make ye. Think ye see
The very persons of our noble story
As they were living; think you see them great,
And followed with the general throng and sweat
Of thousand friends: then, in a moment, see
30   How soon this mightiness meets misery.
And if you can be merry then, I'll say
A man may weep upon his wedding day.

Enter the Duke of Norfolk at one door; at the other,   I.1
the Duke of Buckingham and the Lord Abergavenny

BUCKINGHAM
Good morrow, and well met. How have ye done
Since last we saw in France?

NORFOLK   I thank your grace,
Healthful, and ever since a fresh admirer
Of what I saw there.

BUCKINGHAM   An untimely ague
Stayed me a prisoner in my chamber when
Those suns of glory, those two lights of men,
Met in the vale of Andren.

NORFOLK   'Twixt Guynes and Arde.
I was then present, saw them salute on horseback,
Beheld them when they lighted, how they clung
In their embracement, as they grew together;   10
Which had they, what four throned ones could have
     weighed
Such a compounded one?

BUCKINGHAM   All the whole time
I was my chamber's prisoner.

NORFOLK   Then you lost
The view of earthly glory; men might say,
Till this time pomp was single, but now married

To one above itself. Each following day
Became the next day's master, till the last
Made former wonders its. Today the French,
All clinquant, all in gold, like heathen gods,
20   Shone down the English; and tomorrow they
Made Britain India; every man that stood
Showed like a mine. Their dwarfish pages were
As cherubins, all gilt; the madams too,
Not used to toil, did almost sweat to bear
The pride upon them, that their very labour
Was to them as a painting. Now this masque
Was cried incomparable; and th'ensuing night
Made it a fool and beggar. The two Kings,
Equal in lustre, were now best, now worst,
30   As presence did present them: him in eye
Still him in praise; and being present both,
'Twas said they saw but one, and no discerner
Durst wag his tongue in censure. When these suns –
For so they phrase 'em – by their heralds challenged
The noble spirits to arms, they did perform
Beyond thought's compass, that former fabulous story,
Being now seen possible enough, got credit,
That Bevis was believed.

BUCKINGHAM   O, you go far!

NORFOLK
As I belong to worship, and affect
40   In honour honesty, the tract of everything
Would by a good discourser lose some life
Which action's self was tongue to. All was royal;
To the disposing of it naught rebelled.
Order gave each thing view; the office did
Distinctly his full function.

BUCKINGHAM   Who did guide –
I mean, who set the body and the limbs

Of this great sport together, as you guess?

NORFOLK

One, certes, that promises no element
In such a business.

BUCKINGHAM   I pray you, who, my lord?

NORFOLK

All this was ordered by the good discretion   50
Of the right reverend Cardinal of York.

BUCKINGHAM

The devil speed him! No man's pie is freed
From his ambitious finger. What had he
To do in these fierce vanities? I wonder
That such a keech can with his very bulk
Take up the rays o'th'beneficial sun,
And keep it from the earth.

NORFOLK   Surely, sir,
There's in him stuff that puts him to these ends;
For, being not propped by ancestry, whose grace
Chalks successors their way, nor called upon   60
For high feats done to th'crown, neither allied
To eminent assistants, but spider-like,
Out of his self-drawing web, 'a gives us note,
The force of his own merit makes his way –
A gift that heaven gives for him, which buys
A place next to the King.

ABERGAVENNY   I cannot tell
What heaven hath given him – let some graver eye
Pierce into that; but I can see his pride
Peep through each part of him. Whence has he that?
If not from hell, the devil is a niggard,   70
Or has given all before, and he begins
A new hell in himself.

BUCKINGHAM   Why the devil,
Upon this French going out, took he upon him –

Without the privity o'th'King – t'appoint
Who should attend on him? He makes up the file
Of all the gentry, for the most part such
To whom as great a charge as little honour
He meant to lay upon; and his own letter,
The honourable board of Council out,
80   Must fetch him in he papers.

ABERGAVENNY   I do know
Kinsmen of mine, three at the least, that have
By this so sickened their estates that never
They shall abound as formerly.

BUCKINGHAM   O, many
Have broke their backs with laying manors on 'em
For this great journey. What did this vanity
But minister communication of
A most poor issue?

NORFOLK   Grievingly I think
The peace between the French and us not values
The cost that did conclude it.

BUCKINGHAM   Every man,
90   After the hideous storm that followed, was
A thing inspired, and, not consulting, broke
Into a general prophecy – that this tempest,
Dashing the garment of this peace, aboded
The sudden breach on't.

NORFOLK   Which is budded out;
For France hath flawed the league, and hath attached
Our merchants' goods at Bordeaux.

ABERGAVENNY   Is it therefore
Th'ambassador is silenced?

NORFOLK   Marry, is't.

ABERGAVENNY
A proper title of a peace, and purchased
At a superfluous rate!

BUCKINGHAM   Why, all this business
Our reverend Cardinal carried.

NORFOLK   Like it your grace,   100
The state takes notice of the private difference
Betwixt you and the Cardinal. I advise you –
And take it from a heart that wishes towards you
Honour and plenteous safety – that you read
The Cardinal's malice and his potency
Together; to consider further, that
What his high hatred would effect wants not
A minister in his power. You know his nature,
That he's revengeful; and I know his sword
Hath a sharp edge – it's long, and't may be said   110
It reaches far, and where 'twill not extend,
Thither he darts it. Bosom up my counsel;
You'll find it wholesome. Lo, where comes that rock
That I advise your shunning.

        Enter Cardinal Wolsey, the purse borne before him,
        certain of the guard, and two Secretaries with papers.
        The Cardinal in his passage fixeth his eye on Bucking-
        ham, and Buckingham on him, both full of disdain

WOLSEY
The Duke of Buckingham's surveyor, ha?
Where's his examination?

SECRETARY   Here, so please you.

WOLSEY
Is he in person ready?

SECRETARY   Ay, please your grace.

WOLSEY
Well, we shall then know more, and Buckingham
Shall lessen this big look.

                        Exeunt Cardinal and his train

BUCKINGHAM
This butcher's cur is venom-mouthed, and I   120

Have not the power to muzzle him; therefore best
Not wake him in his slumber. A beggar's book
Outworths a noble's blood.

NORFOLK   What, are you chafed?
Ask God for temperance; that's th'appliance only
Which your disease requires.

BUCKINGHAM   I read in's looks
Matter against me, and his eye reviled
Me as his abject object. At this instant
He bores me with some trick. He's gone to th'King.
I'll follow, and outstare him.

NORFOLK   Stay, my lord,
130   And let your reason with your choler question
What 'tis you go about. To climb steep hills
Requires slow pace at first. Anger is like
A full hot horse, who being allowed his way,
Self-mettle tires him. Not a man in England
Can advise me like you: be to yourself
As you would to your friend.

BUCKINGHAM   I'll to the King,
And from a mouth of honour quite cry down
This Ipswich fellow's insolence, or proclaim
There's difference in no persons.

NORFOLK   Be advised:
140   Heat not a furnace for your foe so hot
That it do singe yourself. We may outrun
By violent swiftness that which we run at,
And lose by over-running. Know you not
The fire that mounts the liquor till't run o'er
In seeming to augment it wastes it? Be advised.
I say again there is no English soul
More stronger to direct you than yourself,
If with the sap of reason you would quench
Or but allay the fire of passion.

BUCKINGHAM   Sir,
   I am thankful to you, and I'll go along   150
   By your prescription; but this top-proud fellow –
   Whom from the flow of gall I name not, but
   From sincere motions – by intelligence,
   And proofs as clear as founts in July when
   We see each grain of gravel, I do know
   To be corrupt and treasonous.
NORFOLK   Say not treasonous.
BUCKINGHAM
   To th'King I'll say't, and make my vouch as strong
   As shore of rock. Attend: this holy fox,
   Or wolf, or both – for he is equal ravenous
   As he is subtle, and as prone to mischief   160
   As able to perform't, his mind and place
   Infecting one another, yea, reciprocally –
   Only to show his pomp, as well in France
   As here at home, suggests the King our master
   To this last costly treaty, th'interview
   That swallowed so much treasure, and like a glass
   Did break i'th'wrenching.
NORFOLK   Faith, and so it did.
BUCKINGHAM
   Pray give me favour, sir. This cunning Cardinal
   The articles o'th'combination drew
   As himself pleased; and they were ratified   170
   As he cried 'Thus let be', to as much end
   As give a crutch to th'dead. But our Count-Cardinal
   Has done this, and 'tis well; for worthy Wolsey,
   Who cannot err, he did it. Now this follows –
   Which, as I take it, is a kind of puppy
   To th'old dam, treason – Charles the Emperor,
   Under pretence to see the Queen his aunt –
   For 'twas indeed his colour, but he came

To whisper Wolsey – here makes visitation.
His fears were that the interview betwixt
England and France might through their amity
Breed him some prejudice, for from this league
Peeped harms that menaced him. He privily
Deals with our Cardinal, and, as I trow –
Which I do well, for I am sure the Emperor
Paid ere he promised, whereby his suit was granted
Ere it was asked – but when the way was made,
And paved with gold, the Emperor thus desired
That he would please to alter the King's course
And break the foresaid peace. Let the King know,
As soon he shall by me, that thus the Cardinal
Does buy and sell his honour as he pleases,
And for his own advantage.

NORFOLK   I am sorry
To hear this of him, and could wish he were
Something mistaken in't.

BUCKINGHAM   No, not a syllable:
I do pronounce him in that very shape
He shall appear in proof.

Enter Brandon, a Sergeant-at-Arms before him, and
two or three of the guard

BRANDON
Your office, sergeant: execute it.

SERGEANT   Sir,
My lord the Duke of Buckingham, and Earl
Of Hereford, Stafford, and Northampton, I
Arrest thee of high treason, in the name
Of our most sovereign King.

BUCKINGHAM   Lo you, my lord,
The net has fall'n upon me! I shall perish
Under device and practice.

BRANDON   I am sorry

To see you ta'en from liberty, to look on
The business present. 'Tis his highness' pleasure
You shall to th'Tower.

BUCKINGHAM   It will help me nothing
To plead mine innocence, for that dye is on me
Which makes my whit'st part black. The will of heaven
Be done in this and all things! I obey.   210
O my Lord Aberga'nny, fare you well!

BRANDON
Nay, he must bear you company. (*To Abergavenny*) The
        King
Is pleased you shall to th'Tower, till you know
How he determines further.

ABERGAVENNY   As the Duke said,
The will of heaven be done, and the King's pleasure
By me obeyed.

BRANDON   Here is a warrant from
The King, t'attach Lord Montacute, and the bodies
Of the Duke's confessor, John de la Car,
One Gilbert Perk, his chancellor –

BUCKINGHAM   So, so;
These are the limbs o'th'plot: no more, I hope.   220

BRANDON
A monk o'th'Chartreux.

BUCKINGHAM   O, Nicholas Hopkins?

BRANDON   He.

BUCKINGHAM
My surveyor is false. The o'er-great Cardinal
Hath showed him gold. My life is spanned already.
I am the shadow of poor Buckingham,
Whose figure even this instant cloud puts on
By darkening my clear sun. My lord, farewell. *Exeunt*

I.2   *Cornets. Enter King Henry, leaning on the Cardinal's*
             shoulder, the nobles, and Sir Thomas Lovell. The
             Cardinal places himself under the King's feet on his
             right side. Wolsey's Secretary in attendance

KING HENRY
             My life itself, and the best heart of it,
             Thanks you for this great care. I stood i'th'level
             Of a full-charged confederacy, and give thanks
             To you that choked it. Let be called before us
             That gentleman of Buckingham's. In person
             I'll hear him his confessions justify,
             And point by point the treasons of his master
             He shall again relate.

             A noise within, crying 'Room for the Queen!'
             Enter the Queen, ushered by the Dukes of Norfolk
             and Suffolk. She kneels. The King riseth from his
             state, takes her up, kisses and placeth her by him

QUEEN KATHERINE
             Nay, we must longer kneel: I am a suitor.

KING HENRY
10   Arise, and take place by us. Half your suit
             Never name to us: you have half our power.
             The other moiety ere you ask is given.
             Repeat your will, and take it.

QUEEN KATHERINE   Thank your majesty.
             That you would love yourself, and in that love
             Not unconsiderèd leave your honour nor
             The dignity of your office, is the point
             Of my petition.

KING HENRY   Lady mine, proceed.

QUEEN KATHERINE
             I am solicited, not by a few,
             And those of true condition, that your subjects
20   Are in great grievance. There have been commissions

Sent down among 'em which hath flawed the heart
Of all their loyalties; wherein, although,
My good lord Cardinal, they vent reproaches
Most bitterly on you as putter-on
Of these exactions, yet the King our master –
Whose honour heaven shield from soil! – even he
    escapes not
Language unmannerly, yea, such which breaks
The sides of loyalty, and almost appears
In loud rebellion.

NORFOLK   Not 'almost appears' –
It doth appear; for, upon these taxations,   30
The clothiers all, not able to maintain
The many to them 'longing, have put off
The spinsters, carders, fullers, weavers, who,
Unfit for other life, compelled by hunger
And lack of other means, in desperate manner
Daring th'event to th'teeth, are all in uproar,
And danger serves among them.

KING HENRY   Taxation?
Wherein? and what taxation? My lord Cardinal,
You that are blamed for it alike with us,
Know you of this taxation?

WOLSEY   Please you, sir,   40
I know but of a single part in aught
Pertains to th'state, and front but in that file
Where others tell steps with me.

QUEEN KATHERINE   No, my lord?
You know no more than others? But you frame
Things that are known alike, which are not wholesome
To those which would not know them, and yet must
Perforce be their acquaintance. These exactions,
Whereof my sovereign would have note, they are
Most pestilent to th'hearing, and to bear 'em

50   The back is sacrifice to th'load. They say
        They are devised by you, or else you suffer
        Too hard an exclamation.
        KING HENRY   Still exaction!
        The nature of it? In what kind, let's know,
        Is this exaction?
        QUEEN KATHERINE I am much too venturous
        In tempting of your patience, but am boldened
        Under your promised pardon. The subject's grief
        Comes through commissions, which compels from each
        The sixth part of his substance, to be levied
        Without delay; and the pretence for this
60   Is named your wars in France. This makes bold mouths,
        Tongues spit their duties out, and cold hearts freeze
        Allegiance in them. Their curses now
        Live where their prayers did, and it's come to pass
        This tractable obedience is a slave
        To each incensèd will. I would your highness
        Would give it quick consideration, for
        There is no primer business.
        KING HENRY   By my life,
        This is against our pleasure.
        WOLSEY   And for me,
        I have no further gone in this than by
70   A single voice, and that not passed me but
        By learnèd approbation of the judges. If I am
        Traduced by ignorant tongues, which neither know
        My faculties nor person, yet will be
        The chronicles of my doing, let me say
        'Tis but the fate of place, and the rough brake
        That virtue must go through. We must not stint
        Our necessary actions in the fear
        To cope malicious censurers, which ever,

As ravenous fishes, do a vessel follow
That is new-trimmed, but benefit no further   80
Than vainly longing. What we oft do best,
By sick interpreters, once weak ones, is
Not ours, or not allowed; what worst, as oft
Hitting a grosser quality, is cried up
For our best act. If we shall stand still,
In fear our motion will be mocked or carped at,
We should take root here where we sit,
Or sit state-statues only.

KING HENRY   Things done well,
And with a care, exempt themselves from fear;
Things done without example, in their issue   90
Are to be feared. Have you a precedent
Of this commission? I believe, not any.
We must not rend our subjects from our laws,
And stick them in our will. Sixth part of each?
A trembling contribution! Why, we take
From every tree lop, bark, and part o'th'timber,
And though we leave it with a root, thus hacked,
The air will drink the sap. To every county
Where this is questioned send our letters with
Free pardon to each man that has denied   100
The force of this commission. Pray look to't;
I put it to your care.

WOLSEY (aside to Secretary) A word with you.
Let there be letters writ to every shire
Of the King's grace and pardon. The grievèd commons
Hardly conceive of me – let it be noised
That through our intercession this revokement
And pardon comes. I shall anon advise you
Further in the proceeding.

                                        Exit Secretary

Enter Surveyor

QUEEN KATHERINE

    I am sorry that the Duke of Buckingham
110 Is run in your displeasure.

KING HENRY   It grieves many.

    The gentleman is learned, and a most rare speaker,
    To nature none more bound; his training such
    That he may furnish and instruct great teachers,
    And never seek for aid out of himself. Yet see,
    When these so noble benefits shall prove
    Not well disposed, the mind growing once corrupt,
    They turn to vicious forms, ten times more ugly
    Than ever they were fair. This man so complete,
    Who was enrolled 'mongst wonders, and when we
120 Almost with ravished listening, could not find
    His hour of speech a minute – he, my lady,
    Hath into monstrous habits put the graces
    That once were his, and is become as black
    As if besmeared in hell. Sit by us. You shall hear –
    This was his gentleman in trust – of him
    Things to strike honour sad. Bid him recount
    The fore-recited practices, whereof
    We cannot feel too little, hear too much.

WOLSEY

    Stand forth, and with bold spirit relate what you,
130 Most like a careful subject, have collected
    Out of the Duke of Buckingham.

KING HENRY   Speak freely.

SURVEYOR

    First, it was usual with him – every day
    It would infect his speech – that if the King
    Should without issue die, he'll carry it so
    To make the sceptre his. These very words
    I've heard him utter to his son-in-law,

Lord Aberga'nny, to whom by oath he menaced
Revenge upon the Cardinal.

WOLSEY   Please your highness, note
This dangerous conception in this point:
Not friended by his wish to your high person,   140
His will is most malignant, and it stretches
Beyond you to your friends.

QUEEN KATHERINE   My learned lord Cardinal,
Deliver all with charity.

KING HENRY   Speak on.
How grounded he his title to the crown
Upon our fail? To this point hast thou heard him
At any time speak aught?

SURVEYOR   He was brought to this
By a vain prophecy of Nicholas Henton.

KING HENRY
What was that Henton?

SURVEYOR   Sir, a Chartreux friar,
His confessor, who fed him every minute
With words of sovereignty.

KING HENRY   How know'st thou this?   150

SURVEYOR
Not long before your highness sped to France,
The Duke being at the Rose, within the parish
Saint Lawrence Poultney, did of me demand
What was the speech among the Londoners
Concerning the French journey. I replied
Men feared the French would prove perfidious,
To the King's danger. Presently the Duke
Said 'twas the fear indeed, and that he doubted
'Twould prove the verity of certain words
Spoke by a holy monk, 'that oft', says he,   160
'Hath sent to me, wishing me to permit
John de la Car, my chaplain, a choice hour

To hear from him a matter of some moment;
Whom after under the confession's seal
He solemnly had sworn that what he spoke
My chaplain to no creature living but
To me should utter, with demure confidence
This pausingly ensued: "Neither the King nor's heirs,
Tell you the Duke, shall prosper. Bid him strive
To win the love o'th'commonalty. The Duke
Shall govern England.'"

QUEEN KATHERINE   If I know you well,
You were the Duke's surveyor, and lost your office
On the complaint o'th'tenants. Take good heed
You charge not in your spleen a noble person
And spoil your nobler soul — I say, take heed;
Yes, heartily beseech you.

KING HENRY   Let him on.
Go forward.

SURVEYOR   On my soul, I'll speak but truth.
I told my lord the Duke, by th'devil's illusions
The monk might be deceived, and that 'twas dangerous
For him to ruminate on this so far, until
It forged him some design, which, being believed,
It was much like to do. He answered, 'Tush,
It can do me no damage'; adding further
That, had the King in his last sickness failed,
The Cardinal's and Sir Thomas Lovell's heads
Should have gone off.

KING HENRY   Ha! What, so rank? Ah, ha!
There's mischief in this man. Canst thou say further?

SURVEYOR
I can, my liege.

KING HENRY   Proceed.

SURVEYOR   Being at Greenwich,
After your highness had reproved the Duke

About Sir William Bulmer —

KING HENRY   I remember   190
Of such a time; being my sworn servant,
The Duke retained him his. But on; what hence?

SURVEYOR
'If', quoth he, 'I for this had been committed,
As to the Tower I thought, I would have played
The part my father meant to act upon
Th'usurper Richard; who, being at Salisbury,
Made suit to come in's presence, which if granted,
As he made semblance of his duty, would
Have put his knife into him.'

KING HENRY   A giant traitor!

WOLSEY
Now, madam, may his highness live in freedom,   200
And this man out of prison?

QUEEN KATHERINE   God mend all!

KING HENRY
There's something more would out of thee: what sayst?

SURVEYOR
After 'the Duke his father', with the 'knife',
He stretched him, and, with one hand on his dagger,
Another spread on's breast, mounting his eyes,
He did discharge a horrible oath, whose tenor
Was, were he evil used, he would outgo
His father by as much as a performance
Does an irresolute purpose.

KING HENRY   There's his period,
To sheathe his knife in us. He is attached;   210
Call him to present trial. If he may
Find mercy in the law, 'tis his; if none,
Let him not seek't of us. By day and night!
He's traitor to th'height!   *Exeunt*

I.3   *Enter the Lord Chamberlain and Lord Sands*

LORD CHAMBERLAIN
    Is't possible the spells of France should juggle
    Men into such strange mysteries?

SANDS   New customs,
    Though they be never so ridiculous,
    Nay, let 'em be unmanly, yet are followed.

LORD CHAMBERLAIN
    As far as I see, all the good our English
    Have got by the late voyage is but merely
    A fit or two o'th'face – but they are shrewd ones;
    For when they hold 'em, you would swear directly
    Their very noses had been counsellors
10 To Pepin or Clotharius, they keep state so.

SANDS
    They have all new legs, and lame ones. One would take
        it,
    That never see 'em pace before, the spavin
    Or springhalt reigned among 'em.

LORD CHAMBERLAIN   Death, my lord!
    Their clothes are after such a pagan cut to't
    That sure they've worn out Christendom.
        Enter Sir Thomas Lovell
                                             How now?
    What news, Sir Thomas Lovell?

LOVELL   Faith, my lord,
    I hear of none but the new proclamation
    That's clapped upon the court gate.

LORD CHAMBERLAIN   What is't for?

LOVELL
    The reformation of our travelled gallants,
20 That fill the court with quarrels, talk, and tailors.

LORD CHAMBERLAIN
    I'm glad 'tis there. Now I would pray our monsieurs

To think an English courtier may be wise,
And never see the Louvre.

LOVELL   They must either,
For so run the conditions, leave those remnants
Of fool and feather that they got in France,
With all their honourable points of ignorance
Pertaining thereunto, as fights and fireworks,
Abusing better men than they can be
Out of a foreign wisdom, renouncing clean
The faith they have in tennis and tall stockings,   30
Short blistered breeches, and those types of travel,
And understand again like honest men,
Or pack to their old playfellows. There, I take it,
They may, *cum privilegio*, *'oui'* away
The lag end of their lewdness, and be laughed at.

SANDS
'Tis time to give 'em physic, their diseases
Are grown so catching.

LORD CHAMBERLAIN   What a loss our ladies
Will have of these trim vanities!

LOVELL   Ay, marry,
There will be woe indeed, lords! The sly whoresons
Have got a speeding trick to lay down ladies.   40
A French song and a fiddle has no fellow.

SANDS
The devil fiddle 'em! I am glad they are going,
For sure there's no converting of 'em. Now
An honest country lord, as I am, beaten
A long time out of play, may bring his plainsong,
And have an hour of hearing, and, by'r lady,
Held current music too.

LORD CHAMBERLAIN   Well said, Lord Sands.
Your colt's tooth is not cast yet?

SANDS   No, my lord,

Nor shall not while I have a stump.

LORD CHAMBERLAIN   Sir Thomas,
50   Whither were you a-going?

LOVELL   To the Cardinal's;
Your lordship is a guest too.

LORD CHAMBERLAIN   O, 'tis true.
This night he makes a supper, and a great one,
To many lords and ladies. There will be
The beauty of this kingdom, I'll assure you.

LOVELL
That churchman bears a bounteous mind indeed,
A hand as fruitful as the land that feeds us.
His dews fall everywhere.

LORD CHAMBERLAIN   No doubt he's noble.
He had a black mouth that said other of him.

SANDS
He may, my lord; has wherewithal: in him
60   Sparing would show a worse sin than ill doctrine.
Men of his way should be most liberal;
They are set here for examples.

LORD CHAMBERLAIN   True, they are so;
But few now give so great ones. My barge stays;
Your lordship shall along. Come, good Sir Thomas,
We shall be late else, which I would not be,
For I was spoke to, with Sir Henry Guilford,
This night to be comptrollers.

SANDS   I am your lordship's.

Exeunt

I.4   *Hautboys. A small table under a state for the Cardinal,*
a longer table for the guests. Then enter Anne Bullen
and divers other ladies and gentlemen as guests, at one
door; at another door enter Sir Henry Guilford

GUILFORD

    Ladies, a general welcome from his grace
    Salutes ye all. This night he dedicates
    To fair content, and you. None here, he hopes,
    In all this noble bevy, has brought with her
    One care abroad. He would have all as merry
    As, first, good company, good wine, good welcome
    Can make good people.

    Enter the Lord Chamberlain, Lord Sands, and Sir
    Thomas Lovell

                     O, my lord, you're tardy.
    The very thought of this fair company
    Clapped wings to me.

LORD CHAMBERLAIN You are young, Sir Harry Guilford.

SANDS

    Sir Thomas Lovell, had the Cardinal   10
    But half my lay thoughts in him, some of these
    Should find a running banquet, ere they rested,
    I think would better please 'em. By my life,
    They are a sweet society of fair ones.

LOVELL

    O that your lordship were but now confessor
    To one or two of these!

SANDS   I would I were;
    They should find easy penance.

LOVELL   Faith, how easy?

SANDS

    As easy as a down bed would afford it.

LORD CHAMBERLAIN

    Sweet ladies, will it please you sit? Sir Harry,
    Place you that side; I'll take the charge of this.   20
    His grace is entering. – Nay, you must not freeze –
    Two women placed together makes cold weather.
    My Lord Sands, you are one will keep 'em waking:

Pray sit between these ladies.

SANDS   By my faith,
And thank your lordship. By your leave, sweet ladies.
If I chance to talk a little wild, forgive me;
I had it from my father.

ANNE   Was he mad, sir?

SANDS
O, very mad, exceeding mad, in love too;
But he would bite none. Just as I do now,
30   He would kiss you twenty with a breath.

        He kisses her

LORD CHAMBERLAIN   Well said, my lord.
So, now you're fairly seated. Gentlemen,
The penance lies on you if these fair ladies
Pass away frowning.

SANDS   For my little cure,
Let me alone.

        Hautboys. Enter Cardinal Wolsey and takes his state

WOLSEY
You're welcome, my fair guests. That noble lady
Or gentleman that is not freely merry
Is not my friend. This, to confirm my welcome –
And to you all, good health!

        He drinks

SANDS   Your grace is noble.
Let me have such a bowl may hold my thanks,
40   And save me so much talking.

WOLSEY   My Lord Sands,
I am beholding to you. Cheer your neighbours.
Ladies, you are not merry! Gentlemen,
Whose fault is this?

SANDS   The red wine first must rise
In their fair cheeks, my lord; then we shall have 'em
Talk us to silence.

ANNE   You are a merry gamester,
  My Lord Sands.

SANDS   Yes, if I make my play.
  Here's to your ladyship; and pledge it, madam,
  For 'tis to such a thing —

ANNE   You cannot show me.

SANDS
  I told your grace they would talk anon.
    Drum and trumpet. Chambers discharged

WOLSEY   What's that?

LORD CHAMBERLAIN
  Look out there, some of ye.   *Exit a Servant*

WOLSEY   What warlike voice,   50
  And to what end, is this? Nay, ladies, fear not;
  By all the laws of war you're privileged.
    Enter Servant

LORD CHAMBERLAIN
  How now, what is't?

SERVANT   A noble troop of strangers,
  For so they seem. They've left their barge and landed,
  And hither make, as great ambassadors
  From foreign princes.

WOLSEY   Good Lord Chamberlain,
  Go, give 'em welcome — you can speak the French
      tongue;
  And pray receive 'em nobly, and conduct 'em
  Into our presence, where this heaven of beauty
  Shall shine at full upon them. Some attend him.   60
              Exit Lord Chamberlain, attended
    All rise, and tables removed
  You have now a broken banquet, but we'll mend it.
  A good digestion to you all; and once more
  I shower a welcome on ye — welcome all!
    Hautboys. Enter the King and others as masquers,

habited like shepherds, ushered by the Lord Chamber-
lain. They pass directly before the Cardinal, and
gracefully salute him

A noble company! What are their pleasures?

LORD CHAMBERLAIN

Because they speak no English, thus they prayed
To tell your grace, that, having heard by fame
Of this so noble and so fair assembly
This night to meet here, they could do no less,
Out of the great respect they bear to beauty,
70   But leave their flocks, and, under your fair conduct,
Crave leave to view these ladies, and entreat
An hour of revels with 'em.

WOLSEY   Say, Lord Chamberlain,
They have done my poor house grace; for which I pay
'em
A thousand thanks, and pray 'em take their pleasures.

They choose ladies; the King chooses Anne Bullen

KING HENRY

The fairest hand I ever touched! O beauty,
Till now I never knew thee.

Music. Dance

WOLSEY

My lord!

LORD CHAMBERLAIN

Your grace?

WOLSEY   Pray tell 'em thus much from me:
There should be one amongst 'em, by his person,
More worthy this place than myself, to whom,
80   If I but knew him, with my love and duty
I would surrender it.

LORD CHAMBERLAIN I will, my lord.

He whispers with the masquers

WOLSEY
What say they?

LORD CHAMBERLAIN Such a one, they all confess,
There is indeed, which they would have your grace
Find out, and he will take it.

WOLSEY   Let me see then.
He comes from his state
By all your good leaves, gentlemen; here I'll make
My royal choice.
The King unmasks

KING HENRY   Ye have found him, Cardinal.
You hold a fair assembly; you do well, lord.
You are a churchman, or I'll tell you, Cardinal,
I should judge now unhappily.

WOLSEY   I am glad
Your grace is grown so pleasant.

KING HENRY   My Lord Chamberlain,   90
Prithee come hither: what fair lady's that?

LORD CHAMBERLAIN
An't please your grace, Sir Thomas Bullen's daughter,
The Viscount Rochford, one of her highness' women.

KING HENRY
By heaven, she is a dainty one. Sweetheart,
I were unmannerly to take you out
And not to kiss you. A health, gentlemen!
Let it go round.

WOLSEY
Sir Thomas Lovell, is the banquet ready
I'th'privy chamber?

LOVELL   Yes, my lord.

WOLSEY   Your grace,
I fear, with dancing is a little heated.   100

KING HENRY
I fear, too much.

WOLSEY   There's fresher air, my lord,
In the next chamber.
KING HENRY
Lead in your ladies every one. Sweet partner,
I must not yet forsake you. Let's be merry,
Good my lord Cardinal: I have half a dozen healths
To drink to these fair ladies, and a measure
To lead 'em once again; and then let's dream
Who's best in favour. Let the music knock it.

Exeunt, with trumpets

*

II.1   *Enter two Gentlemen, at several doors*
FIRST GENTLEMAN
Whither away so fast?
SECOND GENTLEMAN   O, God save ye!
Even to the Hall, to hear what shall become
Of the great Duke of Buckingham.
FIRST GENTLEMAN   I'll save you
That labour, sir. All's now done but the ceremony
Of bringing back the prisoner.
SECOND GENTLEMAN   Were you there?
FIRST GENTLEMAN
Yes, indeed was I.
SECOND GENTLEMAN Pray speak what has happened.
FIRST GENTLEMAN
You may guess quickly what.
SECOND GENTLEMAN   Is he found guilty?
FIRST GENTLEMAN
Yes, truly is he, and condemned upon't.
SECOND GENTLEMAN
I am sorry for't.

FIRST GENTLEMAN So are a number more.
SECOND GENTLEMAN
    But pray, how passed it?   10
FIRST GENTLEMAN
    I'll tell you in a little. The great Duke
    Came to the bar, where to his accusations
    He pleaded still not guilty, and allegèd
    Many sharp reasons to defeat the law.
    The King's attorney, on the contrary,
    Urged on the examinations, proofs, confessions,
    Of divers witnesses, which the Duke desired
    To have brought *viva voce* to his face;
    At which appeared against him his surveyor,
    Sir Gilbert Perk his chancellor, and John Car,   20
    Confessor to him, with that devil-monk,
    Hopkins, that made this mischief.
SECOND GENTLEMAN   That was he
    That fed him with his prophecies.
FIRST GENTLEMAN   The same.
    All these accused him strongly, which he fain
    Would have flung from him; but indeed he could not;
    And so his peers, upon this evidence,
    Have found him guilty of high treason. Much
    He spoke, and learnèdly, for life, but all
    Was either pitied in him or forgotten.
SECOND GENTLEMAN
    After all this, how did he bear himself?   30
FIRST GENTLEMAN
    When he was brought again to th'bar, to hear
    His knell rung out, his judgement, he was stirred
    With such an agony he sweat extremely,
    And something spoke in choler, ill and hasty;
    But he fell to himself again, and sweetly
    In all the rest showed a most noble patience.

SECOND GENTLEMAN
   I do not think he fears death.

FIRST GENTLEMAN   Sure he does not;
   He never was so womanish. The cause
   He may a little grieve at.

SECOND GENTLEMAN   Certainly
40 The Cardinal is the end of this.

FIRST GENTLEMAN   'Tis likely,
   By all conjectures: first, Kildare's attainder,
   Then deputy of Ireland, who removed,
   Earl Surrey was sent thither, and in haste too,
   Lest he should help his father.

SECOND GENTLEMAN   That trick of state
   Was a deep envious one.

FIRST GENTLEMAN   At his return
   No doubt he will requite it. This is noted,
   And generally: whoever the King favours,
   The Cardinal instantly will find employment,
   And far enough from court too.

SECOND GENTLEMAN   All the commons
50 Hate him perniciously, and, o'my conscience,
   Wish him ten fathom deep. This Duke as much
   They love and dote on, call him bounteous Buckingham,
   The mirror of all courtesy –

FIRST GENTLEMAN   Stay there, sir,
   And see the noble ruined man you speak of.

   Enter Buckingham from his arraignment, tipstaves
   before him, the axe with the edge towards him,
   halberds on each side, accompanied with Sir Thomas
   Lovell, Sir Nicholas Vaux, Sir Walter Sands, and
   common people, etc.

SECOND GENTLEMAN
   Let's stand close, and behold him.

BUCKINGHAM   All good people,

You that thus far have come to pity me,
Hear what I say, and then go home and lose me.
I have this day received a traitor's judgement,
And by that name must die. Yet, heaven bear witness,
And if I have a conscience let it sink me,   60
Even as the axe falls, if I be not faithful!
The law I bear no malice for my death:
'T has done, upon the premises, but justice.
But those that sought it I could wish more Christians.
Be what they will, I heartily forgive 'em.
Yet let 'em look they glory not in mischief,
Nor build their evils on the graves of great men,
For then my guiltless blood must cry against 'em.
For further life in this world I ne'er hope,
Nor will I sue, although the King have mercies   70
More than I dare make faults. You few that loved me,
And dare be bold to weep for Buckingham,
His noble friends and fellows, whom to leave
Is only bitter to him, only dying,
Go with me like good angels to my end,
And as the long divorce of steel falls on me
Make of your prayers one sweet sacrifice,
And lift my soul to heaven. Lead on, a God's name!

LOVELL
I do beseech your grace, for charity,
If ever any malice in your heart,   80
Were hid against me, now to forgive me frankly.

BUCKINGHAM
Sir Thomas Lovell, I as free forgive you
As I would be forgiven. I forgive all.
There cannot be those numberless offences
'Gainst me that I cannot take peace with. No black envy
Shall mark my grave. Commend me to his grace,
And if he speak of Buckingham, pray tell him

You met him half in heaven. My vows and prayers
Yet are the King's and, till my soul forsake,
90   Shall cry for blessings on him. May he live
Longer than I have time to tell his years;
Ever beloved and loving may his rule be;
And, when old time shall lead him to his end,
Goodness and he fill up one monument!

LOVELL
To th'waterside I must conduct your grace,
Then give my charge up to Sir Nicholas Vaux,
Who undertakes you to your end.

VAUX   Prepare there;
The Duke is coming. See the barge be ready,
And fit it with such furniture as suits
100 The greatness of his person.

BUCKINGHAM   Nay, Sir Nicholas,
Let it alone; my state now will but mock me.
When I came hither, I was Lord High Constable
And Duke of Buckingham; now, poor Edward Bohun.
Yet I am richer than my base accusers
That never knew what truth meant. I now seal it,
And with that blood will make 'em one day groan for't.
My noble father, Henry of Buckingham,
Who first raised head against usurping Richard,
Flying for succour to his servant Banister,
110 Being distressed, was by that wretch betrayed,
And without trial fell. God's peace be with him!
Henry the Seventh succeeding, truly pitying
My father's loss, like a most royal prince
Restored me to my honours, and out of ruins
Made my name once more noble. Now his son,
Henry the Eighth, life, honour, name, and all
That made me happy, at one stroke has taken
For ever from the world. I had my trial,

And must needs say a noble one; which makes me
A little happier than my wretched father;   120
Yet thus far we are one in fortunes: both
Fell by our servants, by those men we loved most —
A most unnatural and faithless service.
Heaven has an end in all. Yet, you that hear me,
This from a dying man receive as certain:
Where you are liberal of your loves and counsels
Be sure you be not loose; for those you make friends
And give your hearts to, when they once perceive
The least rub in your fortunes, fall away
Like water from ye, never found again   130
But where they mean to sink ye. All good people,
Pray for me! I must now forsake ye; the last hour
Of my long weary life is come upon me.
Farewell;
And when you would say something that is sad,
Speak how I fell. I have done; and God forgive me.

Exeunt Duke and train

FIRST GENTLEMAN
    O, this is full of pity! Sir, it calls,
    I fear, too many curses on their heads
    That were the authors.

SECOND GENTLEMAN   If the Duke be guiltless,
    'Tis full of woe; yet I can give you inkling   140
    Of an ensuing evil, if it fall,
    Greater than this.

FIRST GENTLEMAN Good angels keep it from us!
    What may it be? You do not doubt my faith, sir?

SECOND GENTLEMAN
    This secret is so weighty, 'twill require
    A strong faith to conceal it.

FIRST GENTLEMAN   Let me have it;
    I do not talk much.

SECOND GENTLEMAN I am confident;
    You shall, sir. Did you not of late days hear
    A buzzing of a separation
    Between the King and Katherine?
FIRST GENTLEMAN   Yes, but it held not;
150   For when the King once heard it, out of anger
    He sent command to the Lord Mayor straight
    To stop the rumour and allay those tongues
    That durst disperse it.
SECOND GENTLEMAN   But that slander, sir,
    Is found a truth now, for it grows again
    Fresher than e'er it was, and held for certain
    The King will venture at it. Either the Cardinal
    Or some about him near have, out of malice
    To the good Queen, possessed him with a scruple
    That will undo her. To confirm this too,
160   Cardinal Campeius is arrived, and lately,
    As all think, for this business.
FIRST GENTLEMAN   'Tis the Cardinal;
    And merely to revenge him on the Emperor
    For not bestowing on him at his asking
    The archbishopric of Toledo, this is purposed.
SECOND GENTLEMAN
    I think you have hit the mark; but is't not cruel
    That she should feel the smart of this? The Cardinal
    Will have his will, and she must fall.
FIRST GENTLEMAN   'Tis woeful.
    We are too open here to argue this;
    Let's think in private more.   *Exeunt*

II.2   *Enter the Lord Chamberlain, reading this letter*
    LORD CHAMBERLAIN *My lord, the horses your lordship*
    sent for, with all the care I had I saw well chosen, ridden,

and furnished. They were young and handsome, and of the
best breed in the north. When they were ready to set out for
London, a man of my lord Cardinal's, by commission and
main power, took 'em from me, with this reason: his
master would be served before a subject, if not before the
King; which stopped our mouths, sir.

I fear he will indeed. Well, let him have them.

He will have all, I think.   10

Enter to the Lord Chamberlain the Dukes of Norfolk
and Suffolk

NORFOLK
Well met, my Lord Chamberlain.

LORD CHAMBERLAIN
Good day to both your graces.

SUFFOLK
How is the King employed?

LORD CHAMBERLAIN   I left him private,
Full of sad thoughts and troubles.

NORFOLK   What's the cause?

LORD CHAMBERLAIN
It seems the marriage with his brother's wife
Has crept too near his conscience.

SUFFOLK (*aside*)   No, his conscience
Has crept too near another lady.

NORFOLK   'Tis so;
This is the Cardinal's doing; the King-Cardinal,
That blind priest, like the eldest son of fortune,
Turns what he list. The King will know him one day.   20

SUFFOLK
Pray God he do! He'll never know himself else.

NORFOLK
How holily he works in all his business,
And with what zeal! For, now he has cracked the league

Between us and the Emperor, the Queen's great
    nephew,
He dives into the King's soul and there scatters
Dangers, doubts, wringing of the conscience,
Fears, and despairs – and all these for his marriage.
And out of all these to restore the King,
He counsels a divorce, a loss of her
30 That like a jewel has hung twenty years
About his neck, yet never lost her lustre;
Of her that loves him with that excellence
That angels love good men with; even of her
That, when the greatest stroke of fortune falls,
Will bless the King – and is not this course pious?

LORD CHAMBERLAIN
Heaven keep me from such counsel! 'Tis most true
These news are everywhere, every tongue speaks 'em,
And every true heart weeps for't. All that dare
Look into these affairs see this main end,
40 The French King's sister. Heaven will one day open
The King's eyes, that so long have slept upon
This bold bad man.

SUFFOLK   And free us from his slavery.

NORFOLK
We had need pray,
And heartily, for our deliverance,
Or this imperious man will work us all
From princes into pages. All men's honours
Lie like one lump before him, to be fashioned
Into what pitch he please.

SUFFOLK   For me, my lords,
I love him not, nor fear him – there's my creed.
50 As I am made without him, so I'll stand,
If the King please. His curses and his blessings
Touch me alike; they're breath I not believe in.

I knew him, and I know him; so I leave him
To him that made him proud – the Pope.

NORFOLK   Let's in,
And with some other business put the King
From these sad thoughts that work too much upon him.
My lord, you'll bear us company?

LORD CHAMBERLAIN   Excuse me,
The King has sent me otherwhere. Besides,
You'll find a most unfit time to disturb him.
Health to your lordships!

NORFOLK   Thanks, my good Lord Chamberlain.   60
                                Exit Lord Chamberlain
    The King draws the curtain and sits reading pensively

SUFFOLK
How sad he looks; sure he is much afflicted.

KING HENRY
Who's there, ha?

NORFOLK   Pray God he be not angry.

KING HENRY
Who's there, I say? How dare you thrust yourselves
Into my private meditations?
Who am I, ha?

NORFOLK
A gracious king that pardons all offences
Malice ne'er meant. Our breach of duty this way
Is business of estate, in which we come
To know your royal pleasure.

KING HENRY   Ye are too bold.
Go to; I'll make ye know your times of business.   70
Is this an hour for temporal affairs, ha?
    Enter Wolsey and Campeius with a commission
Who's there? My good lord Cardinal? O my Wolsey,
The quiet of my wounded conscience,

Thou art a cure fit for a king. (*To Campeius*) You're
        welcome,
Most learnèd reverend sir, into our kingdom;
Use us, and it. (*To Wolsey*) My good lord, have great
        care
I be not found a talker.

WOLSEY   Sir, you cannot.
I would your grace would give us but an hour
Of private conference.

KING HENRY (*to Norfolk and Suffolk*) We are busy; go.

NORFOLK (*aside to Suffolk*)
80   This priest has no pride in him!

SUFFOLK (*aside to Norfolk*)   Not to speak of!
I would not be so sick though for his place.
But this cannot continue.

NORFOLK (*aside to Suffolk*) If it do,
I'll venture one have-at-him.

SUFFOLK (*aside to Norfolk*)   I another.

                                   Exeunt Norfolk and Suffolk

WOLSEY
Your grace has given a precedent of wisdom
Above all princes, in committing freely
Your scruple to the voice of Christendom.
Who can be angry now? What envy reach you?
The Spaniard, tied by blood and favour to her,
Must now confess, if they have any goodness,
90   The trial just and noble. All the clerks –
I mean the learnèd ones in Christian kingdoms –
Have their free voices. Rome, the nurse of judgement,
Invited by your noble self, hath sent
One general tongue unto us, this good man,
This just and learnèd priest, Cardinal Campeius,
Whom once more I present unto your highness.

KING HENRY

And once more in mine arms I bid him welcome,
And thank the holy conclave for their loves.
They have sent me such a man I would have wished for.

CAMPEIUS

Your grace must needs deserve all strangers' loves,   100
You are so noble. To your highness' hand
I tender my commission, by whose virtue,
The court of Rome commanding, you, my lord
Cardinal of York, are joined with me their servant
In the unpartial judging of this business.

KING HENRY

Two equal men. The Queen shall be acquainted
Forthwith for what you come. Where's Gardiner?

WOLSEY

I know your majesty has always loved her
So dear in heart not to deny her that
A woman of less place might ask by law —   110
Scholars allowed freely to argue for her.

KING HENRY

Ay, and the best she shall have, and my favour
To him that does best, God forbid else. Cardinal,
Prithee call Gardiner to me, my new secretary;
I find him a fit fellow.   *Exit Wolsey*
        Enter Wolsey with Gardiner

WOLSEY (*aside to Gardiner*)

Give me your hand: much joy and favour to you.
You are the King's now.

GARDINER (*aside to Wolsey*)   But to be commanded
For ever by your grace, whose hand has raised me.

KING HENRY

Come hither, Gardiner.
        Walks and whispers

CAMPEIUS

120   My lord of York, was not one Doctor Pace
       In this man's place before him?

WOLSEY   Yes, he was.

CAMPEIUS

       Was he not held a learnèd man?

WOLSEY   Yes, surely.

CAMPEIUS

       Believe me, there's an ill opinion spread then,
       Even of yourself, lord Cardinal.

WOLSEY   How? Of me?

CAMPEIUS

       They will not stick to say you envied him,
       And fearing he would rise, he was so virtuous,
       Kept him a foreign man still, which so grieved him
       That he ran mad and died.

WOLSEY   Heaven's peace be with him!
       That's Christian care enough. For living murmurers

130   There's places of rebuke. He was a fool,
       For he would needs be virtuous. That good fellow,
       If I command him, follows my appointment;
       I will have none so near else. Learn this, brother,
       We live not to be griped by meaner persons.

KING HENRY

       Deliver this with modesty to th'Queen.

                                        Exit Gardiner

       The most convenient place that I can think of
       For such receipt of learning is Blackfriars;
       There ye shall meet about this weighty business.
       My Wolsey, see it furnished. O, my lord,

140   Would it not grieve an able man to leave
       So sweet a bedfellow? But conscience, conscience!
       O, 'tis a tender place, and I must leave her.   *Exeunt*

Enter Anne Bullen and an Old Lady   II.3

ANNE

    Not for that neither. Here's the pang that pinches:
    His highness having lived so long with her, and she
    So good a lady that no tongue could ever
    Pronounce dishonour of her – by my life,
    She never knew harm-doing – O, now, after
    So many courses of the sun enthronèd,
    Still growing in a majesty and pomp, the which
    To leave a thousand-fold more bitter than
    'Tis sweet at first t'acquire – after this process,
    To give her the avaunt, it is a pity   10
    Would move a monster.

OLD LADY   Hearts of most hard temper
    Melt and lament for her.

ANNE   O, God's will! Much better
    She ne'er had known pomp; though't be temporal,
    Yet, if that quarrel, Fortune, do divorce
    It from the bearer, 'tis a sufferance panging
    As soul and body's severing.

OLD LADY   Alas, poor lady!
    She's a stranger now again.

ANNE   So much the more
    Must pity drop upon her. Verily,
    I swear, 'tis better to be lowly born,
    And range with humble livers in content,
    Than to be perked up in a glistering grief   20
    And wear a golden sorrow.

OLD LADY   Our content
    Is our best having.

ANNE   By my troth and maidenhead,
    I would not be a queen.

OLD LADY   Beshrew me, I would,
    And venture maidenhead for't; and so would you,

For all this spice of your hypocrisy.
You that have so fair parts of woman on you
Have too a woman's heart, which ever yet
Affected eminence, wealth, sovereignty;
30   Which, to say sooth, are blessings; and which gifts,
Saving your mincing, the capacity
Of your soft cheveril conscience would receive
If you might please to stretch it.

ANNE   Nay, good troth.

OLD LADY

Yes, troth and troth. You would not be a queen?

ANNE

No, not for all the riches under heaven.

OLD LADY

'Tis strange: a threepence bowed would hire me,
Old as I am, to queen it. But, I pray you,
What think you of a duchess? Have you limbs
To bear that load of title?

ANNE   No, in truth.

OLD LADY

40   Then you are weakly made. Pluck off a little;
I would not be a young count in your way
For more than blushing comes to. If your back
Cannot vouchsafe this burden, 'tis too weak
Ever to get a boy.

ANNE   How you do talk!
I swear again, I would not be a queen
For all the world.

OLD LADY   In faith, for little England
You'd venture an emballing. I myself
Would for Caernarvonshire, although there 'longed
No more to th'crown but that. Lo, who comes here?

Enter the Lord Chamberlain

LORD CHAMBERLAIN
　　Good morrow, ladies. What were't worth to know   50
　　The secret of your conference?
ANNE   My good lord,
　　Not your demand; it values not your asking.
　　Our mistress' sorrows we were pitying.
LORD CHAMBERLAIN
　　It was a gentle business, and becoming
　　The action of good women. There is hope
　　All will be well.
ANNE   Now I pray God, amen!
LORD CHAMBERLAIN
　　You bear a gentle mind, and heavenly blessings
　　Follow such creatures. That you may, fair lady,
　　Perceive I speak sincerely, and high note's
　　Ta'en of your many virtues, the King's majesty   60
　　Commends his good opinion of you, and
　　Does purpose honour to you no less flowing
　　Than Marchioness of Pembroke; to which title
　　A thousand pound a year, annual support,
　　Out of his grace he adds.
ANNE   I do not know
　　What kind of my obedience I should tender.
　　More than my all is nothing; nor my prayers
　　Are not words duly hallowed, nor my wishes
　　More worth than empty vanities; yet prayers and wishes
　　Are all I can return. Beseech your lordship,   70
　　Vouchsafe to speak my thanks and my obedience,
　　As from a blushing handmaid, to his highness,
　　Whose health and royalty I pray for.
LORD CHAMBERLAIN   Lady,
　　I shall not fail t'approve the fair conceit
　　The King hath of you. (Aside) I have perused her well;
　　Beauty and honour in her are so mingled

That they have caught the King; and who knows yet
But from this lady may proceed a gem
To lighten all this isle? (*To them*) I'll to the King,
80   And say I spoke with you.

ANNE   My honoured lord!
                                        Exit Lord Chamberlain

OLD LADY
Why, this it is: see, see!
I have been begging sixteen years in court,
Am yet a courtier beggarly, nor could
Come pat betwixt too early and too late
For any suit of pounds; and you – O fate! –
A very fresh fish here – fie, fie, fie upon
This compelled fortune! – have your mouth filled up
Before you open it.

ANNE   This is strange to me.

OLD LADY
How tastes it? Is it bitter? Forty pence, no.
90   There was a lady once – 'tis an old story –
That would not be a queen, that would she not,
For all the mud in Egypt. Have you heard it?

ANNE
Come, you are pleasant.

OLD LADY   With your theme I could
O'ermount the lark. The Marchioness of Pembroke!
A thousand pounds a year, for pure respect!
No other obligation! By my life,
That promises more thousands: honour's train
Is longer than his foreskirt. By this time
I know your back will bear a duchess. Say,
100   Are you not stronger than you were?

ANNE   Good lady,
Make yourself mirth with your particular fancy,
And leave me out on't. Would I had no being,

If this salute my blood a jot; it faints me
To think what follows.
The Queen is comfortless, and we forgetful
In our long absence. Pray do not deliver
What here you've heard to her.

OLD LADY   What do you think me?

Exeunt

> *Trumpets, sennet, and cornets. Enter two Vergers,*   II.4
> *with short silver wands; next them two Scribes, in*
> *the habit of doctors; after them, the Archbishop of*
> *Canterbury alone; after him, the Bishops of Lincoln,*
> *Ely, Rochester, and Saint Asaph; next them, with*
> *some small distance, follows a Gentleman bearing the*
> *purse, with the great seal, and a cardinal's hat; then*
> *two Priests bearing each a silver cross; then Griffith,*
> *a Gentleman Usher, bare-headed, accompanied with a*
> *Sergeant-at-Arms bearing a silver mace; then two*
> *Gentlemen bearing two great silver pillars; after*
> *them, side by side, the two Cardinals; two noblemen*
> *with the sword and mace. The King takes place under*
> *the cloth of state. The two Cardinals sit under him as*
> *judges. The Queen takes place some distance from the*
> *King. The Bishops place themselves on each side the*
> *court in manner of a consistory; below them the*
> *Scribes. The Lords sit next the Bishops. The rest of the*
> *attendants stand in convenient order about the stage*

WOLSEY
Whilst our commission from Rome is read,
Let silence be commanded.

KING HENRY   What's the need?
It hath already publicly been read,
And on all sides th'authority allowed.

You may then spare that time.

WOLSEY   Be't so, proceed.

SCRIBE Say 'Henry, King of England, come into the court'.

CRIER Henry, King of England, come into the court.

KING HENRY Here.

10 SCRIBE Say 'Katherine, Queen of England, come into the court'.

CRIER Katherine, Queen of England, come into the court.

The Queen makes no answer, rises out of her chair, goes about the court, comes to the King, and kneels at his feet; then speaks

QUEEN KATHERINE
  Sir, I desire you do me right and justice,
  And to bestow your pity on me; for
  I am a most poor woman, and a stranger,
  Born out of your dominions, having here
  No judge indifferent, nor no more assurance
  Of equal friendship and proceeding. Alas, sir,
  In what have I offended you? What cause
20 Hath my behaviour given to your displeasure
  That thus you should proceed to put me off
  And take your good grace from me? Heaven witness,
  I have been to you a true and humble wife,
  At all times to your will conformable,
  Ever in fear to kindle your dislike,
  Yea, subject to your countenance, glad or sorry
  As I saw it inclined. When was the hour
  I ever contradicted your desire,
  Or made it not mine too? Or which of your friends
30 Have I not strove to love, although I knew
  He were mine enemy? What friend of mine
  That had to him derived your anger did I
  Continue in my liking, nay, gave notice

He was from thence discharged? Sir, call to mind
That I have been your wife in this obedience
Upward of twenty years, and have been blessed
With many children by you. If, in the course
And process of this time, you can report,
And prove it too, against mine honour aught,
My bond to wedlock, or my love and duty   40
Against your sacred person, in God's name
Turn me away, and let the foul'st contempt
Shut door upon me, and so give me up
To the sharp'st kind of justice. Please you, sir,
The King your father was reputed for
A prince most prudent, of an excellent
And unmatched wit and judgement. Ferdinand
My father, King of Spain, was reckoned one
The wisest prince that there had reigned, by many
A year before. It is not to be questioned   50
That they had gathered a wise council to them
Of every realm, that did debate this business,
Who deemed our marriage lawful. Wherefore I humbly
Beseech you, sir, to spare me, till I may
Be by my friends in Spain advised, whose counsel
I will implore. If not, i'th'name of God,
Your pleasure be fulfilled.

WOLSEY   You have here, lady,
And of your choice, these reverend fathers, men
Of singular integrity and learning,
Yea, the elect o'th'land, who are assembled   60
To plead your cause. It shall be therefore bootless
That longer you desire the court, as well
For your own quiet, as to rectify
What is unsettled in the King.

CAMPEIUS   His grace
Hath spoken well and justly. Therefore, madam,

It's fit this royal session do proceed,
And that without delay their arguments
Be now produced and heard.

QUEEN KATHERINE   Lord Cardinal,
To you I speak.

WOLSEY   Your pleasure, madam.

QUEEN KATHERINE   Sir,
70   I am about to weep; but, thinking that
We are a queen, or long have dreamed so, certain
The daughter of a king, my drops of tears
I'll turn to sparks of fire.

WOLSEY   Be patient yet.

QUEEN KATHERINE
I will, when you are humble; nay, before,
Or God will punish me. I do believe,
Induced by potent circumstances, that
You are mine enemy, and make my challenge
You shall not be my judge; for it is you
Have blown this coal betwixt my lord and me —
80   Which God's dew quench! Therefore I say again,
I utterly abhor, yea, from my soul
Refuse you for my judge, whom yet once more
I hold my most malicious foe, and think not
At all a friend to truth.

WOLSEY   I do profess
You speak not like yourself, who ever yet
Have stood to charity and displayed th'effects
Of disposition gentle and of wisdom
O'ertopping woman's power. Madam, you do me
                wrong:
I have no spleen against you, nor injustice
90   For you or any. How far I have proceeded,
Or how far further shall, is warranted
By a commission from the consistory,

Yea, the whole consistory of Rome. You charge me
That I have blown this coal. I do deny it.
The King is present. If it be known to him
That I gainsay my deed, how may he wound,
And worthily, my falsehood — yea, as much
As you have done my truth. If he know
That I am free of your report, he knows
I am not of your wrong. Therefore in him   100
It lies to cure me, and the cure is to
Remove these thoughts from you; the which before
His highness shall speak in, I do beseech
You, gracious madam, to unthink your speaking
And to say so no more.
QUEEN KATHERINE   My lord, my lord,
I am a simple woman, much too weak
T'oppose your cunning. You're meek and humble
        mouthed;
You sign your place and calling, in full seeming,
With meekness and humility; but your heart
Is crammed with arrogancy, spleen, and pride.   110
You have, by fortune and his highness' favours,
Gone slightly o'er low steps, and now are mounted
Where powers are your retainers, and your words,
Domestics to you, serve your will as't please
Yourself pronounce their office. I must tell you,
You tender more your person's honour than
Your high profession spiritual, that again
I do refuse you for my judge, and here,
Before you all, appeal unto the Pope,
To bring my whole cause 'fore his holiness,   120
And to be judged by him.
        She curtsies to the King, and offers to depart
CAMPEIUS   The Queen is obstinate,
Stubborn to justice, apt to accuse it, and

Disdainful to be tried by't; 'tis not well.
She's going away.

KING HENRY Call her again.

CRIER Katherine, Queen of England, come into the court.

GRIFFITH Madam, you are called back.

QUEEN KATHERINE

What need you note it? Pray you keep your way;
When you are called, return. Now the Lord help!
130 They vex me past my patience. Pray you, pass on.
I will not tarry; no, nor ever more
Upon this business my appearance make
In any of their courts.

Exeunt Queen and her attendants

KING HENRY   Go thy ways, Kate.
That man i'th'world who shall report he has
A better wife, let him in naught be trusted
For speaking false in that. Thou art alone –
If thy rare qualities, sweet gentleness,
Thy meekness saint-like, wife-like government,
Obeying in commanding, and thy parts
140 Sovereign and pious else, could speak thee out –
The queen of earthly queens. She's noble born,
And like her true nobility she has
Carried herself towards me.

WOLSEY   Most gracious sir,
In humblest manner I require your highness
That it shall please you to declare in hearing
Of all these ears – for where I am robbed and bound,
There must I be unloosed, although not there
At once and fully satisfied – whether ever I
Did broach this business to your highness, or
150 Laid any scruple in your way which might
Induce you to the question on't, or ever
Have to you, but with thanks to God for such

A royal lady, spake one the least word that might
Be to the prejudice of her present state,
Or touch of her good person?

KING HENRY   My lord Cardinal,
I do excuse you; yea, upon mine honour,
I free you from't. You are not to be taught
That you have many enemies that know not
Why they are so, but, like to village curs,
Bark when their fellows do. By some of these   160
The Queen is put in anger. You're excused.
But will you be more justified? You ever
Have wished the sleeping of this business, never desired
It to be stirred, but oft have hindered, oft,
The passages made toward it. On my honour,
I speak my good lord Cardinal to this point,
And thus far clear him. Now, what moved me to't,
I will be bold with time and your attention.
Then mark th'inducement. Thus it came – give heed
     to't:
My conscience first received a tenderness,   170
Scruple, and prick, on certain speeches uttered
By th'Bishop of Bayonne, then French ambassador,
Who had been hither sent on the debating
A marriage 'twixt the Duke of Orleans and
Our daughter Mary. I'th'progress of this business,
Ere a determinate resolution, he –
I mean the Bishop – did require a respite,
Wherein he might the King his lord advertise
Whether our daughter were legitimate,
Respecting this our marriage with the dowager,   180
Sometimes our brother's wife. This respite shook
The bosom of my conscience, entered me,
Yea, with a spitting power, and made to tremble
The region of my breast; which forced such way

That many mazed considerings did throng
And pressed in with this caution. First, methought
I stood not in the smile of heaven, who had
Commanded nature that my lady's womb,
If it conceived a male child by me, should
190   Do no more offices of life to't than
The grave does to th'dead; for her male issue
Or died where they were made, or shortly after
This world had aired them. Hence I took a thought
This was a judgement on me, that my kingdom,
Well worthy the best heir o'th'world, should not
Be gladded in't by me. Then follows that
I weighed the danger which my realms stood in
By this my issue's fail, and that gave to me
Many a groaning throe. Thus hulling in
200   The wild sea of my conscience, I did steer
Toward this remedy, whereupon we are
Now present here together; that's to say,
I meant to rectify my conscience, which
I then did feel full sick, and yet not well,
By all the reverend fathers of the land
And doctors learned. First I began in private
With you, my lord of Lincoln. You remember
How under my oppression I did reek
When I first moved you.

LINCOLN   Very well, my liege.

KING HENRY
210   I have spoke long; be pleased yourself to say
How far you satisfied me.

LINCOLN   So please your highness,
The question did at first so stagger me —
Bearing a state of mighty moment in't,
And consequence of dread — that I committed
The daring'st counsel which I had to doubt,

And did entreat your highness to this course
Which you are running here.
KING HENRY   I then moved you,
My lord of Canterbury, and got your leave
To make this present summons. Unsolicited
I left no reverend person in this court,   220
But by particular consent proceeded
Under your hands and seals. Therefore, go on,
For no dislike i'th'world against the person
Of the good Queen, but the sharp thorny points
Of my allegèd reasons, drives this forward.
Prove but our marriage lawful, by my life
And kingly dignity, we are contented
To wear our mortal state to come with her,
Katherine our Queen, before the primest creature
That's paragoned o'th'world.
CAMPEIUS   So please your highness,   230
The Queen being absent, 'tis a needful fitness
That we adjourn this court till further day.
Meanwhile must be an earnest motion
Made to the Queen to call back her appeal
She intends unto his holiness.
KING HENRY (aside)   I may perceive
These Cardinals trifle with me. I abhor
This dilatory sloth and tricks of Rome.
My learned and well-belovèd servant, Cranmer,
Prithee return. With thy approach I know
My comfort comes along. (To them) Break up the court;   240
I say, set on.

                              Exeunt in manner as they entered

                                        *

III.I   *Enter the Queen and her women, as at work*

QUEEN KATHERINE

Take thy lute, wench. My soul grows sad with troubles;
Sing, and disperse 'em if thou canst. Leave working.

GENTLEWOMAN *(sings)*

Orpheus with his lute made trees,
And the mountain tops that freeze,
Bow themselves when he did sing.
To his music plants and flowers
Ever sprung, as sun and showers
There had made a lasting spring.

Everything that heard him play,
10   Even the billows of the sea,
Hung their heads, and then lay by.
In sweet music is such art,
Killing care and grief of heart
Fall asleep, or hearing die.

Enter a Gentleman

QUEEN KATHERINE

How now?

GENTLEMAN

An't please your grace, the two great Cardinals
Wait in the presence.

QUEEN KATHERINE   Would they speak with me?

GENTLEMAN

They willed me say so, madam.

QUEEN KATHERINE   Pray their graces
To come near.   *Exit Gentleman*

What can be their business
20   With me, a poor weak woman, fall'n from favour?
I do not like their coming. Now I think on't,

They should be good men, their affairs as righteous:
But all hoods make not monks.

Enter the two Cardinals, Wolsey and Campeius

WOLSEY   Peace to your highness!

QUEEN KATHERINE
Your graces find me here part of a housewife —
I would be all, against the worst may happen.
What are your pleasures with me, reverend lords?

WOLSEY
May it please you, noble madam, to withdraw
Into your private chamber, we shall give you
The full cause of our coming.

QUEEN KATHERINE   Speak it here.
There's nothing I have done yet, o'my conscience,   30
Deserves a corner. Would all other women
Could speak this with as free a soul as I do!
My lords, I care not — so much I am happy
Above a number — if my actions
Were tried by every tongue, every eye saw 'em,
Envy and base opinion set against 'em,
I know my life so even. If your business
Seek me out, and that way I am wife in,
Out with it boldly. Truth loves open dealing.

WOLSEY *Tanta est erga te mentis integritas, Regina serenis-*   40
sima —

QUEEN KATHERINE
O, good my lord, no Latin!
I am not such a truant since my coming
As not to know the language I have lived in.
A strange tongue makes my cause more strange, sus-
        picious;
Pray speak in English. Here are some will thank you,
If you speak truth, for their poor mistress' sake.
Believe me, she has had much wrong. Lord Cardinal,

The willing'st sin I ever yet committed
50   May be absolved in English.
WOLSEY   Noble lady,
I am sorry my integrity should breed –
And service to his majesty and you –
So deep suspicion, where all faith was meant.
We come not by the way of accusation,
To taint that honour every good tongue blesses,
Nor to betray you any way to sorrow –
You have too much, good lady – but to know
How you stand minded in the weighty difference
Between the King and you, and to deliver,
60   Like free and honest men, our just opinions
And comforts to your cause.
CAMPEIUS   Most honoured madam,
My lord of York, out of his noble nature,
Zeal and obedience he still bore your grace,
Forgetting, like a good man, your late censure
Both of his truth and him – which was too far –
Offers, as I do, in a sign of peace,
His service, and his counsel.
QUEEN KATHERINE (aside)   To betray me. –
My lords, I thank you both for your good wills.
Ye speak like honest men – pray God ye prove so!
70   But how to make ye suddenly an answer
In such a point of weight, so near mine honour,
More near my life, I fear, with my weak wit,
And to such men of gravity and learning,
In truth I know not. I was set at work
Among my maids, full little – God knows – looking
Either for such men or such business.
For her sake that I have been – for I feel
The last fit of my greatness – good your graces,
Let me have time and counsel for my cause.

Alas, I am a woman friendless, hopeless!   80

WOLSEY

Madam, you wrong the King's love with these fears;
Your hopes and friends are infinite.

QUEEN KATHERINE   In England
But little for my profit. Can you think, lords,
That any Englishman dare give me counsel,
Or be a known friend, 'gainst his highness' pleasure –
Though he be grown so desperate to be honest –
And live a subject? Nay, forsooth, my friends,
They that must weigh out my afflictions,
They that my trust must grow to, live not here.
They are, as all my other comforts, far hence,   90
In mine own country, lords.

CAMPEIUS   I would your grace
Would leave your griefs, and take my counsel.

QUEEN KATHERINE   How, sir?

CAMPEIUS

Put your main cause into the King's protection;
He's loving and most gracious. 'Twill be much
Both for your honour better and your cause;
For if the trial of the law o'ertake ye
You'll part away disgraced.

WOLSEY   He tells you rightly.

QUEEN KATHERINE

Ye tell me what ye wish for both – my ruin.
Is this your Christian counsel? Out upon ye!
Heaven is above all yet; there sits a judge   100
That no king can corrupt.

CAMPEIUS   Your rage mistakes us.

QUEEN KATHERINE

The more shame for ye! Holy men I thought ye,
Upon my soul, two reverend cardinal virtues;
But cardinal sins and hollow hearts I fear ye.

Mend 'em for shame, my lords. Is this your comfort?
The cordial that ye bring a wretched lady,
A woman lost among ye, laughed at, scorned?
I will not wish ye half my miseries;
I have more charity. But say I warned ye;
110   Take heed, for heaven's sake take heed, lest at once
The burden of my sorrows fall upon ye.

WOLSEY
Madam, this is a mere distraction.
You turn the good we offer into envy.

QUEEN KATHERINE
Ye turn me into nothing. Woe upon ye,
And all such false professors! Would you have me –
If you have any justice, any pity,
If ye be anything but churchmen's habits –
Put my sick cause into his hands that hates me?
Alas, 'has banished me his bed already,
120   His love too long ago! I am old, my lords,
And all the fellowship I hold now with him
Is only my obedience. What can happen
To me above this wretchedness? All your studies
Make me a curse like this!

CAMPEIUS   Your fears are worse.

QUEEN KATHERINE
Have I lived thus long – let me speak myself,
Since virtue finds no friends – a wife, a true one?
A woman, I dare say without vainglory,
Never yet branded with suspicion?
Have I with all my full affections
130   Still met the King, loved him next heaven, obeyed him,
Been, out of fondness, superstitious to him,
Almost forgot my prayers to content him,
And am I thus rewarded? 'Tis not well, lords.
Bring me a constant woman to her husband,

One that ne'er dreamed a joy beyond his pleasure,
And to that woman, when she has done most,
Yet will I add an honour – a great patience.

WOLSEY
Madam, you wander from the good we aim at.

QUEEN KATHERINE
My lord, I dare not make myself so guilty
To give up willingly that noble title   140
Your master wed me to. Nothing but death
Shall e'er divorce my dignities.

WOLSEY   Pray hear me.

QUEEN KATHERINE
Would I had never trod this English earth,
Or felt the flatteries that grow upon it!
Ye have angels' faces, but heaven knows your hearts.
What will become of me now, wretched lady?
I am the most unhappy woman living.
(To her women)
Alas, poor wenches, where are now your fortunes?
Shipwrecked upon a kingdom where no pity,
No friends, no hope, no kindred weep for me;   150
Almost no grave allowed me. Like the lily
That once was mistress of the field and flourished,
I'll hang my head, and perish.

WOLSEY   If your grace
Could but be brought to know our ends are honest,
You'd feel more comfort. Why should we, good lady,
Upon what cause, wrong you? Alas, our places,
The way of our profession is against it.
We are to cure such sorrows, not to sow 'em.
For goodness' sake, consider what you do,
How you may hurt yourself, ay, utterly   160
Grow from the King's acquaintance, by this carriage.
The hearts of princes kiss obedience,

So much they love it; but to stubborn spirits
They swell, and grow as terrible as storms.
I know you have a gentle, noble temper,
A soul as even as a calm. Pray think us
Those we profess, peace-makers, friends, and servants.

CAMPEIUS

Madam, you'll find it so. You wrong your virtues
With these weak women's fears. A noble spirit,
170 As yours was put into you, ever casts
Such doubts as false coin from it. The King loves you;
Beware you lose it not. For us, if you please
To trust us in your business, we are ready
To use our utmost studies in your service.

QUEEN KATHERINE

Do what ye will, my lords, and pray forgive me
If I have used myself unmannerly.
You know I am a woman, lacking wit
To make a seemly answer to such persons.
Pray do my service to his majesty;
180 He has my heart yet, and shall have my prayers
While I shall have my life. Come, reverend fathers,
Bestow your counsels on me. She now begs
That little thought, when she set footing here,
She should have bought her dignities so dear.

Exeunt

III.2   *Enter the Duke of Norfolk, Duke of Suffolk, Lord*
              Surrey, and the Lord Chamberlain

NORFOLK

If you will now unite in your complaints
And force them with a constancy, the Cardinal
Cannot stand under them. If you omit
The offer of this time, I cannot promise

But that you shall sustain more new disgraces
With these you bear already.

SURREY   I am joyful
To meet the least occasion that may give me
Remembrance of my father-in-law, the Duke,
To be revenged on him.

SUFFOLK   Which of the peers
Have uncontemned gone by him, or at least   10
Strangely neglected? When did he regard
The stamp of nobleness in any person
Out of himself?

LORD CHAMBERLAIN
                              My lords, you speak your pleasures.
What he deserves of you and me I know;
What we can do to him – though now the time
Gives way to us – I much fear. If you cannot
Bar his access to th'King, never attempt
Anything on him, for he hath a witchcraft
Over the King in's tongue.

NORFOLK   O, fear him not;
His spell in that is out. The King hath found   20
Matter against him that for ever mars
The honey of his language. No, he's settled,
Not to come off, in his displeasure.

SURREY   Sir,
I should be glad to hear such news as this
Once every hour.

NORFOLK   Believe it, this is true.
In the divorce his contrary proceedings
Are all unfolded, wherein he appears
As I would wish mine enemy.

SURREY   How came
His practices to light?

SUFFOLK   Most strangely.

SURREY   O, how, how?

SUFFOLK

30   The Cardinal's letters to the Pope miscarried,
        And came to th'eye o'th'King, wherein was read
        How that the Cardinal did entreat his holiness
        To stay the judgement o'th'divorce; for if
        It did take place, 'I do' – quoth he – 'perceive
        My King is tangled in affection to
        A creature of the Queen's, Lady Anne Bullen.'

SURREY

Has the King this?

SUFFOLK   Believe it.

SURREY   Will this work?

LORD CHAMBERLAIN

        The King in this perceives him how he coasts
        And hedges his own way. But in this point
40   All his tricks founder, and he brings his physic
        After his patient's death: the King already
        Hath married the fair lady.

SURREY   Would he had!

SUFFOLK

        May you be happy in your wish, my lord,
        For I profess you have it.

SURREY   Now all my joy

Trace the conjunction!

SUFFOLK   My amen to't!

NORFOLK   All men's!

SUFFOLK

        There's order given for her coronation.
        Marry, this is yet but young, and may be left
        To some ears unrecounted. But, my lords,
        She is a gallant creature, and complete
50   In mind and feature. I persuade me, from her
        Will fall some blessing to this land, which shall

In it be memorized.

SURREY   But will the King
Digest this letter of the Cardinal's?
The Lord forbid!

NORFOLK   Marry, amen!

SUFFOLK   No, no.
There be more wasps that buzz about his nose
Will make this sting the sooner. Cardinal Campeius
Is stol'n away to Rome; hath ta'en no leave;
Has left the cause o'th'King unhandled, and
Is posted as the agent of our Cardinal
To second all his plot. I do assure you   60
The King cried 'Ha!' at this.

LORD CHAMBERLAIN   Now God incense him,
And let him cry 'Ha!' louder!

NORFOLK   But, my lord,
When returns Cranmer?

SUFFOLK
He is returned in his opinions, which
Have satisfied the King for his divorce,
Together with all famous colleges
Almost in Christendom. Shortly, I believe,
His second marriage shall be published, and
Her coronation. Katherine no more
Shall be called Queen, but Princess Dowager,   70
And widow to Prince Arthur.

NORFOLK   This same Cranmer's
A worthy fellow, and hath ta'en much pain
In the King's business.

SUFFOLK   He has, and we shall see him
For it an archbishop.

NORFOLK   So I hear.

SUFFOLK   'Tis so.
    Enter Wolsey and Cromwell

The Cardinal!

NORFOLK   Observe, observe, he's moody.

WOLSEY
The packet, Cromwell,
Gave't you the King?

CROMWELL   To his own hand, in's bedchamber.

WOLSEY
Looked he o'th'inside of the paper?

CROMWELL   Presently
He did unseal them, and the first he viewed
He did it with a serious mind; a heed
Was in his countenance. You he bade
Attend him here this morning.

WOLSEY   Is he ready
To come abroad?

CROMWELL   I think by this he is.

WOLSEY
Leave me awhile.   *Exit Cromwell*
(*Aside*) It shall be to the Duchess of Alençon,
The French King's sister; he shall marry her.
Anne Bullen? No, I'll no Anne Bullens for him;
There's more in't than fair visage. Bullen!
No, we'll no Bullens. Speedily I wish
To hear from Rome. The Marchioness of Pembroke?

NORFOLK
He's discontented.

SUFFOLK   Maybe he hears the King
Does whet his anger to him.

SURREY   Sharp enough,
Lord, for Thy justice!

WOLSEY (*aside*)
The late Queen's gentlewoman, a knight's daughter,
To be her mistress' mistress? the Queen's Queen?
This candle burns not clear; 'tis I must snuff it,

Then out it goes. What though I know her virtuous
And well deserving? Yet I know her for
A spleeny Lutheran, and not wholesome to
Our cause, that she should lie i'th'bosom of   100
Our hard-ruled King. Again, there is sprung up
An heretic, an arch-one, Cranmer, one
Hath crawled into the favour of the King,
And is his oracle.

NORFOLK   He is vexed at something.

SURREY

I would 'twere something that would fret the string,
The master-cord on's heart!

Enter the King, reading of a schedule, and Lovell

SUFFOLK   The King, the King!

KING HENRY

What piles of wealth hath he accumulated
To his own portion! And what expense by th'hour
Seems to flow from him! How, i'th'name of thrift,
Does he rake this together? – Now, my lords,   110
Saw you the Cardinal?

NORFOLK   My lord, we have
Stood here observing him. Some strange commotion
Is in his brain; he bites his lip, and starts,
Stops on a sudden, looks upon the ground,
Then lays his finger on his temple; straight
Springs out into fast gait; then stops again,
Strikes his breast hard, and anon he casts
His eye against the moon. In most strange postures
We have seen him set himself.

KING HENRY   It may well be,
There is a mutiny in's mind. This morning   120
Papers of state he sent me to peruse,
As I required; and wot you what I found
There, on my conscience, put unwittingly?

Forsooth, an inventory, thus importing
The several parcels of his plate, his treasure,
Rich stuffs, and ornaments of household, which
I find at such proud rate that it outspeaks
Possession of a subject.

NORFOLK   It's heaven's will;
Some spirit put this paper in the packet
130   To bless your eye withal.

KING HENRY   If we did think
His contemplation were above the earth
And fixed on spiritual object, he should still
Dwell in his musings; but I am afraid
His thinkings are below the moon, not worth
His serious considering.

*The King takes his seat, whispers to Lovell, who goes
to the Cardinal*

WOLSEY   Heaven forgive me!
Ever God bless your highness!

KING HENRY   Good my lord,
You are full of heavenly stuff, and bear the inventory
Of your best graces in your mind, the which
You were now running o'er. You have scarce time
140   To steal from spiritual leisure a brief span
To keep your earthly audit. Sure, in that
I deem you an ill husband, and am glad
To have you therein my companion.

WOLSEY   Sir,
For holy offices I have a time; a time
To think upon the part of business which
I bear i'th'state; and nature does require
Her times of preservation, which perforce
I, her frail son, amongst my brethren mortal,
Must give my tendance to.

KING HENRY   You have said well.

WOLSEY
    And ever may your highness yoke together,   150
    As I will lend you cause, my doing well
    With my well saying!
KING HENRY   'Tis well said again,
    And 'tis a kind of good deed to say well;
    And yet words are no deeds. My father loved you;
    He said he did, and with his deed did crown
    His word upon you. Since I had my office,
    I have kept you next my heart, have not alone
    Employed you where high profits might come home,
    But pared my present havings to bestow
    My bounties upon you.
WOLSEY (aside)   What should this mean?   160
SURREY (aside)
    The Lord increase this business!
KING HENRY   Have I not made you
    The prime man of the state? I pray you tell me
    If what I now pronounce you have found true;
    And, if you may confess it, say withal
    If you are bound to us or no. What say you?
WOLSEY
    My sovereign, I confess your royal graces,
    Showered on me daily, have been more than could
    My studied purposes requite, which went
    Beyond all man's endeavours. My endeavours
    Have ever come too short of my desires,   170
    Yet filed with my abilities. Mine own ends
    Have been mine so that evermore they pointed
    To th'good of your most sacred person and
    The profit of the state. For your great graces
    Heaped upon me, poor undeserver, I
    Can nothing render but allegiant thanks,
    My prayers to heaven for you, my loyalty,

Which ever has and ever shall be growing,
Till death, that winter, kill it.

KING HENRY   Fairly answered!
180 A loyal and obedient subject is
Therein illustrated. The honour of it
Does pay the act of it, as, i'th'contrary,
The foulness is the punishment. I presume
That as my hand has opened bounty to you,
My heart dropped love, my power rained honour, more
On you than any, so your hand and heart,
Your brain and every function of your power,
Should, notwithstanding that your bond of duty,
As 'twere in love's particular, be more
190 To me, your friend, than any.

WOLSEY   I do profess
That for your highness' good I ever laboured
More than mine own; that am, have, and will be —
Though all the world should crack their duty to you,
And throw it from their soul; though perils did
Abound, as thick as thought could make 'em, and
Appear in forms more horrid — yet my duty,
As doth a rock against the chiding flood,
Should the approach of this wild river break,
And stand unshaken yours.

KING HENRY   'Tis nobly spoken.
200 Take notice, lords, he has a loyal breast,
For you have seen him open't. Read o'er this,
          (*he gives him papers*)
And after, this; and then to breakfast with
What appetite you have.

                    Exit King, frowning upon the Cardinal; the nobles
                    throng after him, smiling and whispering

WOLSEY   What should this mean?
What sudden anger's this? How have I reaped it?

He parted frowning from me, as if ruin
Leaped from his eyes. So looks the chafèd lion
Upon the daring huntsman that has galled him,
Then makes him nothing. I must read this paper:
I fear, the story of his anger. 'Tis so;
This paper has undone me. 'Tis th'account   210
Of all that world of wealth I have drawn together
For mine own ends – indeed, to gain the popedom,
And fee my friends in Rome. O negligence,
Fit for a fool to fall by! What cross devil
Made me put this main secret in the packet
I sent the King? Is there no way to cure this?
No new device to beat this from his brains?
I know 'twill stir him strongly; yet I know
A way, if it take right, in spite of fortune
Will bring me off again. What's this? 'To th'Pope'?   220
The letter, as I live, with all the business
I writ to's holiness. Nay then, farewell!
I have touched the highest point of all my greatness,
And from that full meridian of my glory
I haste now to my setting. I shall fall
Like a bright exhalation in the evening,
And no man see me more.

Enter to Wolsey the Dukes of Norfolk and Suffolk, the
Earl of Surrey, and the Lord Chamberlain

NORFOLK

Hear the King's pleasure, Cardinal, who commands you
To render up the great seal presently
Into our hands, and to confine yourself   230
To Asher House, my lord of Winchester's,
Till you hear further from his highness.

WOLSEY   Stay:
Where's your commission, lords? Words cannot carry
Authority so weighty.

SUFFOLK   Who dare cross 'em,
Bearing the King's will from his mouth expressly?

WOLSEY
Till I find more than will or words to do it –
I mean your malice – know, officious lords,
I dare, and must deny it. Now I feel
Of what coarse metal ye are moulded – envy;

240 How eagerly ye follow my disgraces
As if it fed ye! And how sleek and wanton
Ye appear in everything may bring my ruin!
Follow your envious courses, men of malice;
You have Christian warrant for 'em, and no doubt
In time will find their fit rewards. That seal
You ask with such a violence, the King,
Mine and your master, with his own hand gave me;
Bade me enjoy it, with the place and honours,
During my life; and, to confirm his goodness,

250 Tied it by letters patents. Now, who'll take it?

SURREY
The King that gave it.

WOLSEY   It must be himself then.

SURREY
Thou art a proud traitor, priest.

WOLSEY   Proud lord, thou liest.
Within these forty hours Surrey durst better
Have burnt that tongue than said so.

SURREY   Thy ambition,
Thou scarlet sin, robbed this bewailing land
Of noble Buckingham, my father-in-law.
The heads of all thy brother Cardinals,
With thee and all thy best parts bound together,
Weighed not a hair of his. Plague of your policy!

260 You sent me deputy for Ireland,
Far from his succour, from the King, from all

That might have mercy on the fault thou gav'st him;
Whilst your great goodness, out of holy pity,
Absolved him with an axe.

WOLSEY   This, and all else
This talking lord can lay upon my credit,
I answer is most false. The Duke by law
Found his deserts. How innocent I was
From any private malice in his end
His noble jury and foul cause can witness.
If I loved many words, lord, I should tell you   270
You have as little honesty as honour,
That in the way of loyalty and truth
Toward the King, my ever royal master,
Dare mate a sounder man than Surrey can be,
And all that love his follies.

SURREY   By my soul,
Your long coat, priest, protects you; thou shouldst feel
My sword i'th'life-blood of thee else. My lords,
Can ye endure to hear this arrogance,
And from this fellow? If we live thus tamely,
To be thus jaded by a piece of scarlet,   280
Farewell nobility! Let his grace go forward,
And dare us with his cap, like larks.

WOLSEY   All goodness
Is poison to thy stomach.

SURREY   Yes, that goodness
Of gleaning all the land's wealth into one,
Into your own hands, Cardinal, by extortion –
The goodness of your intercepted packets
You writ to th'Pope against the King! Your goodness,
Since you provoke me, shall be most notorious.
My lord of Norfolk, as you are truly noble,
As you respect the common good, the state   290
Of our despised nobility, our issues –

Who, if he live, will scarce be gentlemen –
Produce the grand sum of his sins, the articles
Collected from his life. I'll startle you
Worse than the sacring bell, when the brown wench
Lay kissing in your arms, lord Cardinal.

WOLSEY
How much, methinks, I could despise this man,
But that I am bound in charity against it!

NORFOLK
Those articles, my lord, are in the King's hand;
300 But thus much, they are foul ones.

WOLSEY   So much fairer
And spotless shall mine innocence arise
When the King knows my truth.

SURREY   This cannot save you.
I thank my memory, I yet remember
Some of these articles, and out they shall.
Now, if you can blush and cry 'Guilty', Cardinal,
You'll show a little honesty.

WOLSEY   Speak on, sir;
I dare your worst objections. If I blush,
It is to see a nobleman want manners.

SURREY
I had rather want those than my head. Have at you!
310 First, that without the King's assent or knowledge
You wrought to be a legate, by which power
You maimed the jurisdiction of all bishops.

NORFOLK
Then, that in all you writ to Rome, or else
To foreign princes, *Ego et Rex meus*
Was still inscribed; in which you brought the King
To be your servant.

SUFFOLK   Then, that without the knowledge
Either of King or Council, when you went

Ambassador to the Emperor, you made bold
To carry into Flanders the great seal.

SURREY

Item, you sent a large commission   320
To Gregory de Cassado, to conclude,
Without the King's will or the state's allowance,
A league between his highness and Ferrara.

SUFFOLK

That out of mere ambition you have caused
Your holy hat to be stamped on the King's coin.

SURREY

Then, that you have sent innumerable substance –
By what means got I leave to your own conscience –
To furnish Rome, and to prepare the ways
You have for dignities, to the mere undoing
Of all the kingdom. Many more there are,   330
Which since they are of you, and odious,
I will not taint my mouth with.

LORD CHAMBERLAIN   O my lord,
Press not a falling man too far! 'Tis virtue.
His faults lie open to the laws; let them,
Not you, correct him. My heart weeps to see him
So little of his great self.

SURREY   I forgive him.

SUFFOLK

Lord Cardinal, the King's further pleasure is –
Because all those things you have done of late
By your power legatine within this kingdom
Fall into th'compass of a praemunire –   340
That therefore such a writ be sued against you:
To forfeit all your goods, lands, tenements,
Chattels, and whatsoever, and to be
Out of the King's protection. This is my charge.

NORFOLK

And so we'll leave you to your meditations
How to live better. For your stubborn answer
About the giving back the great seal to us,
The King shall know it and, no doubt, shall thank you.
So fare you well, my little good lord Cardinal.

Exeunt all but Wolsey

WOLSEY

350   So farewell – to the little good you bear me.
Farewell, a long farewell, to all my greatness!
This is the state of man: today he puts forth
The tender leaves of hopes, tomorrow blossoms,
And bears his blushing honours thick upon him.
The third day comes a frost, a killing frost,
And when he thinks, good easy man, full surely
His greatness is a-ripening, nips his root,
And then he falls, as I do. I have ventured,
Like little wanton boys that swim on bladders,
360   This many summers in a sea of glory,
But far beyond my depth. My high-blown pride
At length broke under me, and now has left me
Weary, and old with service, to the mercy
Of a rude stream that must for ever hide me.
Vain pomp and glory of this world, I hate ye.
I feel my heart new opened. O, how wretched
Is that poor man that hangs on princes' favours!
There is betwixt that smile we would aspire to,
That sweet aspect of princes, and their ruin,
370   More pangs and fears than wars or women have;
And when he falls, he falls like Lucifer,
Never to hope again.

Enter Cromwell, standing amazed

Why, how now, Cromwell?

CROMWELL
    I have no power to speak, sir.

WOLSEY   What, amazed
    At my misfortunes? Can thy spirit wonder
    A great man should decline? Nay, an you weep
    I am fall'n indeed.

CROMWELL   How does your grace?

WOLSEY   Why, well;
    Never so truly happy, my good Cromwell.
    I know myself now, and I feel within me
    A peace above all earthly dignities,
    A still and quiet conscience. The King has cured me,   380
    I humbly thank his grace, and from these shoulders,
    These ruined pillars, out of pity, taken
    A load would sink a navy – too much honour.
    O, 'tis a burden, Cromwell, 'tis a burden
    Too heavy for a man that hopes for heaven!

CROMWELL
    I am glad your grace has made that right use of it.

WOLSEY
    I hope I have: I am able now, methinks,
    Out of a fortitude of soul I feel,
    To endure more miseries and greater far
    Than my weak-hearted enemies dare offer.   390
    What news abroad?

CROMWELL   The heaviest, and the worst,
    Is your displeasure with the King.

WOLSEY   God bless him!

CROMWELL
    The next is that Sir Thomas More is chosen
    Lord Chancellor in your place.

WOLSEY   That's somewhat sudden.
    But he's a learnèd man. May he continue
    Long in his highness' favour, and do justice

For truth's sake, and his conscience, that his bones,
When he has run his course and sleeps in blessings,
May have a tomb of orphans' tears wept on him.

400   What more?

CROMWELL   That Cranmer is returned with welcome,
Installed lord Archbishop of Canterbury.

WOLSEY
That's news indeed.

CROMWELL   Last, that the Lady Anne,
Whom the King hath in secrecy long married,
This day was viewed in open as his queen,
Going to chapel, and the voice is now
Only about her coronation.

WOLSEY
There was the weight that pulled me down. O
       Cromwell,
The King has gone beyond me. All my glories
In that one woman I have lost for ever.

410   No sun shall ever usher forth mine honours,
Or gild again the noble troops that waited
Upon my smiles. Go get thee from me, Cromwell;
I am a poor fall'n man, unworthy now
To be thy lord and master. Seek the King –
That sun, I pray, may never set! I have told him
What and how true thou art. He will advance thee;
Some little memory of me will stir him –
I know his noble nature – not to let
Thy hopeful service perish too. Good Cromwell,

420   Neglect him not; make use now, and provide
For thine own future safety.

CROMWELL   O my lord,
Must I then leave you? Must I needs forgo
So good, so noble, and so true a master?
Bear witness, all that have not hearts of iron,

With what a sorrow Cromwell leaves his lord.
The King shall have my service, but my prayers
For ever and for ever shall be yours.

WOLSEY

Cromwell, I did not think to shed a tear
In all my miseries, but thou hast forced me,
Out of thy honest truth, to play the woman.   430
Let's dry our eyes, and thus far hear me, Cromwell,
And when I am forgotten, as I shall be,
And sleep in dull cold marble, where no mention
Of me more must be heard of, say I taught thee —
Say Wolsey, that once trod the ways of glory,
And sounded all the depths and shoals of honour,
Found thee a way, out of his wreck, to rise in,
A sure and safe one, though thy master missed it.
Mark but my fall, and that that ruined me.
Cromwell, I charge thee, fling away ambition: 440
By that sin fell the angels. How can man then,
The image of his Maker, hope to win by it?
Love thyself last, cherish those hearts that hate thee;
Corruption wins not more than honesty.
Still in thy right hand carry gentle peace
To silence envious tongues. Be just, and fear not.
Let all the ends thou aim'st at be thy country's,
Thy God's, and truth's. Then if thou fall'st, O Crom-
        well,
Thou fall'st a blessèd martyr. Serve the King;
And prithee, lead me in.   450
There take an inventory of all I have,
To the last penny; 'tis the King's. My robe,
And my integrity to heaven, is all
I dare now call mine own. O Cromwell, Cromwell,
Had I but served my God with half the zeal
I served my King, He would not in mine age

Have left me naked to mine enemies.

CROMWELL

Good sir, have patience.

WOLSEY   So I have. Farewell,
The hopes of court! My hopes in heaven do dwell.

Exeunt

*

IV.1   *Enter two Gentlemen, meeting one another*

FIRST GENTLEMAN

You're well met once again.

SECOND GENTLEMAN   So are you.

FIRST GENTLEMAN

You come to take your stand here and behold
The Lady Anne pass from her coronation?

SECOND GENTLEMAN

'Tis all my business. At our last encounter
The Duke of Buckingham came from his trial.

FIRST GENTLEMAN

'Tis very true. But that time offered sorrow,
This, general joy.

SECOND GENTLEMAN 'Tis well. The citizens,
I am sure, have shown at full their royal minds —
As, let 'em have their rights, they are ever forward —
In celebration of this day with shows,
Pageants, and sights of honour.

FIRST GENTLEMAN   Never greater,
Nor, I'll assure you, better taken, sir.

SECOND GENTLEMAN

May I be bold to ask what that contains,
That paper in your hand?

FIRST GENTLEMAN   Yes, 'tis the list

Of those that claim their offices this day,
By custom of the coronation.
The Duke of Suffolk is the first, and claims
To be High Steward; next, the Duke of Norfolk,
He to be Earl Marshal. You may read the rest.

SECOND GENTLEMAN
I thank you, sir; had I not known those customs,   20
I should have been beholding to your paper.
But I beseech you, what's become of Katherine,
The Princess Dowager? How goes her business?

FIRST GENTLEMAN
That I can tell you too. The Archbishop
Of Canterbury, accompanied with other
Learnèd and reverend fathers of his order,
Held a late court at Dunstable, six miles off
From Ampthill, where the Princess lay; to which
She was often cited by them, but appeared not.
And, to be short, for not appearance, and   30
The King's late scruple, by the main assent
Of all these learnèd men, she was divorced,
And the late marriage made of none effect;
Since which she was removed to Kimbolton,
Where she remains now sick.

SECOND GENTLEMAN   Alas, good lady!

    Trumpets
The trumpets sound. Stand close, the Queen is coming.
    Hautboys
    The Order of the Coronation:
    1. A lively flourish of trumpets
    2. Then two Judges
    3. Lord Chancellor, with purse and mace before him
    4. Choristers singing
        Music
    5. Mayor of London, bearing the mace. Then Garter,

in his coat of arms, and on his head he wore a gilt
copper crown

6. Marquis Dorset, bearing a sceptre of gold, on his
head a demi-coronal of gold. With him the Earl of
Surrey, bearing the rod of silver with the dove,
crowned with an earl's coronet. Collars of Esses

7. Duke of Suffolk, in his robe of estate, his coronet
on his head, bearing a long white wand, as High
Steward. With him the Duke of Norfolk, with the rod
of marshalship, a coronet on his head. Collars of Esses

8. A canopy borne by four of the Cinque Ports;
under it the Queen in her robe; in her hair, richly
adorned with pearl, crowned. On each side her the
Bishops of London and Winchester

9. The old Duchess of Norfolk, in a coronal of gold
wrought with flowers, bearing the Queen's train

10. Certain ladies or Countesses, with plain circlets
of gold without flowers

The procession passes over the stage in order and state

SECOND GENTLEMAN
A royal train, believe me. These I know.
Who's that that bears the sceptre?

FIRST GENTLEMAN   Marquis Dorset;
And that the Earl of Surrey, with the rod.

SECOND GENTLEMAN
40   A bold brave gentleman. That should be
The Duke of Suffolk?

FIRST GENTLEMAN   'Tis the same: High Steward.

SECOND GENTLEMAN
And that my Lord of Norfolk?

FIRST GENTLEMAN   Yes.

SECOND GENTLEMAN (*looking at the Queen*)
                                        Heaven bless thee!
Thou hast the sweetest face I ever looked on.

Sir, as I have a soul, she is an angel;
Our King has all the Indies in his arms,
And more, and richer, when he strains that lady.
I cannot blame his conscience.
FIRST GENTLEMAN   They that bear
The cloth of honour over her are four barons
Of the Cinque Ports.
SECOND GENTLEMAN
Those men are happy, and so are all are near her.   50
I take it, she that carries up the train
Is that old noble lady, Duchess of Norfolk.
FIRST GENTLEMAN
It is, and all the rest are countesses.
SECOND GENTLEMAN
Their coronets say so. These are stars indeed –
FIRST GENTLEMAN
And sometimes falling ones.
SECOND GENTLEMAN   No more of that.
    The end of the procession leaves; and then a great
    flourish of trumpets
    Enter a third Gentleman
FIRST GENTLEMAN
God save you, sir! Where have you been broiling?
THIRD GENTLEMAN
Among the crowd i'th'Abbey, where a finger
Could not be wedged in more; I am stifled
With the mere rankness of their joy.
SECOND GENTLEMAN   You saw
The ceremony?
THIRD GENTLEMAN That I did.
FIRST GENTLEMAN   How was it?   60
THIRD GENTLEMAN
Well worth the seeing.
SECOND GENTLEMAN   Good sir, speak it to us.

THIRD GENTLEMAN

As well as I am able. The rich stream
Of lords and ladies, having brought the Queen
To a prepared place in the choir, fell off
A distance from her, while her grace sat down
To rest awhile, some half an hour or so,
In a rich chair of state, opposing freely
The beauty of her person to the people.
Believe me, sir, she is the goodliest woman
70   That ever lay by man; which when the people
Had the full view of, such a noise arose
As the shrouds make at sea in a stiff tempest,
As loud, and to as many tunes. Hats, cloaks –
Doublets, I think – flew up, and had their faces
Been loose, this day they had been lost. Such joy
I never saw before. Great-bellied women,
That had not half a week to go, like rams
In the old time of war, would shake the press,
And make 'em reel before 'em. No man living
80   Could say 'This is my wife' there, all were woven
So strangely in one piece.

SECOND GENTLEMAN   But what followed?

THIRD GENTLEMAN

At length her grace rose, and with modest paces
Came to the altar, where she kneeled, and saint-like
Cast her fair eyes to heaven, and prayed devoutly,
Then rose again, and bowed her to the people;
When by the Archbishop of Canterbury
She had all the royal makings of a queen,
As holy oil, Edward Confessor's crown,
The rod, and bird of peace, and all such emblems
90   Laid nobly on her: which performed, the choir,
With all the choicest music of the kingdom,
Together sung *Te Deum*. So she parted,

And with the same full state paced back again
To York Place, where the feast is held.

FIRST GENTLEMAN   Sir,
You must no more call it York Place; that's past,
For since the Cardinal fell that title's lost:
'Tis now the King's, and called Whitehall.

THIRD GENTLEMAN   I know it,
But 'tis so lately altered that the old name
Is fresh about me.

SECOND GENTLEMAN What two reverend bishops
Were those that went on each side of the Queen?   100

THIRD GENTLEMAN
Stokesley and Gardiner, the one of Winchester,
Newly preferred from the King's secretary,
The other, London.

SECOND GENTLEMAN He of Winchester
Is held no great good lover of the Archbishop's,
The virtuous Cranmer.

THIRD GENTLEMAN   All the land knows that;
However, yet there is no great breach. When it comes,
Cranmer will find a friend will not shrink from him.

SECOND GENTLEMAN
Who may that be, I pray you?

THIRD GENTLEMAN   Thomas Cromwell,
A man in much esteem with th'King, and truly
A worthy friend. The King has made him Master   110
O'th'Jewel House,
And one, already, of the Privy Council.

SECOND GENTLEMAN
He will deserve more.

THIRD GENTLEMAN   Yes, without all doubt.
Come, gentlemen, ye shall go my way, which
Is to th'court, and there ye shall be my guests:
Something I can command. As I walk thither,

I'll tell ye more.
SECOND *and* THIRD GENTLEMEN
                              You may command us, sir.   *Exeunt*

IV.2   *Enter Katherine, Dowager, sick, led between*
              Griffith, her gentleman usher, and Patience, her
              woman

GRIFFITH
  How does your grace?
KATHERINE   O Griffith, sick to death.
  My legs like loaden branches bow to th'earth,
  Willing to leave their burden. Reach a chair.
  So: now, methinks, I feel a little ease.
  Didst thou not tell me, Griffith, as thou ledst me,
  That the great child of honour, Cardinal Wolsey,
  Was dead?
GRIFFITH   Yes, madam; but I think your grace,
  Out of the pain you suffered, gave no ear to't.
KATHERINE
  Prithee, good Griffith, tell me how he died.
10 If well, he stepped before me happily
  For my example.
GRIFFITH   Well, the voice goes, madam;
  For after the stout Earl Northumberland
  Arrested him at York, and brought him forward,
  As a man sorely tainted, to his answer,
  He fell sick suddenly, and grew so ill
  He could not sit his mule.
KATHERINE   Alas, poor man.
GRIFFITH
  At last, with easy roads, he came to Leicester,
  Lodged in the abbey, where the reverend abbot,

With all his covent, honourably received him;
To whom he gave these words: 'O father abbot,   20
An old man, broken with the storms of state,
Is come to lay his weary bones among ye;
Give him a little earth for charity.'
So went to bed, where eagerly his sickness
Pursued him still, and three nights after this,
About the hour of eight, which he himself
Foretold should be his last, full of repentance,
Continual meditations, tears, and sorrows,
He gave his honours to the world again,
His blessèd part to heaven, and slept in peace.   30

KATHERINE
So may he rest; his faults lie gently on him!
Yet thus far, Griffith, give me leave to speak him,
And yet with charity. He was a man
Of an unbounded stomach, ever ranking
Himself with princes; one that by suggestion
Tied all the kingdom. Simony was fair play;
His own opinion was his law. I'th'presence
He would say untruths, and be ever double
Both in his words and meaning. He was never,
But where he meant to ruin, pitiful.   40
His promises were as he then was, mighty,
But his performance as he is now, nothing.
Of his own body he was ill, and gave
The clergy ill example.

GRIFFITH   Noble madam,
Men's evil manners live in brass; their virtues
We write in water. May it please your highness
To hear me speak his good now?

KATHERINE   Yes, good Griffith,
I were malicious else.

GRIFFITH   This Cardinal,

Though from an humble stock, undoubtedly
50   Was fashioned to much honour. From his cradle
He was a scholar, and a ripe and good one,
Exceeding wise, fair-spoken, and persuading;
Lofty and sour to them that loved him not,
But, to those men that sought him, sweet as summer.
And though he were unsatisfied in getting –
Which was a sin – yet in bestowing, madam,
He was most princely: ever witness for him
Those twins of learning that he raised in you,
Ipswich and Oxford! – one of which fell with him,
60   Unwilling to outlive the good that did it;
The other, though unfinished, yet so famous,
So excellent in art, and still so rising,
That Christendom shall ever speak his virtue.
His overthrow heaped happiness upon him,
For then, and not till then, he felt himself,
And found the blessèdness of being little;
And, to add greater honours to his age
Than man could give him, he died fearing God.

KATHERINE
After my death I wish no other herald,
70   No other speaker of my living actions,
To keep mine honour from corruption
But such an honest chronicler as Griffith.
Whom I most hated living, thou hast made me,
With thy religious truth and modesty,
Now in his ashes honour. Peace be with him!
Patience, be near me still, and set me lower;
I have not long to trouble thee. Good Griffith,
Cause the musicians play me that sad note
I named my knell, whilst I sit meditating
80   On that celestial harmony I go to.

        Sad and solemn music

GRIFFITH

She is asleep. Good wench, let's sit down quiet,
For fear we wake her. Softly, gentle Patience.

The Vision:
Enter, solemnly tripping one after another, six per-
sonages clad in white robes, wearing on their heads
garlands of bays, and golden vizards on their faces;
branches of bays or palm in their hands. They first
congee unto her, then dance; and, at certain changes,
the first two hold a spare garland over her head, at
which the other four make reverent curtsies. Then the
two that held the garland deliver the same to the other
next two, who observe the same order in their
changes, and holding the garland over her head;
which done, they deliver the same garland to the last
two, who likewise observe the same order. At which,
as it were by inspiration, she makes in her sleep signs
of rejoicing, and holdeth up her hands to heaven; and
so in their dancing vanish, carrying the garland with
them. The music continues

KATHERINE

Spirits of peace, where are ye? Are ye all gone,
And leave me here in wretchedness behind ye?

GRIFFITH

Madam, we are here.

KATHERINE   It is not you I call for.
Saw ye none enter since I slept?

GRIFFITH   None, madam.

KATHERINE

No? Saw you not even now a blessèd troop
Invite me to a banquet, whose bright faces
Cast thousand beams upon me, like the sun?
They promised me eternal happiness,   90
And brought me garlands, Griffith, which I feel

I am not worthy yet to wear; I shall, assuredly.

GRIFFITH
I am most joyful, madam, such good dreams
Possess your fancy.

KATHERINE   Bid the music leave,
They are harsh and heavy to me.
        Music ceases

PATIENCE   Do you note
How much her grace is altered on the sudden?
How long her face is drawn? How pale she looks?
And of an earthy colour? Mark her eyes.

GRIFFITH
She is going, wench. Pray, pray.

PATIENCE   Heaven comfort her!
        Enter a Messenger

MESSENGER
100 An't like your grace —

KATHERINE   You are a saucy fellow!
Deserve we no more reverence?

GRIFFITH (*to Messenger*)   You are to blame,
Knowing she will not lose her wonted greatness,
To use so rude behaviour. Go to, kneel.

MESSENGER
I humbly do entreat your highness' pardon;
My haste made me unmannerly. There is staying
A gentleman sent from the King, to see you.

KATHERINE
Admit him entrance, Griffith; but this fellow
Let me ne'er see again.   *Exit Messenger*
        Enter Lord Capuchius
                          If my sight fail not,
You should be lord ambassador from the Emperor,
110 My royal nephew, and your name Capuchius.

CAPUCHIUS
Madam, the same: your servant.

KATHERINE   O my lord,
The times and titles now are altered strangely
With me since first you knew me. But I pray you,
What is your pleasure with me?

CAPUCHIUS   Noble lady,
First, mine own service to your grace; the next,
The King's request that I would visit you,
Who grieves much for your weakness, and by me
Sends you his princely commendations,
And heartily entreats you take good comfort.

KATHERINE
O my good lord, that comfort comes too late,   120
'Tis like a pardon after execution.
That gentle physic, given in time, had cured me,
But now I am past all comforts here but prayers.
How does his highness?

CAPUCHIUS   Madam, in good health.

KATHERINE
So may he ever do, and ever flourish,
When I shall dwell with worms, and my poor name
Banished the kingdom. Patience, is that letter
I caused you write yet sent away?

PATIENCE   No, madam.
    She gives it to Katherine

KATHERINE
Sir, I most humbly pray you to deliver
This to my lord the King.

CAPUCHIUS   Most willing, madam.   130

KATHERINE
In which I have commended to his goodness
The model of our chaste loves, his young daughter –
The dews of heaven fall thick in blessings on her! –

Beseeching him to give her virtuous breeding.
She is young, and of a noble modest nature;
I hope she will deserve well – and a little
To love her for her mother's sake, that loved him,
Heaven knows how dearly. My next poor petition
Is that his noble grace would have some pity
140   Upon my wretched women, that so long
Have followed both my fortunes faithfully;
Of which there is not one, I dare avow –
And now I should not lie – but will deserve,
For virtue and true beauty of the soul,
For honesty and decent carriage,
A right good husband, let him be a noble;
And sure those men are happy that shall have 'em.
The last is for my men – they are the poorest,
But poverty could never draw 'em from me –
150   That they may have their wages duly paid 'em,
And something over to remember me by.
If heaven had pleased to have given me longer life
And able means, we had not parted thus.
These are the whole contents; and, good my lord,
By that you love the dearest in this world,
As you wish Christian peace to souls departed,
Stand these poor people's friend, and urge the King
To do me this last right.

CAPUCHIUS   By heaven, I will,
Or let me lose the fashion of a man!

KATHERINE
160   I thank you, honest lord. Remember me
In all humility unto his highness.
Say his long trouble now is passing
Out of this world. Tell him in death I blessed him,
For so I will. Mine eyes grow dim. Farewell,
My lord. Griffith, farewell. Nay, Patience,

You must not leave me yet. I must to bed;
Call in more women. When I am dead, good wench,
Let me be used with honour; strew me over
With maiden flowers, that all the world may know
I was a chaste wife to my grave. Embalm me,   170
Then lay me forth; although unqueened, yet like
A queen, and daughter to a king, inter me.
I can no more.   *Exeunt, leading Katherine*

*

Enter Gardiner, Bishop of Winchester, a Page with a   V.1
torch before him, met by Sir Thomas Lovell

GARDINER
It's one o'clock, boy, is't not?
PAGE   It hath struck.
GARDINER
These should be hours for necessities,
Not for delights, times to repair our nature
With comforting repose, and not for us
To waste these times. Good hour of night, Sir Thomas!
Whither so late?
LOVELL   Came you from the King, my lord?
GARDINER
I did, Sir Thomas, and left him at primero
With the Duke of Suffolk.
LOVELL   I must to him too,
Before he go to bed. I'll take my leave.
GARDINER
Not yet, Sir Thomas Lovell. What's the matter?   10
It seems you are in haste. An if there be
No great offence belongs to't, give your friend
Some touch of your late business. Affairs that walk,

As they say spirits do, at midnight, have
In them a wilder nature than the business
That seeks dispatch by day.

LOVELL   My lord, I love you,
And durst commend a secret to your ear
Much weightier than this work. The Queen's in labour,
They say, in great extremity, and feared
20   She'll with the labour end.

GARDINER   The fruit she goes with
I pray for heartily, that it may find
Good time, and live; but, for the stock, Sir Thomas,
I wish it grubbed up now.

LOVELL   Methinks I could
Cry the amen, and yet my conscience says
She's a good creature and, sweet lady, does
Deserve our better wishes.

GARDINER   But, sir, sir,
Hear me, Sir Thomas. You're a gentleman
Of mine own way; I know you wise, religious;
And let me tell you, it will ne'er be well —
30   'Twill not, Sir Thomas Lovell, take't of me —
Till Cranmer, Cromwell — her two hands — and she
Sleep in their graves.

LOVELL   Now, sir, you speak of two
The most remarked i'th'kingdom. As for Cromwell,
Beside that of the Jewel House, is made Master
O'th'Rolls, and the King's secretary; further, sir,
Stands in the gap and trade of more preferments,
With which the time will load him. Th'Archbishop
Is the King's hand and tongue, and who dare speak
One syllable against him?

GARDINER   Yes, yes, Sir Thomas,
40   There are that dare, and I myself have ventured
To speak my mind of him; and indeed this day,

Sir – I may tell it you – I think I have
Incensed the lords o'th'Council that he is –
For so I know he is, they know he is –
A most arch heretic, a pestilence
That does infect the land; with which they, movèd,
Have broken with the King, who hath so far
Given ear to our complaint, of his great grace
And princely care, foreseeing those fell mischiefs
Our reasons laid before him, hath commanded   50
Tomorrow morning to the Council board
He be convented. He's a rank weed, Sir Thomas,
And we must root him out. From your affairs
I hinder you too long. Good night, Sir Thomas.

LOVELL
    Many good nights, my lord; I rest your servant.
                                    Exeunt Gardiner and Page
        Enter the King and Suffolk

KING HENRY
    Charles, I will play no more tonight.
    My mind's not on't; you are too hard for me.

SUFFOLK
    Sir, I did never win of you before.

KING HENRY
                            But little, Charles,
    Nor shall not, when my fancy's on my play.
    Now, Lovell, from the Queen what is the news?   60

LOVELL
    I could not personally deliver to her
    What you commanded me, but by her woman
    I sent your message, who returned her thanks
    In the great'st humbleness, and desired your highness
    Most heartily to pray for her.

KING HENRY   What sayst thou, ha?
    To pray for her? What, is she crying out?

LOVELL

So said her woman, and that her sufferance made
Almost each pang a death.

KING HENRY   Alas, good lady!

SUFFOLK

70   God safely quit her of her burden, and
With gentle travail, to the gladding of
Your highness with an heir!

KING HENRY   'Tis midnight, Charles;
Prithee to bed, and in thy prayers remember
Th'estate of my poor Queen. Leave me alone,
For I must think of that which company
Would not be friendly to.

SUFFOLK   I wish your highness
A quiet night, and my good mistress will
Remember in my prayers.

KING HENRY   Charles, good night.

Exit Suffolk

Enter Sir Anthony Denny

Well, sir, what follows?

DENNY

80   Sir, I have brought my lord the Archbishop,
As you commanded me.

KING HENRY   Ha? Canterbury?

DENNY

Ay, my good lord.

KING HENRY   'Tis true. Where is he, Denny?

DENNY

He attends your highness' pleasure.

KING HENRY   Bring him to us.

Exit Denny

LOVELL (*aside*)

This is about that which the Bishop spake;
I am happily come hither.

Enter Cranmer and Denny

KING HENRY

Avoid the gallery.

Lovell seems to stay

                  Ha! I have said. Be gone.

What?   *Exeunt Lovell and Denny*

CRANMER (*aside*)

      I am fearful – wherefore frowns he thus?

'Tis his aspect of terror. All's not well.

KING HENRY

How now, my lord? You do desire to know

Wherefore I sent for you.

CRANMER (*kneeling*)   It is my duty

T'attend your highness' pleasure.   90

KING HENRY   Pray you, arise,

My good and gracious lord of Canterbury.

Come, you and I must walk a turn together;

I have news to tell you. Come, come, give me your

    hand.

Ah, my good lord, I grieve at what I speak,

And am right sorry to repeat what follows.

I have, and most unwillingly, of late

Heard many grievous – I do say, my lord,

Grievous – complaints of you; which, being considered,

Have moved us and our Council that you shall

This morning come before us, where I know   100

You cannot with such freedom purge yourself

But that, till further trial in those charges

Which will require your answer, you must take

Your patience to you and be well contented

To make your house our Tower. You a brother of us,

It fits we thus proceed, or else no witness

Would come against you.

CRANMER (*kneeling*)   I humbly thank your highness,
And am right glad to catch this good occasion
110 Most throughly to be winnowed, where my chaff
And corn shall fly asunder, for I know
There's none stands under more calumnious tongues
Than I myself, poor man.

KING HENRY   Stand up, good Canterbury;
Thy truth and thy integrity is rooted
In us, thy friend. Give me thy hand, stand up;
Prithee let's walk. Now, by my holidame,
What manner of man are you? My lord, I looked
You would have given me your petition that
I should have ta'en some pains to bring together
120 Yourself and your accusers, and to have heard you
Without indurance further.

CRANMER   Most dread liege,
The good I stand on is my truth and honesty.
If they shall fail, I with mine enemies
Will triumph o'er my person, which I weigh not,
Being of those virtues vacant. I fear nothing
What can be said against me.

KING HENRY   Know you not
How your state stands i'th'world, with the whole world?
Your enemies are many, and not small; their practices
Must bear the same proportion, and not ever
130 The justice and the truth o'th'question carries
The due o'th'verdict with it. At what ease
Might corrupt minds procure knaves as corrupt
To swear against you? Such things have been done.
You are potently opposed, and with a malice
Of as great size. Ween you of better luck,
I mean in perjured witness, than your Master,
Whose minister you are, whiles here He lived
Upon this naughty earth? Go to, go to;

You take a precipice for no leap of danger,
And woo your own destruction.

CRANMER   God and your majesty   140
Protect mine innocence, or I fall into
The trap is laid for me!

KING HENRY   Be of good cheer;
They shall no more prevail than we give way to.
Keep comfort to you, and this morning see
You do appear before them. If they shall chance,
In charging you with matters, to commit you,
The best persuasions to the contrary
Fail not to use, and with what vehemency
Th'occasion shall instruct you. If entreaties
Will render you no remedy, this ring   150
Deliver them, and your appeal to us
There make before them. Look, the good man weeps!
He's honest, on mine honour. God's blest mother!
I swear he is true-hearted, and a soul
None better in my kingdom. Get you gone,
And do as I have bid you.   *Exit Cranmer*
                        He has strangled
His language in his tears.
    Enter Old Lady

LOVELL (*within*)   Come back! What mean you?
    Enter Lovell, following her

OLD LADY
I'll not come back; the tidings that I bring
Will make my boldness manners. Now good angels
Fly o'er thy royal head, and shade thy person
Under their blessèd wings!   160

KING HENRY   Now by thy looks
I guess thy message. Is the Queen delivered?
Say 'Ay, and of a boy'.

OLD LADY   Ay, ay, my liege,
  And of a lovely boy. The God of heaven
  Both now and ever bless her! 'Tis a girl
  Promises boys hereafter. Sir, your Queen
  Desires your visitation, and to be
  Acquainted with this stranger. 'Tis as like you
  As cherry is to cherry.

KING HENRY   Lovell!

LOVELL   Sir?

KING HENRY

170   Give her an hundred marks. I'll to the Queen.   *Exit*

OLD LADY
  An hundred marks? By this light, I'll ha' more.
  An ordinary groom is for such payment.
  I will have more, or scold it out of him.
  Said I for this the girl was like to him? I'll
  Have more, or else unsay't; and now, while 'tis hot,
  I'll put it to the issue.   *Exeunt*

V.2   *Pursuivants, pages, and others, attending before the*
           Council Chamber
           Enter Cranmer, Archbishop of Canterbury

CRANMER
  I hope I am not too late, and yet the gentleman
  That was sent to me from the Council prayed me
  To make great haste. All fast? What means this? Ho!
  Who waits there?

           Enter Keeper

                       Sure you know me?

KEEPER   Yes, my lord,
  But yet I cannot help you.

CRANMER   Why?

           Enter Doctor Butts

KEEPER   Your grace
  Must wait till you be called for.
CRANMER   So!
BUTTS (*aside*)
  This is a piece of malice. I am glad
  I came this way so happily; the King
  Shall understand it presently.   *Exit*
CRANMER (*aside*)   'Tis Butts,
  The King's physician. As he passed along,   10
  How earnestly he cast his eyes upon me!
  Pray heaven he sound not my disgrace! For certain
  This is of purpose laid by some that hate me –
  God turn their hearts! I never sought their malice –
  To quench mine honour. They would shame to make
      me
  Wait else at door, a fellow Councillor,
  'Mong boys, grooms, and lackeys. But their pleasures
  Must be fulfilled, and I attend with patience.
      Enter the King and Butts, at a window above
BUTTS
  I'll show your grace the strangest sight –
KING HENRY   What's that, Butts?
BUTTS
  I think your highness saw this many a day.   20
KING HENRY
  Body o'me, where is it?
BUTTS   There, my lord –
  The high promotion of his grace of Canterbury,
  Who holds his state at door, 'mongst pursuivants,
  Pages, and footboys.
KING HENRY   Ha? 'Tis he indeed.
  Is this the honour they do one another?
  'Tis well there's one above 'em yet. I had thought
  They had parted so much honesty among 'em –

At least good manners – as not thus to suffer
A man of his place, and so near our favour,
30   To dance attendance on their lordships' pleasures,
And at the door too, like a post with packets.
By holy Mary, Butts, there's knavery!
Let 'em alone, and draw the curtain close;
We shall hear more anon.

*They partly close the curtain, but remain watching;
Cranmer withdraws to wait without*

V.3   *A council-table brought in with chairs and stools, and
placed under the state. Enter Lord Chancellor, places
himself at the upper end of the table on the left hand,
a seat being left void above him, as for Canterbury's
seat. Duke of Suffolk, Duke of Norfolk, Surrey, Lord
Chamberlain, Gardiner, seat themselves in order on
each side; Cromwell at lower end, as secretary.
Keeper at the door*

LORD CHANCELLOR
Speak to the business, master secretary:
Why are we met in council?
CROMWELL   Please your honours,
The chief cause concerns his grace of Canterbury.
GARDINER
Has he had knowledge of it?
CROMWELL   Yes.
NORFOLK   Who waits there?
KEEPER
Without, my noble lords?
GARDINER   Yes.
KEEPER   My lord Archbishop,
And has done half an hour, to know your pleasures.

LORD CHANCELLOR
    Let him come in.
KEEPER   Your grace may enter now.
    Cranmer approaches the council-table
LORD CHANCELLOR
    My good lord Archbishop, I'm very sorry
    To sit here at this present and behold
    That chair stand empty, but we all are men   10
    In our own natures frail, and capable
    Of our flesh; few are angels; out of which frailty
    And want of wisdom, you, that best should teach us,
    Have misdemeaned yourself, and not a little,
    Toward the King first, then his laws, in filling
    The whole realm, by your teaching and your chaplains' —
    For so we are informed — with new opinions,
    Diverse and dangerous, which are heresies,
    And, not reformed, may prove pernicious.
GARDINER
    Which reformation must be sudden too,   20
    My noble lords; for those that tame wild horses
    Pace 'em not in their hands to make 'em gentle,
    But stop their mouths with stubborn bits and spur 'em
    Till they obey the manage. If we suffer,
    Out of our easiness and childish pity
    To one man's honour, this contagious sickness,
    Farewell all physic — and what follows then?
    Commotions, uproars, with a general taint
    Of the whole state, as of late days our neighbours,
    The upper Germany, can dearly witness,   30
    Yet freshly pitied in our memories.
CRANMER
    My good lords, hitherto in all the progress
    Both of my life and office, I have laboured,
    And with no little study, that my teaching

And the strong course of my authority
Might go one way, and safely; and the end
Was ever to do well. Nor is there living –
I speak it with a single heart, my lords –
A man that more detests, more stirs against,
40   Both in his private conscience and his place,
Defacers of a public peace than I do.
Pray heaven the King may never find a heart
With less allegiance in it! Men that make
Envy and crookèd malice nourishment
Dare bite the best. I do beseech your lordships
That, in this case of justice, my accusers,
Be what they will, may stand forth face to face,
And freely urge against me.

SUFFOLK   Nay, my lord,
That cannot be; you are a Councillor,
50   And by that virtue no man dare accuse you.

GARDINER
My lord, because we have business of more moment,
We will be short with you. 'Tis his highness' pleasure
And our consent, for better trial of you,
From hence you be committed to the Tower;
Where, being but a private man again,
You shall know many dare accuse you boldly,
More than, I fear, you are provided for.

CRANMER
Ah, my good lord of Winchester, I thank you;
You are always my good friend. If your will pass,
60   I shall both find your lordship judge and juror,
You are so merciful. I see your end:
'Tis my undoing. Love and meekness, lord,
Become a churchman better than ambition.
Win straying souls with modesty again;
Cast none away. That I shall clear myself,

Lay all the weight ye can upon my patience,
I make as little doubt as you do conscience
In doing daily wrongs. I could say more,
But reverence to your calling makes me modest.

GARDINER
My lord, my lord, you are a sectary,   70
That's the plain truth. Your painted gloss discovers,
To men that understand you, words and weakness.

CROMWELL
My lord of Winchester, you are a little,
By your good favour, too sharp. Men so noble,
However faulty, yet should find respect
For what they have been. 'Tis a cruelty
To load a falling man.

GARDINER   Good master secretary,
I cry your honour mercy; you may worst
Of all this table say so.

CROMWELL   Why, my lord?

GARDINER
Do not I know you for a favourer   80
Of this new sect? Ye are not sound.

CROMWELL   Not sound?

GARDINER
Not sound, I say.

CROMWELL   Would you were half so honest!
Men's prayers then would seek you, not their fears.

GARDINER
I shall remember this bold language.

CROMWELL   Do.
Remember your bold life too.

LORD CHANCELLOR   This is too much;
Forbear, for shame, my lords.

GARDINER   I have done.

CROMWELL   And I.

LORD CHANCELLOR
Then thus for you, my lord: it stands agreed,
I take it, by all voices, that forthwith
You be conveyed to th'Tower a prisoner,
90 There to remain till the King's further pleasure
Be known unto us. Are you all agreed, lords?

ALL
We are.

CRANMER Is there no other way of mercy,
But I must needs to th'Tower, my lords?

GARDINER   What other
Would you expect? You are strangely troublesome.
Let some o'th'guard be ready there.

Enter the Guard

CRANMER   For me?
Must I go like a traitor thither?

GARDINER   Receive him,
And see him safe i'th'Tower.

CRANMER   Stay, good my lords,
I have a little yet to say. Look there, my lords.
By virtue of that ring I take my cause
100 Out of the gripes of cruel men, and give it
To a most noble judge, the King my master.

LORD CHAMBERLAIN
This is the King's ring.

SURREY   'Tis no counterfeit.

SUFFOLK
'Tis the right ring, by heaven. I told ye all,
When we first put this dangerous stone a-rolling,
'Twould fall upon ourselves.

NORFOLK   Do you think, my lords,
The King will suffer but the little finger
Of this man to be vexed?

LORD CHAMBERLAIN   'Tis now too certain.

How much more is his life in value with him!
Would I were fairly out on't!   *Exit King above*

CROMWELL   My mind gave me,
In seeking tales and informations   110
Against this man, whose honesty the devil
And his disciples only envy at,
Ye blew the fire that burns ye. Now have at ye!
    Enter the King frowning on them; takes his seat

GARDINER
Dread sovereign, how much are we bound to heaven
In daily thanks, that gave us such a prince,
Not only good and wise, but most religious;
One that in all obedience makes the church
The chief aim of his honour, and, to strengthen
That holy duty, out of dear respect,
His royal self in judgement comes to hear   120
The cause betwixt her and this great offender.

KING HENRY
You were ever good at sudden commendations,
Bishop of Winchester. But know I come not
To hear such flattery now, and in my presence
They are too thin and bare to hide offences;
To me you cannot reach. You play the spaniel,
And think with wagging of your tongue to win me;
But whatsoe'er thou tak'st me for, I'm sure
Thou hast a cruel nature and a bloody.
    (*To Cranmer*)
Good man, sit down. Now let me see the proudest,   130
He that dares most, but wag his finger at thee.
By all that's holy, he had better starve
Than but once think this place becomes thee not.

SURREY
May it please your grace —

KING HENRY   No, sir, it does not please me.

I had thought I had had men of some understanding
And wisdom of my Council, but I find none.
Was it discretion, lords, to let this man,
This good man — few of you deserve that title —
This honest man, wait like a lousy footboy

140   At chamber door? — and one as great as you are?
Why, what a shame was this! Did my commission
Bid ye so far forget yourselves? I gave ye
Power as he was a Councillor to try him,
Not as a groom. There's some of ye, I see,
More out of malice than integrity,
Would try him to the utmost, had ye mean;
Which ye shall never have while I live.

LORD CHANCELLOR   Thus far,
My most dread sovereign, may it like your grace
To let my tongue excuse all. What was purposed

150   Concerning his imprisonment was rather —
If there be faith in men — meant for his trial
And fair purgation to the world than malice,
I'm sure, in me.

KING HENRY   Well, well, my lords, respect him.
Take him and use him well; he's worthy of it.
I will say thus much for him: if a prince
May be beholding to a subject, I
Am, for his love and service, so to him.
Make me no more ado, but all embrace him;
Be friends, for shame, my lords! My lord of Canterbury,

160   I have a suit which you must not deny me:
That is, a fair young maid that yet wants baptism;
You must be godfather, and answer for her.

CRANMER
The greatest monarch now alive may glory
In such an honour. How may I deserve it,
That am a poor and humble subject to you?

KING HENRY Come, come, my lord, you'd spare your
    spoons. You shall have two noble partners with you,
    the old Duchess of Norfolk and Lady Marquis Dorset.
    Will these please you?
    Once more, my lord of Winchester, I charge you   170
    Embrace and love this man.
GARDINER   With a true heart
    And brother-love I do it.
CRANMER   And let heaven
    Witness how dear I hold this confirmation.
KING HENRY
    Good man, those joyful tears show thy true heart.
    The common voice, I see, is verified
    Of thee, which says thus: 'Do my lord of Canterbury
    A shrewd turn and he's your friend for ever.'
    Come, lords, we trifle time away; I long
    To have this young one made a Christian.
    As I have made ye one, lords, one remain;   180
    So I grow stronger, you more honour gain.   *Exeunt*

Noise and tumult within. Enter Porter and his Man   V.4
PORTER You'll leave your noise anon, ye rascals. Do you
    take the court for Parish Garden? Ye rude slaves, leave
    your gaping.
SERVANT (*within*) Good master porter, I belong to
    th'larder.
PORTER Belong to th'gallows, and be hanged, ye rogue!
    Is this a place to roar in? Fetch me a dozen crab-tree
    staves, and strong ones: these are but switches to 'em.
    I'll scratch your heads. You must be seeing christen-
    ings? Do you look for ale and cakes here, you rude   10
    rascals?

MAN
Pray, sir, be patient. 'Tis as much impossible,
Unless we sweep 'em from the door with cannons,
To scatter 'em as 'tis to make 'em sleep
On May-day morning; which will never be.
We may as well push against Paul's as stir 'em.

PORTER How got they in, and be hanged?

MAN
Alas, I know not. How gets the tide in?
As much as one sound cudgel of four foot –
20   You see the poor remainder – could distribute,
I made no spare, sir.

PORTER   You did nothing, sir.

MAN
I am not Samson, nor Sir Guy, nor Colbrand,
To mow 'em down before me; but if I spared any
That had a head to hit, either young or old,
He or she, cuckold or cuckold-maker,
Let me ne'er hope to see a chine again –
And that I would not for a cow, God save her!

SERVANT (within) Do you hear, master porter?

PORTER I shall be with you presently, good master
30   puppy. Keep the door close, sirrah.

MAN What would you have me do?

PORTER What should you do, but knock 'em down by
th'dozens? Is this Moorfields to muster in? Or have we
some strange Indian with the great tool come to court,
the women so besiege us? Bless me, what a fry of
fornication is at door! On my Christian conscience, this
one christening will beget a thousand: here will be
father, godfather, and all together.

MAN The spoons will be the bigger, sir. There is a fellow
40   somewhat near the door, he should be a brazier by his
face, for, o'my conscience, twenty of the dog-days now

reign in's nose; all that stand about him are under the
line, they need no other penance. That fire-drake did I
hit three times on the head, and three times was his
nose discharged against me; he stands there like a
mortar-piece, to blow us. There was a haberdasher's
wife of small wit near him, that railed upon me till her
pinked porringer fell off her head, for kindling such a
combustion in the state. I missed the meteor once, and
hit that woman, who cried out 'Clubs!', when I might   50
see from far some forty truncheoners draw to her
succour, which were the hope o'th'Strand, where she
was quartered. They fell on; I made good my place. At
length they came to th'broomstaff to me; I defied 'em
still; when suddenly a file of boys behind 'em, loose
shot, delivered such a shower of pebbles that I was fain
to draw mine honour in, and let 'em win the work. The
devil was amongst 'em, I think, surely.

PORTER These are the youths that thunder at a playhouse,
and fight for bitten apples, that no audience but the   60
tribulation of Tower Hill or the limbs of Limehouse,
their dear brothers, are able to endure. I have some of
'em in *Limbo Patrum*, and there they are like to dance
these three days, besides the running banquet of two
beadles that is to come.

Enter the Lord Chamberlain

LORD CHAMBERLAIN
Mercy o'me, what a multitude are here!
They grow still, too; from all parts they are coming,
As if we kept a fair here! Where are these porters,
These lazy knaves? You've made a fine hand, fellows!
There's a trim rabble let in: are all these   70
Your faithful friends o'th'suburbs? We shall have
Great store of room, no doubt, left for the ladies,
When they pass back from the christening.

PORTER   An't please your honour,
We are but men, and what so many may do,
Not being torn a-pieces, we have done.
An army cannot rule 'em.

LORD CHAMBERLAIN   As I live,
If the King blame me for't, I'll lay ye all
By th'heels, and suddenly; and on your heads
Clap round fines for neglect. You're lazy knaves,
80   And here ye lie baiting of bombards, when
Ye should do service.

Trumpets

                              Hark! The trumpets sound;
They're come already from the christening.
Go break among the press, and find a way out
To let the troop pass fairly, or I'll find
A Marshalsea shall hold ye play these two months.

PORTER
Make way there for the Princess!

MAN   You great fellow,
Stand close up, or I'll make your head ache.

PORTER
You i'th'camlet, get up o'th'rail;
I'll peck you o'er the pales else.   *Exeunt*

V.5   *Enter trumpets, sounding; then two Aldermen, Lord
               Mayor, Garter, Cranmer, Duke of Norfolk with his
               marshal's staff, Duke of Suffolk, two noblemen
               bearing great standing bowls for the christening gifts;
               then four noblemen bearing a canopy, under which the
               Duchess of Norfolk, godmother, bearing the child
               richly habited in a mantle, etc., train borne by a lady;
               then follows the Marchioness Dorset, the other god-*

mother, and ladies. The troop pass once about the
stage, and Garter speaks

GARTER Heaven, from thy endless goodness, send prosperous life, long, and ever happy, to the high and
mighty Princess of England, Elizabeth!
    Flourish. Enter the King and Guard

CRANMER (*kneeling*)
    And to your royal grace, and the good Queen!
    My noble partners and myself thus pray
    All comfort, joy, in this most gracious lady,
    Heaven ever laid up to make parents happy,
    May hourly fall upon ye!

KING HENRY   Thank you, good lord Archbishop.
    What is her name?

CRANMER   Elizabeth.

KING HENRY   Stand up, lord.
    The King kisses the child
    With this kiss take my blessing: God protect thee!   10
    Into Whose hand I give thy life.

CRANMER   Amen.

KING HENRY
    My noble gossips, you've been too prodigal;
    I thank ye heartily. So shall this lady
    When she has so much English.

CRANMER   Let me speak, sir,
    For heaven now bids me, and the words I utter
    Let none think flattery, for they'll find 'em truth.
    This royal infant – heaven still move about her! –
    Though in her cradle, yet now promises
    Upon this land a thousand thousand blessings,
    Which time shall bring to ripeness. She shall be –   20
    But few now living can behold that goodness –
    A pattern to all princes living with her,

And all that shall succeed. Saba was never
More covetous of wisdom and fair virtue
Than this pure soul shall be. All princely graces
That mould up such a mighty piece as this is,
With all the virtues that attend the good,
Shall still be doubled on her. Truth shall nurse her,
Holy and heavenly thoughts still counsel her;
30   She shall be loved and feared. Her own shall bless her;
Her foes shake like a field of beaten corn,
And hang their heads with sorrow. Good grows with
          her;
In her days every man shall eat in safety
Under his own vine what he plants, and sing
The merry songs of peace to all his neighbours.
God shall be truly known, and those about her
From her shall read the perfect ways of honour,
And by those claim their greatness, not by blood.
Nor shall this peace sleep with her; but as when
40   The bird of wonder dies, the maiden phoenix,
Her ashes new-create another heir
As great in admiration as herself,
So shall she leave her blessèdness to one –
When heaven shall call her from this cloud of dark-
          ness –
Who from the sacred ashes of her honour
Shall star-like rise, as great in fame as she was,
And so stand fixed. Peace, plenty, love, truth, terror,
That were the servants to this chosen infant,
Shall then be his, and like a vine grow to him.
50   Wherever the bright sun of heaven shall shine,
His honour and the greatness of his name
Shall be, and make new nations. He shall flourish,
And like a mountain cedar reach his branches
To all the plains about him; our children's children

Shall see this, and bless heaven.

KING HENRY   Thou speakest wonders.

CRANMER

She shall be, to the happiness of England,
An agèd princess; many days shall see her,
And yet no day without a deed to crown it.
Would I had known no more! But she must die –
She must, the saints must have her – yet a virgin;   60
A most unspotted lily shall she pass
To th'ground, and all the world shall mourn her.

KING HENRY

O lord Archbishop,
Thou hast made me now a man; never before
This happy child did I get anything.
This oracle of comfort has so pleased me
That when I am in heaven I shall desire
To see what this child does, and praise my Maker.
I thank ye all. To you, my good Lord Mayor,
And you, good brethren, I am much beholding: 70
I have received much honour by your presence,
And ye shall find me thankful. Lead the way, lords;
Ye must all see the Queen, and she must thank ye;
She will be sick else. This day, no man think
'Has business at his house, for all shall stay:
This little one shall make it holiday.   *Exeunt*

THE EPILOGUE

'Tis ten to one this play can never please
All that are here. Some come to take their ease,
And sleep an act or two; but those, we fear,
We've frighted with our trumpets; so, 'tis clear,
They'll say 'tis naught. Others to hear the city

Abused extremely, and to cry 'That's witty!' —
Which we have not done neither; that, I fear,
All the expected good we're like to hear
For this play at this time is only in
The merciful construction of good women,
For such a one we showed 'em. If they smile,
And say 'twill do, I know within a while
All the best men are ours; for 'tis ill hap
If they hold when their ladies bid 'em clap.

An Account of the Text

The earliest text is that in the first Folio (1623), *Mr. William Shakespeares Comedies, Histories, & Tragedies*. In the list of contents (or 'Catalogue of the seuerall Comedies, Histories, and Tragedies contained in this Volume') it is called *The Life of King Henry the Eight*; on its individual title-page it is *The Famous History of the Life of King Henry the Eight*.

The text is a good one, presenting only minor problems, and not many even of these. It is divided into acts and scenes at the points followed in modern editions, save that it runs together as the second scene of Act V what is now generally divided as scenes 2 and 3; consequently its subsequent scene numbers are one lower than in most modern editions.

The copy from which the text was set up was carefully prepared. Entrances and exits, except for a few self-evident ones, are duly marked and need little readjustment. Forms of speech prefixes show only unimportant variations, and indicate care to be fairly uniform: Queen Katherine appears as '*Queen*' (or abbreviations thereof) until, after her dethronement, she is '*Katherine Dowager*' in the entry direction for IV.2 and speaks as '*Kath.*'. The Lord Chamberlain appears in various abbreviations of his title; in V.3.85 and 87 the Folio reads '*Cham.*' where presumably '*Chan.*' (Lord Chancellor) is meant. But this is a very minor error.

The stage directions – which are retained in this edition except as indicated below (List 2) – offer interesting features. Some of them reflect stage terminology or the imperatives of practical instructions, and might seem to have originated in a prompt-book (for example, I.1.0, '*Enter the Duke of Norfolke at one doore. At the other, the Duke of Buckingham*'; or I.4.49, '*Drum and Trumpet, Chambers dischargd*'; see also, in the text, I.4.76, II.1.0, and II.2.119, and, in the collations, I.4.74 and 81). Some express what looks like authorial imprecision rather than prompt-book specificity (for example, I.1.114, '*certaine of the Guard*'; I.1.197, '*two or theee* [*sic*] *of the Guard*'; I.4.0, '*diuers other Ladies, & Gentlemen*'). Some suggest the author indicating effects or situations (for example, I.1.114, '*The Cardinall in his passage, fixeth his eye on Buckingham, and Buckingham on him, both full of disdaine*'; I.4.63, '*They passe directly before the Cardinall, and gracefully salute him*'; II.2.0, '*... reading this Letter*'; IV.1.36, '*A liuely Flourish ...*'; see also II.1.54, II.2.60, III.2.203 and 372, and V.3.113). This kind of descriptive particularity includes a striking attention to details of behaviour or position (for example, I.2.0, '*Cornets. Enter King Henry, leaning on the Cardinals shoulder ... the Cardinall places himselfe vnder the Kings feete on his right side*'; see also I.2.8, and such details as '*with some small distance*' in the entry direction for II.4). In the account of Katherine's vision (IV.2.82) there is an evident desire for interpretative description: '*... (as it were by inspiration) she makes (in her sleepe) signes of reioycing*'.

Particularly noticeable are the long descriptions of ceremonial arrangements, for the Queen's trial in II.4, the coronation procession in IV.1, the vision in IV.2, the Council assembly in V.3, and the christening in V.5. The curious past tense in section 5 of the coronation procession, where the Garter King-of-Arms '*wore a gilt copper crowne*', suggests that the writer was influenced by Holinshed's past-tense narration, in which 'every king-of-arms put on a crown of copper and gilt, all which were worn till night' (III.784), rather than that he had his mind on the stage.

The reliability and uniformity of the text and speech prefixes might suggest that the Folio text was printed from a prompt-book; but the frequent narrative descriptions of actions and manners, and the graphic particularity with which processions and other spectacles are related, would be unusual in a prompt-book. These considerations together suggest that the Folio text was printed from a fair copy made by a scribe from an author's manuscript that had been carefully prepared as a text for reading rather than for stage production.

COLLATIONS

The following lists are selective, not comprehensive; they record significant variants, including variant punctuation where any change of sense is involved, but they do not include regularizations such as the correction of misprints or small changes in stage directions. 'F' indicates the first Folio (1623). Its readings are given here unmodernized, except that 'long s' (ʃ) is printed as 's'.

1 Accepted readings later than F

The following readings in the present text (given first, and terminating in a square bracket) originate in editions later than F; if proposed by a modern editor, they are identified. The rejected F reading follows.

I.I

    33 censure. When] censure, when

    42–7 All was royal; . . . together,] *Buc.* All was Royall, . . . together?

    45 function. BUCKINGHAM Who] Function: who

    47–8 as you guess? | NORFOLK One] *Nor.* As you guesse: | One

    63 web, 'a] (*G. L. Kittredge, 1936*); Web. O

    69–70 that? | If not from hell, the] that, | If not from Hell? The

    78–80 letter, | . . . in he papers.] Letter | The Honourable Boord of Councell, out | Must fetch him in, he Papers.

    87 issue?] issue.

    120 venom-mouthed] venom'd-mouth'd

    123 chafed] chaff'd

    159–62 – for . . . perform't, his . . . reciprocally –] (for . . . perform't) his . . . reciprocally,

    183 him. He privily] him. Priuily

    200 Hereford] *Hertford*

    219 Perk] (*R. A. Foakes, 1957, from Holinshed's* Perke); *Pecke*

chancellor] (*from Holinshed*); Councellour
221 Nicholas] (*from Holinshed*); *Michaell*
226 lord] Lords

I.2

67 business] basenesse
139–40 point: | ... person,] point, | ... person;
156 feared] feare
164 confession's] (*from Holinshed*); Commissions
170 To win] (*C. J. Sisson, 1954*); To
179–80 dangerous | For him] dangerous | For this
190 Bulmer] (*from Holinshed*); *Blumer*

I.3

13 Or] A
34 '*oui*'] wee
59 wherewithal: in him] wherewithall in him;

II.1

18 have] him
20 Perk] (*as at* I.1.219)
42–3 who removed, | Earl Surrey was] who remou'd |
Earle *Surrey*, was
86 mark] make

II.2

83 one have-at-him] one; haue at him

II.3

14 quarrel, Fortune,] quarrell. Fortune,
59 note's] notes
61 of you,] of you, to you;

II.4

127 GRIFFITH] *Gent. Vsh.*
174 A] And
219 summons. Unsolicited] Summons vnsolicited.
239 return. With thy approach] returne, with thy
approch:

III.1

3 GENTLEWOMAN (*sings*)] SONG.
61 your] our
82–3 England | But little for my profit. Can] England, |
But little for my profit can

175-7 forgive me | If ... unmannerly. | You] forgiue
      me; | If ... vnmannerly, | You

III.2

171 filed] fill'd
209 I fear, the] I feare the
233 commission, lords? Words] Commission? Lords,
    words
292 Who] Whom
339 legatine] (*from Holinshed*); Legatiue
343 Chattels] Castles
351 Farewell, a long] Farewell? A long

IV.1

9-10 forward – | In] forward | In
20 SECOND GENTLEMAN] 1 (*i.e.* FIRST GENTLEMAN)
34 Kimbolton] Kymmalton
54-5 indeed – | FIRST GENTLEMAN And] indeed, | And
101 Stokesley] (*from Holinshed's* Stokesleie); *Stokeley*

IV.2

7 think] thanke
98 colour] cold

V.1

1 PAGE] *Boy.*
37 time] Lime
140 woo] woe
157 LOVELL] *Gent.*

V.2

7 piece] Peere

V.3

0 *no fresh scene number in* F
85, 87 LORD CHANCELLOR] *Cham.*
125 bare] base
130-31 proudest, | He that] proudest | Hee, that
133 this] his
172 brother-love] Brother; loue
174 heart] hearts

V.4

0 *scene numbered* 'Scena Tertia' *in* F
4, 28 SERVANT] *not in* F

V.5

> 0 *scene numbered 'Scena Quarta' in* F
> 4 Queen!] Queen,
> 37 ways] way

2 Stage directions

The following list shows the more important amendments of and additions to F's stage directions. F's reading follows the square bracket. Additions such as 'aside' and indications of the character to whom a speech is addressed are not listed.

I.2

> 0 *Wolsey's Secretary in attendance*] *not in* F
> 8 Queen!' *Enter the Queen, ushered by the Dukes of Norfolk and Suffolk*] Queene, vsher'd by the Duke of Norfolke. Enter the Queene, Norfolke and Suffolke:

I.3

> 15 *Enter Sir Thomas Lovell*] *after* 'Lovell?', *line* 16

I.4

> 30 *He kisses her*] *not in* F
> 38 *He drinks*] *not in* F
> 49 *Drum and trumpet. Chambers discharged*] *after line* 48
> 50 *Exit a Servant*] *not in* F
> 60 *Exit Lord Chamberlain, attended*] *not in* F
> 74 *They choose ladies; the King chooses Anne Bullen*] Choose Ladies, King and An Bullen.
> 81 *He whispers with the masquers*] Whisper. (*after* 'surrender it', *line* 81)
> 84 *He comes from his state*] *not in* F
> 86 *The King unmasks*] *not in* F

II.1

> 54 *Enter . . . people, etc.*] *after* 'courtesy', *line* 53

II.2

> 115 *Exit Wolsey*] *not in* F
> *Enter Wolsey with Gardiner*] Enter Gardiner.

II.3

> 80 *Exit Lord Chamberlain*] *after* 'you', *line* 80

II.4

  0 *Archbishop*] Bishop
     then Griffith, a Gentleman Usher] *Then a*
     Gentleman Vsher

III.1

  19 *Exit Gentleman*] *not in* F

III.2

 106 *Enter . . . Lovell*] *Enter King, reading of a scedule.*
     (*after line* 104)
 201 *he gives him papers*] *not in* F

IV.1

  35 *Trumpets*] *not in* F
  36 (*after the procession*) *The procession passes over the*
     stage in order and state] *Exeunt, first passing ouer the*
     Stage in Order and State, and then, A great Flourish of
     Trumpets.
  42 *looking at the Queen*] *not in* F
  55 *The end of the procession leaves;*] *not in* F
     and then a great flourish of trumpets] *after* 'Order and
     State' (*following section* 10 *of the Order of the Coronation*)

IV.2

 128 *She gives it to Katherine*] *not in* F

V.1

  55 *Exeunt Gardiner and Page*] *Exit Gardiner and Page.*
     (*after line* 54)
  78 *Enter Sir Anthony Denny*] *after line* 79
  83 *Exit Denny*] *not in* F
  90 *kneeling*] *not in* F
 108 *kneeling*] *not in* F
 157 *Enter Lovell, following her*] *not in* F
 176 *Exeunt*] *Exit Ladie.*

V.2

  0 *Pursuivants . . . Chamber*] *not in* F
  4 *Enter Keeper*] *after* 'Sure you know me?'
  5 *Enter Doctor Butts*] *after* 'called for', *line* 6
  34 *They partly . . . wait without*] *not in* F

V.3

  0 *Keeper at the door*] *not in* F
 109 *Exit King above*] *not in* F

V.4

    81 *Trumpets*] *not in* F

V.5

    4 *kneeling*] *not in* F
    9 *The King kisses the child*] *not in* F

3 Rejected variants

The following list contains some of the more interesting variants
proposed or accepted in editions after the first Folio but not
accepted here. The readings of this edition are given first, followed
by a square bracket. The rejected variants follow, separated by a
semi-colon where there is more than one. The source is given of
those that originate in modern editions. Where no source is named,
the reading is one proposed by an earlier editor which has not
gained general acceptance.

I.1

    63 web, 'a] Web. O!; web he; web, O,
   219 Perk] Peck; Parke

I.2

  43–4 lord? | You know no more than others?] lord, | You
       know no more than others:
   120 ravished listening] list'ning ravish'd
   139 This dangerous] His dangerous (*C. J. Sisson, 1954*)
 139–40 point: | Not friended . . . wish to . . . person,] point; |
      Not friended . . . wish, to . . . person
   147 Henton] Hopkins (*see* I.1.221 *and note to* I.2.147)
   170 To win] To gain
 179–80 dangerous | For him to] Dangerous | To; Dangerous
      for him | To

I.3

    12 see] saw
    13 Or] And
    34 '*oui*'] wear

I.4

    6 first, good] first-good; feast, good
 104–5 merry, | Good my lord Cardinal]: merry. Good my
      lord cardinal,

II.1

20   Perk] Peck; Parke
89   forsake] forsake me

II.2

83   one have-at-him] one heave at him

II.3

14   quarrel, Fortune,] quarr'lous Fortune;
     quarr'ler Fortune; cruel Fortune; fortune's quarrel
61   of you,] to you,

II.4

33   gave notice] gave not notice
62   desire] defer
148 At once] Atton'd
182 bosom] bottom
183 spitting] splitting

III.1

21   coming. Now I think on't,] coming, now I think on't.
124 a curse] accursed (*F. D. Hoeniger, 1969*)

III.2

119–20 be, | There] be | There
192 that am, have, and will be] that am I, have been, will
     be; that I am true and will be
305 can blush] can, blush

IV.2

36   Tied] Tyth'd
50   honour. From his cradle] honour from his cradle.
98   colour] coldness

V.1

43   Incensed] Insensed
122 good] ground

V.3

11   frail, and capable] frail, incapable; frail, and culpable
12   Of our flesh] Of frailty
124 presence] presence;
126 reach. You] reach, you
172 brother-love] brother's love

V.5

70   you, good] your good (F *has* 'you good')

Commentary

REFERENCES AND QUOTATIONS

The spelling and punctuation of quotations from sixteenth- and seventeenth-century texts have usually been modernized.

Bishops' Bible	Translation of the Bible (1568), the standard Elizabethan version, from which all biblical quotations are given unless they are otherwise attributed
F	The Folio edition of Shakespeare's plays (1623), the first collected edition
Foakes	*Henry VIII*, revised Arden edition (1957), edited by R. A. Foakes
Foxe	John Foxe, *Acts and Monuments*, edition of 1596
Holinshed	Raphael Holinshed, *Chronicles of England* (second edition, 1587). References are to the edition by Henry Ellis (1807–8)
Rowley	Samuel Rowley, *When You See Me You Know Me* (1605). References are to the Malone Society Reprint (1952), edited by F. P. Wilson and John Crow
Tilley	M. P. Tilley, *Dictionary of the Proverbs in England in the Sixteenth and Seventeenth Centuries* (1950)

THE CHARACTERS IN THE PLAY

No list of these is provided in F. Editions differ somewhat in the
number of very brief parts they include (for instance, servants
or messengers with a few words only). The attempt has been
made here to mention all speaking or singing parts, and to group
them approximately according to function – King, courtiers,
churchmen and their entourage, miscellaneous functionaries,
Queen Katherine and her household, Anne Bullen and her Old
Lady. 'Lord Sands' appears in the II.1.54 stage direction as 'Sir
Walter Sands'; see the note at that point. It is Griffith who in the
trial scene speaks to the Queen (II.4.127): F attributes the speech
to the Queen's Gentleman Usher, but that he and Griffith are
identical is clear from the entry direction of IV.2.

The Setting
The action takes place in London, Westminster, and Kimbolton.

Prologue

The style of the Prologue (which Dr Johnson thought
unShakespearian, and tentatively ascribed to Ben
Jonson) certainly lacks the Shakespearian idiosyncrasy.
It has something of Jonson's derisive challenge, and
something of Fletcher's relaxed persuasiveness, as in
the Prologue and Epilogue of *The Two Noble Kinsmen*
(to which, however, it is superior, though not so pre-
eminently so as to make Fletcher's authorship unlikely).
True Shakespearian Prologues, as in *Henry IV, Part II*,
Henry V, *Romeo and Juliet*, and *Troilus and Cressida*,
engage very closely with their plays, whereas this one
deals vaguely with the play's contents, and indeed gives
a misleading impression of its end. In its favour,
however, is the fact that it offers the speaker the chance
to attract the attention of the audience sympathetically
and seriously to *our chosen truth* (line 18).

1 *I come no more to make you laugh*: The first performance, or early performances, must have followed some

comedy to which audiences would catch the reference, though which one is unknown. The allusion in lines 14–16 may well be to Samuel Rowley's chronicle drama, *When You See Me You Know Me. Or the famous Chronicle History of King Henry the Eighth.*

3 *Sad, high, and working*: Serious, lofty, and moving. *state*: Stateliness.

9 *May here find truth*: This is possibly an allusion to an earlier or alternative title to the play, *All is True*, as in Sir Henry Wotton's letter and Henry Bluett's description. The Prologue repeatedly stresses the historical reality conveyed in the play – see 18, 21, 25–7.

10 *show*: Spectacle. (The play is unusually elaborate in ceremonial.)

12 *their shilling*: Admission to prominent seats near the stage, in which gallants might display themselves, cost one shilling or more by the date of the play. Dekker advises his gull in *The Gull's Hornbook* (1609; page 2) 'When at a new play you take up the twelvepenny room, next the stage (because the lords and you may seem to be hail-fellow-well-met)'; and Overbury writes of 'The Proud Man' in *Characters* (1614) 'If he have but twelvepence in's purse, he will give it for the best room in a playhouse.' Playhouse prices are discussed in detail by E. K. Chambers in *The Elizabethan Stage*, Volume 2, page 534, note 1.

13 *two short hours*: This period bears little relationship to the play itself, though two hours is often mentioned, conventionally, as the time taken by play performances; compare 'the two hours' traffic of our stage' (*Romeo and Juliet*, Prologue, 12), 'these two short hours' (*The Alchemist*, Prologue, 1), and 'scenes ... worth two hours' travel' (*The Two Noble Kinsmen*, Prologue, 28). The actual time taken must often have been longer; the Induction to Jonson's *Bartholomew Fair* refers to 'the space of two hours and an half, and somewhat more'. *Henry VIII* is among the longest of Shakespeare's history plays, and the elaborate ceremonials would in themselves take a considerable time.

14–16 *a merry, bawdy play . . . guarded with yellow*: This refers
probably to Rowley's *When You See Me You Know Me*,
which contains two fools, Patch and Will Summers,
attached respectively to Wolsey and Henry VIII. It
includes a sword-and-buckler fight (cf. *A noise of targets*,
15) between Henry himself, in disguise, and Black Will,
a thief, which ends in their both being seized by the
watch. It is certainly (among other things) *merry*, and,
in regard to Will Summers's witticisms, tolerably *bawdy*.

15 *targets*: Bucklers, shields.

16 *a long motley coat guarded with yellow*: Professional fools
wore long coats of 'motley', a greenish-yellow stuff,
trimmed (*guarded*) with yellow strips.

17 *deceived*: Disappointed.

19–21 *forfeiting | Our own brains, and the opinion that we
bring | To make that only true we now intend*: Giving up
any claim we have to intelligence and our reputation
for presenting truthfully what we are to show.

22 *an understanding friend*: This is probably a quibbling
allusion to the groundlings who stood below the stage;
compare Jonson, *Bartholomew Fair*, Induction, 49: 'the
understanding gentlemen o'the ground there asked my
judgement'. E. K. Chambers, in *The Elizabethan Stage*,
Volume 2, page 527, note 6, gives several examples of
this playhouse jest.

23 *for goodness' sake*: Out of your good nature (not the
modern colloquial sense).

24 *The first and happiest hearers*: The leading and best-
qualified audience.

25 *sad*: Serious.

25–30 *Think ye see . . . mightiness meets misery*: The fact that
this appeal to the audience sketchily resembles that in
the Prologue of *Henry V* –

> Suppose within the girdle of these walls
> Are now confined two mighty monarchies . . .
> Think, when we talk of horses, that you see them
> Printing their proud hoofs i'th'receiving earth

– has sometimes been offered as evidence that Shakespeare wrote this Prologue. It could more properly be offered as evidence to the contrary, the difference in vividness and dramatic quality being so striking.

25–6 *ye see . . . story*: An example of 'laxity in versification', as Dr Johnson calls it, not infrequent in drama; compare Epilogue, 9–10.

I.1

Most of Shakespeare's history plays begin their action in the first scene without any prefatory material, and four of them (*King John, Richard II, Henry IV, Part I*, and *Richard III*) open with the titular character. The argument that the unifying and organizing centre of *Henry VIII* is Henry himself would be stronger were this the case here; instead, one's attention is first drawn to Wolsey. Nevertheless, the scene gives valuable information and suggests viewpoints and themes essential to the play.

J. R. Sutherland, in 'The Language of the Last Plays' (*More Talking of Shakespeare*, edited by J. Garrett, 1959, page 154), suggests that the elliptical and tricky style shows Shakespeare 'putting forth a mighty effort in the opening scene' (as also in *Cymbeline*) and galvanizing himself into a high style – 'The old eagle is soaring with his mighty spread of wing, but he is toiling upwards where once he sailed along the wind'. Yet there is a vivacious energy in the strain of style that seems the outcome of nearly uncontrolled exuberance rather than of willed effort.

0 *one door . . . the other*: Stage directions often refer to the doors, on each side of the stage rear in Elizabethan theatres, for entrances and exits.

2 *saw*: Saw each other, met (cf. *Cymbeline*, I.1.124, 'When shall we see again?').

4–5 *An untimely ague | Stayed me a prisoner*: Henry VIII of England and Francis I of France met on 7 June 1520, and meetings continued until 24 June. Their meeting-place was called the Field of the Cloth of Gold, so splendid was the panoply of the two monarchs and

their followers. Buckingham was in fact present for at
least part of the ceremonies: Holinshed (III.654)
records that 'The Lord Cardinal in stately attire, accompanied with the Duke of Buckingham, and other great
lords, conducted forward the French King, and in their
way they encountered and met the King of England
and his company right in the valley of Andren.'
Norfolk, for his part, was in England. Presumably
Shakespeare's reversal of this is meant to dissociate
Buckingham from Wolsey's extravagant *vanities* as
displayed at the Field of the Cloth of Gold.

6 *Those suns of glory*: The sun metaphor is common for
royalty; cf. 33 and 56. There may also be a quibble on
'sons'.

7 *Andren ... Guynes and Arde*: Guynes, held by the
English, and Arde (modern Ardres), held by the French,
lie each side of the valley of Andren in Picardy.

9 *lighted*: Alighted.

10 *as*: As if.

11 *Which had they*: Had they done so.
   weighed: Equalled.

15–16 *Till this time pomp was single, but now married | To one
above itself*: Pomp has reached a higher pitch in this
conjoined splendour of the two Kings than each ever
had singly.

15 *single*: (1) Unmarried; (2) insignificant (cf. *Macbeth*,
I.6.16, 'poor and single business').

16–18 *Each following day ... Made former wonders its*: Each
successive day taught its lesson (of glory) to the next
one, till the last summed up all the wonders that had
preceded it.

19 *clinquant*: Glittering. Cotgrave's *Dictionary* (1611)
defines the noun as 'Thin plate-lace of gold or silver'.
   like heathen gods: Perhaps a reminiscence of Psalm 115.4,
'their idols are silver and gold, even the work of men's
hands'.

21–2 *India ... Showed like a mine*: The idea of India itself
as a source of untold wealth was reinforced by the gold
mines of the New World (South America and the West

Indies); compare *Henry IV, Part I*, III.1.162–3, 'as
bountiful | As mines of India', and Donne, 'The Sun
Rising', line 17, 'both th'Indias of spice and mine'.

23 *madams*: Ladies of rank.

24–5 *sweat to bear | The pride upon them*: The theme of over-
weening extravagance runs throughout this account,
leading to the attack upon Wolsey as exploiter and
ruiner of the country. Pride is a fault not only socially
ruinous but theologically fatal.

25 *that*: So that.

26 *Was to them as a painting*: Coloured them as if they
were rouged.

26–8 *Now this masque ... a fool and beggar*: Holinshed has
several accounts of brilliant masques presented by both
French and English courts.

30–31 *him in eye | Still him in praise*: The one seen was ever
the one praised.

33 *in censure*: In judging which was the better. *Censure*
bears no sense of condemnation here, as it does at
III.1.64.

36 *that*: So that.

former fabulous story: Old stories hitherto thought fabulous.

38 *Bevis*: A Saxon knight and medieval romance hero, said
to have been made Earl of Southampton by William
the Conqueror.

39–40 *As I belong to worship, and affect | In honour honesty*: As
I am a nobleman and honourably cherish truth.

40–42 *the tract of everything ... Which action's self was tongue
to*: 'The course of these triumphs and pleasures,
however well related, must lose in the description part
of that spirit and energy which were expressed in the
real action' (Dr Johnson).

42–7 *All was royal ... as you guess?*: F starts Buckingham's
speech at *All was Royall*, and ends it at *Of this great
Sport together?* (47); it gives *As you guesse*: (47) to
Norfolk, as if Buckingham showed signs of guessing
the answer. But it is unlikely that Buckingham would
comment so decisively (*All was royal ... full function*)

on an event seen by Norfolk but not by himself, or that he would be credited with a guess he has not made. The alteration, first made by Theobald in the eighteenth century, has been adopted by most editors since then.

44-5 *Order gave each thing view; the office did | Distinctly his full function*: The whole affair was so well ordered as to be easily seen; those in charge carried everything through clearly and properly.

47 *sport*: Entertainment.

48 *certes*: Certainly (here one syllable, though sometimes two, as in *The Tempest*, III.3.31, 'For certes, these are people of the island').

   promises no element: Seems no proper constituent.

51 *Cardinal of York*: Wolsey was appointed Archbishop of York in 1514 and a Cardinal in 1515.

52 *The devil speed him*: May the devil (not God) look after him!

52-3 *No man's pie is freed | From his ambitious finger*: 'To have a finger in the pie' was proverbial; Tilley, F 228.

54 *fierce vanities*: Wild follies.

55 *keech*: Animal fat rolled up into a lump for tallow-making. Wolsey was reputedly a butcher's son (cf. 120, *This butcher's cur*), though his father was in fact a grazier and wool merchant. In *Henry IV, Part II*, II.1.89, a butcher's wife is 'goodwife Keech' and in *Henry IV, Part I*, II.4.224, Prince Hal calls Falstaff 'greasy tallow-catch', probably a variant of the same word.

56 *Take up the rays o'th'beneficial sun*: Absorb in himself all the King's favour.

58 *stuff*: Qualities.

59-60 *whose grace | Chalks successors their way*: Whose virtue marks out the way for those who follow.

61 *high feats*: Great services.

61-2 *allied | To eminent assistants*: Connected with ministers of state.

63 *self-drawing web*: Web spun from his own resources. Since spiders were thought poisonous and sinister, the analogy reflects damagingly upon Wolsey.

   'a gives us note: He lets us know. The F reading, *O gives*

us note, has been defended as an exclamation of passion or as meaning that Wolsey is, by himself, a mere cipher. But it is far more likely to be a misprint of the colloquial "a" meaning 'he'.

65 *A gift that heaven gives for him*: His merits he considers as heaven-sent gifts bestowed on his behalf.

70–72 *If not from hell ... A new hell in himself*: If his pride come not from hell, the devil must, unexpectedly, be tight-fisted – or has already given away all the pride he owned, and Wolsey now originates a new hell of his own, as Lucifer's pride originated the first one. (Throughout the play Wolsey's pride and ambition are condemned on theological grounds; similarly, Thomas Churchyard's poem on Wolsey in *A Mirror for Magistrates* (1559) associates his pride with Lucifer's: 'Your fault not half so great as was my pride, | For which offence fell Lucifer from skies'.)

73 *going out*: Expedition.

74 *privity*: Participation (in secret business).

75 *file*: List.

77–8 *To whom as great a charge as little honour | He meant to lay upon*: On whom he meant to impose expenses as great as the honour intended to them is little.

78–80 *his own letter ... he papers*: This is a striking instance of Shakespeare's late, eccentric, style. The F reading – *his owne Letter | The Honourable Boord of Councell, out | Must fetch him in, he Papers* – verges on the incomprehensible, though A. P. Rossiter argued that it means 'The Cardinal's mere letter, that distinguished and impudent mockery of the whole Council whose rights it usurps, once sent out, had the power to call up and fetch in whomsoever he was pleased to put down on paper' (*The Times Literary Supplement*, 15 July 1949, page 459). But this more-than-telegraphese use of *out*, and the jolting antithesis of *out* and *in*, are syntactically too far-fetched even for late Shakespeare.

79 *The honourable board of Council out*: 'Without consent of the whole board of the Council' (Holinshed, III.644).

80 *Must fetch him in he papers*: Must involve whomever he puts on his list.

84 *Have broke their backs with laying manors on 'em*: Have ruined themselves by pawning or selling their estates so as to dress extravagantly. The idea of breaking one's back financially, or bearing one's birthright on one's back, was proverbial; Tilley, B 16, L 452.

85 *vanity*: Futile extravagance.

86-7 *minister communication of | A most poor issue*: Bring about the disclosure of a fruitless result. This clumsy phrase goes back to Holinshed (III.644): 'he knew not for what cause so much money should be spent . . . and communication to be ministered of things of no importance'.

88 *not values*: Is not worth.

90 *the hideous storm*: The storm – a historical fact – figures appropriately also as a dramatic portent of conflict: Holinshed writes 'On Monday, the eighteenth of June, was such an hideous storm of wind and weather that many conjectured it did prognosticate trouble and hatred shortly after to follow between princes' (III.654).

91 *not consulting*: Without pausing to consult others.

93 *aboded*: Boded, foreboded.

95 *flawed*: Cracked, broken.

   attached: Seized by legal process. (The seizure of English goods at Bordeaux in fact took place in March 1523, but is here anticipated for dramatic effect.)

96 *therefore*: For that reason.

97 *Th'ambassador is silenced*: This detail is probably taken from Edward Hall, who writes 'The ambassador was commanded to keep his house in silence' (*The Union of the Two Noble Families of Lancaster and York* (1548), edited by Henry Ellis, 1809, page 634), rather than Holinshed, who has 'The ambassador ... was commanded to keep his house' (III.676).

98 *A proper title of a peace*: A fine thing to call a peace.

99 *superfluous rate*: Excessive price.

100 *Like it*: May it please.

101 *difference*: Quarrel.

104 *read*: Reckon.

105 *potency*: Power (to harm).

108 *A minister in his power*: An agent to effect it.

109–12 *I know his sword ... Thither he darts it*: A variant on the proverb 'Kings have long arms'; Tilley, K 87.

111–12 *where 'twill not extend, | Thither he darts it*: He makes it wound even though at a distance.

114 *the purse*: The bag containing the great seal (carried before the Lord Chancellor as an emblem of his office).

115 *surveyor*: Overseer of estates. Buckingham's surveyor was his cousin, Charles Knevet.

116 *examination*: Testimony.

120 *butcher's cur*: See note on 55. 'As surly as a butcher's cur' was a proverbial phrase; Tilley, B 764.

121–2 *best | Not wake him*: That is, let sleeping dogs lie.

122–3 *A beggar's book | Outworths a noble's blood*: A beggar's learning has more power than a nobleman's high birth. 'This is a contemptuous exclamation very naturally put into the mouth of one of the ancient, unlettered, martial nobility' (Dr Johnson).

124 *temperance*: Self-control.

appliance only: Sole remedy.

125 *in's*: In his.

127 *abject object*: Object of contempt.

128 *bores*: Fools, cheats. The exact sense is uncertain; editors have suggested 'undermines', 'stabs', 'wounds', or, by connection with the French *bourder*, 'mocks', 'cheats'. 'To bore the nose' or 'bore the nostrils' is found in the sense 'outwit' or 'lead by the nose', and *bore* may derive thence; compare the anonymous *Thomas Lord Cromwell* (reprinted in *The Shakespeare Apocrypha*, edited by C. F. Tucker Brooke, 1908), III.2.167, 'I am no earl but a smith, sir, one Hodge, a smith at Putney, sir; one that hath gulled you, that hath bored you, sir', and Beaumont and Fletcher, *The Spanish Curate*, IV.5.149–50, 'I am abused, betrayed! I am laughed at, scorned, | Baffled, and bored, it seems!'

131–45 *To climb steep hills ... wastes it*: Norfolk delivers a string of proverbial or gnomic phrases; for example, 131–2, 132–4, 140–41, 141–3, 143–5.

133 *full hot*: High-spirited.

134 *Self-mettle*: His own ardour.

137 *from a mouth of honour*: With the voice of a nobleman.

138 *Ipswich*: Wolsey's birthplace.

139 *There's difference in no persons*: Distinctions of rank count for nothing.

    Be advised: Take heed.

140–41 *Heat not a furnace ... singe yourself*: An allusion to Daniel 3.22, 'Therefore because the King's command was strait, and the furnace was exceeding hot, the men that put in Sidrach, Misach, and Abednego, the flame of the fire destroyed them.'

144 *mounts the liquor*: Makes the liquid rise.

147 *More stronger*: An instance of the double comparative or superlative form common in Elizabethan English.

149 *allay*: Moderate.

151 *top-proud*: Proud in the highest degree.

152–3 *Whom from the flow of gall I name not, but | From sincere motions*: Whom I speak of not from personal rancour but from honest motives. By the medieval doctrine of the 'humours', the gall-bladder was held to produce 'choler', the origin of anger and bitterness.

153 *intelligence*: Information.

154–5 *proofs as clear ... gravel*: This resembles a passage in one of the scenes attributed to Shakespeare in *The Two Noble Kinsmen*, I.1.112–13, 'Like wrinkled pebbles in a glassy stream | You may behold 'em'.

157 *vouch*: Assertion.

161 *his mind and place*: His intentions and high position.

164 *suggests*: Prompts (in a bad sense).

167 *wrenching*: (1) Rinsing; (2) twisting. Cf. likewise Gerard Manley Hopkins's poem 'Spring': 'thrush | Through the echoing timber does so rinse and wring | The ear'.

169 *articles o'th'combination*: Terms of the treaty or league.

172 *Count-Cardinal*: Pope's emendation to 'court-cardinal', that is, Cardinal engrossed in court policy, may be right ('r' being easily misread as 'n'). The F reading indicates Wolsey's assumption of lordly rank – the very grounds of Buckingham's hatred.

174–90 *Now this follows ... the foresaid peace*: This is closely derived from Holinshed's account of the connivance between Wolsey and Charles V, who landed in England in May 1520.

176–7 *Charles the Emperor ... the Queen his aunt*: Katherine of Aragon was sister of Joanna, mother of Charles, Emperor of the Holy Roman Empire and King of Spain.

178 *colour*: Pretext.

179 *whisper*: Speak secretly with.

184–7 *as I trow ... the way was made*: The syntax is erratic, but the sense is clear.

184 *trow*: Believe.

192 *buy and sell*: Traffic in (a proverbial phrase, often with implications of ignoble dealing; cf. *Richard III*, V.3.306, 'Dickon thy master is bought and sold', and *Coriolanus*, III.2.9–10, 'woollen vassals, things created | To buy and sell with groats').

195 *mistaken*: Misrepresented.

197 *Brandon*: The Duke of Suffolk's family name was Brandon, but there is no sign that Suffolk is intended here; the name may have occurred to Shakespeare haphazardly. The arrest was actually effected by Sir Henry Marney, captain of the King's guard, on 16 April 1521, as Holinshed relates (III.658).

Sergeant-at-Arms: The monarch is attended by a body of sergeants-at-arms, of knightly rank, charged with his protection and the arrest of traitors.

200 *Hereford*: Pronounced 'Herford'. F by a slip reads *Hertford*.

204 *device and practice*: Tricks and plots.

204–6 *I am sorry ... The business present*: 'I am sorry to see that you are taken prisoner, and to be an eye-witness of the event' (J. M. Berdan and C. T. Brooke, Yale edition, 1925).

207 *th'Tower*: Of London, where traitors were imprisoned.

211 *Aberga'nny*: Abergavenny (spelt 'Aburgany' in F, and so pronounced; 'Aburgauennie' in Holinshed).

216–21 *Here is a warrant ... Nicholas Hopkins*: 'There was also

attached [arrested] the foresaid Chartreux monk
[Nicholas Hopkins], master John de la Car *alias* de la
Court, the Duke's confessor, and Sir Gilbert Perke,
priest, the Duke's chancellor ... After the apprehen-
sion of the Duke, inquisitions were taken in diverse
shires of England of him; so that by the knights and
gentlemen he was indicted of high treason, for certain
words spoken ... by the same Duke at Blechingly, to
the Lord of Abergavenny; and therewith was the same
lord attached for concealment, and so likewise was the
Lord Montacute, and both led to the Tower'
(Holinshed, III.658).

217 *Lord Montacute*: Henry Pole, Lord Montacute
(1492–1539), son-in-law of Abergavenny; he was
pardoned on this occasion but executed for treason in
1539.

219 *Gilbert Perk, his chancellor*: F has *Gilbert Pecke, his
Councellour* for Holinshed's 'Sir Gilbert Perke, priest,
the Duke's chancellor', both changes being easy errors
of transcription or misreading. 'Perke' is probably a
mistake for 'clerk'; contemporary records refer to
'Robert Gilbert, clerk' as Buckingham's chancellor
(*Calendar of State Papers, Henry VIII*, Part I, 490–95).
Shortly after, Holinshed refers correctly to 'Robert
Gilbert, his chancellor' (III.660).

221 *Chartreux*: Carthusian order (introduced into England
late in the twelfth century).

     Nicholas Hopkins: F has *Michaell Hopkins* for
Holinshed's 'Nicholas Hopkins'; perhaps 'Nicholas'
was indicated by 'Nich.', misread 'Mich.'

223–4 *My life is spanned ... I am the shadow*: 'My time is
measured, the length of my life is now determined'
(Dr Johnson). This echoes Psalm 39.6–7 (Prayer Book
version): 'Behold, Thou hast made my days as it were
a span long ... For man walketh in a vain shadow.'

224–6 *I am the shadow ... darkening my clear sun*: I am reduced
to the mere semblance of my substantial self, whose
form this sudden cloud of misfortune has taken,
eclipsing the sun of my life (my own glory, or the King's

favour). (It is impossible to get all the elements of this complicated though expressive figure into focus at once, but the general sense is clear.)

226 *My lord*: F reads *My Lords*, but Norfolk is the only person of whom Buckingham can take farewell, since Abergavenny accompanies him off, with Brandon.

I.2

under the King's feet: At the King's feet (the King's seat or 'state' being raised up).

1 *best heart*: Very essence.

2 *level*: Aim, line of fire.

3 *full-charged*: Fully loaded.

4 *choked*: Suppressed. The word could be used for blotting out a battery of cannon, and so carries on the artillery metaphor of lines 2–3; compare Beaumont and Fletcher, *The Mad Lover*, I.1.96–7, 'If he mount at me, | I may chance choke his battery.'

5 *That gentleman of Buckingham's*: The surveyor referred to at I.1.222–3.

8 *state*: Canopied throne, chair of state.

12 *moiety*: Half.

13 *Repeat your will, and take it*: Say what you desire and it is yours (no sense of repetition is involved).

20–29 *There have been commissions . . . In loud rebellion*: 'By the Cardinal there was devised strange commissions, and sent in the end of March into every shire . . . that the sixth part of every man's substance should be paid in money or plate to the King without delay . . . Hereof followed such cursing, weeping, and exclamation against both King and Cardinal that pity it was to hear' (Holinshed, III.708–9). The date of these events was 1525, but they are predated here so that Katherine can plead for the oppressed and for Buckingham, and stand out at once as an opponent of Wolsey. This is a foretaste of Shakespeare's sympathetic development of Katherine, far beyond the indications Holinshed gave him.

20–21 *commissions . . . which hath flawed*: The use of a singular verb with a plural subject, and vice versa, is common in Elizabethan English.

24 *putter-on*: Instigator.

27-8 *breaks | The sides of loyalty*: Is more than loyalty can
   bear. Shakespeare often presents a violent inner anguish
   as bursting through the body; compare *King Lear*,
   II.4.196-7, 'O sides, you are too tough! | Will you yet
   hold?', and *Antony and Cleopatra*, I.3.16-17, 'the sides
   of nature | Will not sustain it'.

31-7 *The clothiers all . . . serves among them*: 'The Duke of
   Suffolk, sitting in commission about this subsidy in
   Suffolk, persuaded by courteous means the rich clothiers to assent thereto: but when they came home, and
   went about to discharge and put from them their spinners, carders, fullers, weavers, and other artificers,
   which they kept in work aforetime, the people began
   to assemble in companies . . . The Duke . . . commanded
   the constables that every man's harness should be taken
   from him . . . Then the rage of the people increased,
   railing openly on the Duke and Sir Robert Drury, and
   threatening them with death, and the Cardinal also.
   And herewith there assembled together after the manner
   of rebels four thousand men . . . which put themselves
   in harness, and rang the bells' alarm, and began still to
   assemble in great number' (Holinshed, III.709).

32 *'longing*: Belonging.

33 *spinsters, carders, fullers*: Spinners, combers (those who
   remove impurities from wool by combing it), cleansers
   (those who beat wool to clean or thicken it).

37 *danger serves among them*: Danger is welcomed as a
   comrade in arms. The personification may have been
   derived from the answer made by the rebels to the
   Duke of Norfolk: 'Poverty was their captain, the which
   with his cousin Necessity had brought them to that
   doing' (Holinshed, III.709).

41-2 *I know but of a single part in aught | Pertains to th'state*:
   I know only an individual's share in state matters.

42-3 *and front but in that file | Where others tell steps with
   me*: And merely march in the front rank with others
   who step in pace with me (that is, all the Council are
   jointly responsible).

44–7 *you frame* | *Things that are known alike . . . their acquain-*
tance: All members of the Council equally know what
measures are taken, but it is you who frame these measures, which, however harmful, are then imposed on
those who would wish to evade them but cannot.

50 *The back is sacrifice to th'load*: The back must suffer
under its burden.

52 *exclamation*: Protest.

56 *subject's*: F's *Subiects* might be singular or plural: it is
taken here, after *The*, as a generic singular.

grief: Grievance.

57 *commissions, which compels*: See the note on 20–21.

59 *pretence*: Pretext.

62 *Allegiance*: Four syllables.

64–5 *This tractable obedience is a slave* | *To each incensèd will*:
Their willingness to be obedient is mastered by their
anger

67 *primer*: More urgent.

business: F reads *basenesse*, which some editors retain:
'no primer baseness' would mean 'no more pressing
example of wickedness', but the expression would be
awkward. The Queen's point seems to be the urgent
need of attending to this matter of concern.

70 *A single voice*: My individual vote.

71 *approbation of the judges*: Wolsey claims that he
supported only measures whose legality the judges had
justified. 'The Cardinal excused himself and said that
when it was moved in Council how to levy money to
the King's use, the King's Council, and namely the
judges, said that he might lawfully demand any sum
by commission, and that by consent of the whole
Council it was done' (Holinshed, III.710).

73 *faculties*: Qualities.

73–4 *will be* | *The chronicles of my doing*: Presume to expound
all that I do.

75 *place*: High office.

78 *cope*: Encounter (cf. *As You Like It*, II.1.67, 'I love to
cope him in these sullen fits').

80 *new-trimmed*: Newly fitted out (as a seaworthy vessel

is immune from sharks, so honest men are immune from slanderers who try to harm them).

82 *sick interpreters, once weak ones*: Unsound, distorted, commentators, in a word, weak-witted ones. For this sense of *once*, compare *Much Ado About Nothing*, I.1.297, 'Look what will serve is fit. 'Tis once, thou lovest'; *Coriolanus*, II.3.1–2, 'Once, if he do require our voices, we ought not to deny him.'

83 *Not ours, or not allowed*: Not acknowledged as our act, or not approved.

83–4 *as oft | Hitting a grosser quality*: Appealing just as often to cruder minds.

86 *our motion*: Whatever move we make.

88 *state-statues*: Effigies of statesmen.

90 *example*: Precedent.
    issue: Outcome.

93–4 *We must not rend our subjects from our laws, | And stick them in our will*: We must not rend our subjects away from the rule of law and fix them under our arbitrary wills.

95 *trembling*: Fearful.

95–8 *we take … drink the sap*: If we do this it is like lopping off branches, bark, and part of the main timber; even though the root is left, the life-blood (*sap*) of a tree so hacked will dry up.

96 *lop*: Small branches, loppings.

99 *questioned*: Disputed.

104–7 *The grieved commons … pardon comes*: 'The Cardinal, to deliver himself of the evil will of the commons, purchased by procuring and advancing of this demand, affirmed, and caused it to be bruited abroad, that through his intercession the King had pardoned and released all things' (Holinshed, III.710).

105 *Hardly conceive*: Think harshly.
    noised: Reported.

106 *our*: Wolsey uses the royal plural.

110 *Is run in*: Has incurred.

110–28 *It grieves many … hear too much*: Closely though much of this scene follows Holinshed, the King's impressive eulogy does not derive from the source, where Wolsey alone examines Buckingham's surveyor. Shakespeare probably wishes to strengthen the King's dramatic role at this point, in keeping with the power of command Henry has just shown in reproving Wolsey. In each successive crisis the King displays more initiative. Here he follows up and completes the action Wolsey initiated against Buckingham. In the trial of Queen Katherine he exonerates Wolsey from the charge of being the chief mover, and attributes the action to his own scruples of conscience and concern for his realm. In the fall of Wolsey he reveals his independence of his great chancellor. And in favouring Cranmer he acts as the unquestioned and unrivalled ruler.

111 *learned*: One syllable, as also at 142, and II.4.206 and 238; elsewhere two syllables.

112 *bound*: Indebted.

114 *out of himself*: Beyond his own powers.

116 *disposed*: Applied.

118 *complete*: Accented on the first syllable.

120 *with ravished listening*: Ravished with listening. The word order is eccentric or erroneous.

122 *monstrous habits*: Hideous garments.

130 *Most like a careful subject*: Wolsey's Machiavellianism is evident, since far from being a *careful subject* the surveyor is his own bribed ally.

130–31 *collected | Out of*: Gathered from.

139 *This dangerous conception in this point*: 'This particular part of this dangerous design' (Dr Johnson).

140 *Not friended by his wish*: Not successful in his wish (that you should die without issue).

142 *learned*: One syllable; see note on 111.

145 *fail*: (1) Death; but also probably (2) failure to beget an heir (see 133–4 and 168–9, and II.4.198, *By this my issue's fail*).

147 *Nicholas Henton*: The *Nicholas Hopkins* of I.1.221, the confusion arising from Holinshed's sentence 'Nicholas Hopkins, a monk of an house of the Chartreux order beside Bristow, called Henton, sometime his confessor'.

150 *of sovereignty*: About the gaining of the crown.

151 *sped to*: Made your expedition to.

152–71 *The Duke being at the Rose ... Shall govern England*:
'The same Duke, the tenth of May [1520], in the twelfth
year of the King's reign, at London in a place called
the Rose, within the parish of Saint Lawrence Poultney
... demanded of the said Charles Knevet esquire what
was the talk amongst the Londoners concerning the
King's journey beyond the seas? And the said Charles
told him that many stood in doubt of that journey, lest
the Frenchmen meant some deceit towards the King.
Whereto the Duke answered that it was to be feared
lest it would come to pass according to the words of a
certain holy monk. "For there is," saith he, "a Chartreux
monk, that diverse times hath sent to me, willing me
to send unto him my chancellor; and I did send unto
him John de la Court, my chaplain, unto whom he
would not declare anything till de la Court had sworn
unto him to keep all things secret, and to tell no creature living what he should hear of him, except it were
to me. And then the said monk told de la Court that
neither the King nor his heirs should prosper, and that
I should endeavour myself to purchase the good wills
of the commonalty of England; for I the same Duke
and my blood should prosper, and have the rule of the
realm of England"' (Holinshed, III.660–61).

152 *the Rose*: A manor of Buckingham's, converted in 1561
into the Merchant Taylors' School.

157 *Presently*: At once.

158 *doubted*: Feared.

164 *confession's*: F has 'Commissions', but the relevant
passage in Holinshed reads 'he had done very well to
bind his chaplain John de la Court under the seal of
confession to keep secret such matter' (III.659).

167 *with demure confidence*: In solemn trust.

170 *To win the love o'th'commonalty*: The first Folio reads
To the loue o'th'Commonalty. The unauthoritative fourth
Folio inserted 'gain' between 'To' and 'the loue'. The
present emendation is based on Holinshed, who in the

relevant passages has 'to win the favour of the people' (III.658), 'to win their favour and friendships' (III.659) and 'to purchase the good wills of the commonalty' (III.661); these may have coalesced and produced *To win the love o'th'commonalty*.

172–3 *lost your office* | *On the complaint o'th'tenants*: 'Now it chanced that the Duke ... went before into Kent unto a manor place which he had there. And whilst he stayed in that country ... grievous complaints were exhibited to him by his farmers and tenants against Charles Knevet his surveyor, for such bribing as he had used there amongst them. Whereupon the Duke took such displeasure against him that he deprived him of his office, not knowing how that in so doing he procured his own destruction, as after appeared' (Holinshed, III.645).

174 *spleen*: Malice (the spleen being supposedly the source of strong passions).

175 *spoil your nobler soul*: Blot your soul, which is of greater value than any human rank.

178–86 *I told my lord ... Should have gone off*: 'Then said Charles Knevet, "The monk may be deceived through the devil's illusion", and that it was evil to meddle with such matters. "Well," said the Duke, "it cannot hurt me", and so (saith the indictment) the Duke seemed to rejoice in the monk's words. And further, at the same time, the Duke told the said Charles that if the King had miscarried now in his last sickness, he would have chopped off the heads of the Cardinal, of Sir Thomas Lovell, knight, and of others' (Holinshed, III.661).

180 *For him to ruminate on this*: F reads *For this to ruminate on this*. Shakespeare does not elsewhere use the phrase 'to ruminate on', and the intended reading may be 'For him to ruminate this.'

181 *forged him*: Caused him to fashion.

186 *Ha!*: This exclamation, frequent in Henry's mouth, may derive from Rowley's *When You See Me You Know Me*, where the King so repeatedly uses it that it is recognized almost as his slogan; for example:

> KING Am I not Harry, am I not England's king, ha?
> WILL SUMMERS So la, now, the watchword's given,
>   nay, and he once cry 'Ha!', ne'er a man in the court
>   dare for his head speak again.   (lines 657–60)

This trait, together with a threatening countenance,
seems to have been part of the received portrait of
Henry. Foxe's *Acts and Monuments* (page 1025) reports
that when Henry examined the martyr John Lambert
he turned to him 'with his brows bent, as it were threatening some grievous thing unto him, [and] said these
words, "Ho, good fellow, what is thy name?"' See also
the Roman Catholic life of Saint John Fisher (Harleian
MSS. 6382, edited by R. Bayne, 1921, page 62), '"No,
ah!" quoth the King, and therewith looking upon my
lord of Rochester with a frowning countenance'.
so rank: (1) So gross, corrupt; (2) grown so high (with
reference to Buckingham's plotting).

188–209 *Being at Greenwich . . . an irresolute purpose*: 'The same
Duke on the fourth of November [1519], in the eleventh
year of the King's reign, at east Greenwich in the
country of Kent, said unto one Charles Knevet esquire,
after that the King had reproved the Duke for retaining
William Bulmer, knight, into his service, that if he had
perceived that he should have been committed to the
Tower (as he doubted he should have been) he would
so have wrought that the principal doers therein should
not have had cause of great rejoicing; for he would
have played the part which his father intended to have
put in practice against King Richard the Third at
Salisbury, who made earnest suit to have come unto
the presence of the said King Richard; which suit if he
might have obtained, he, having a knife secretly about
him, would have thrust it into the body of King
Richard, as he had made semblance to kneel down
before him. And, in speaking these words, he maliciously laid his hand upon his dagger, and said that if
he were so evil used he would do his best to accomplish

his pretended purpose, swearing to confirm his word
by the blood of our Lord' (Holinshed, III.660).

190–91 *remember | Of:* Have memory of (a usage not found
elsewhere in Shakespeare).

191 *sworn:* Two syllables.

195 *my father:* Henry Stafford, Duke of Buckingham,
figures in *Richard III*, first as Richard's ally, then as his
foe, captured and executed.

198 *semblance of his duty:* A show of dutifully kneeling.

199 *A giant traitor:* Maxwell (in the New Cambridge edition,
1962) suggests that this phrase, and *Hamlet*, IV.5.118,
'That thy rebellion looks so giant-like', may glance at
the Titans' rebellion against the gods in Greek
mythology.

201 *And this man out of prison:* While this man is at liberty.

204 *stretched him:* Raised himself to his full height.

209 *irresolute:* Unaccomplished.

    his period: The end he aims at.

210 *attached:* Arrested.

I.3

2 *strange mysteries:* Outlandish freaks.

6 *the late voyage:* Elizabethan dramatists often satirize
gallants who affect foreign fashions: for example,
Chapman, *Bussy D'Ambois* (1607), I.2.42–50:

> Never were men so weary of their skins,
> And apt to leap out of themselves as they;
> Who, when they travel to bring forth rare men,
> Come home, delivered of a fine French suit.
> Their brains lie with their tailors.
>   . . . he's sole heir
> To all the moral virtues that first greets
> The light with a new fashion, which becomes them
> Like apes, disfigured with the attires of men.

Holinshed's account (III.635) of foolish antics on a
mission in February 1520, some months before the Field
of the Cloth of Gold, has been adapted here to make
them a consequence of that extravagant episode:

'During this time remained in the French court diverse
young gentlemen of England, and they with the French
King rode daily disguised through Paris, throwing eggs,
stones, and other foolish trifles at the people . . . And
when these young gentlemen came again into England,
they were all French in eating, drinking, and apparel,
yea, and in French vices and brags, so that all the estates
in England were by them laughed at, the ladies and
gentlewomen were dispraised, but if it were after the
French turn.'

7 *A fit or two o'th'face*: A grimace or two.
   shrewd: Acute.

10 *Pepin or Clotharius*: Early Frankish kings, of the eighth
   and sixth centuries respectively; the implication is of
   French affectations, but grotesque and barbarous ones.
   keep state: Affect (an awkward) grandeur.

11 *new legs*: New ways of walking and bowing.

12 *see*: Pope altered to 'saw' and most editors follow, but
   see was not infrequent as a past tense, and still can be
   so in dialect or popular idiom.
   spavin: Disease of horses, making the hock swell and
   causing lameness.

13 *Or*: F reads *A*, which most editors change to 'Or' or
   'And'.
   springhalt: Nervous twitching of the hind-legs in horses;
   from 'stringhalt', 'an unnatural binding of the sinews'
   as Gervase Markham's *Cheap and Good Husbandry*
   (1614), F3ʳ, describes it.
   Death: By God's death (an oath).

14 *to't*: As well.

15 *worn out Christendom*: Exhausted every Christian fashion.

17 *the new proclamation*: After describing the travellers'
   follies (see note on 6), Holinshed writes (III.640), 'The
   King's Council caused the Lord Chamberlain to call
   before them diverse of the privy chamber, which had
   been in the French court, and banished them the court
   for diverse considerations . . . Which discharge out of
   court grieved sore the hearts of these young men.'

18 *court gate*: In Ralph Agas's map of London (*c.* 1560),

one of the gates of Whitehall is so named, probably
the one designed by Holbein facing Charing Cross to
the south of the banqueting house.

23 *the Louvre*: The seat of the French court.

25 *fool and feather*: Folly and foppery (apparently a set
phrase for fashionable gallants: extravagant plumes
worn in headgear were often satirized).

26 *honourable points of ignorance*: Points of empty-headed
etiquette.

27 *as*: Such as.

    fireworks: As well as the usual sense there is probably
    a quibble on whores, the source of venereal disease, so
    often referred to in terms of burning etc.

28-9 *Abusing better men than they can be | Out of a foreign
wisdom*: Mocking better men than themselves, through
the 'wisdom' they have gained abroad. (The sense
continues from *points of ignorance*.)

29-31 *renouncing clean ... types of travel*: The grammatical
construction goes back to *leave those remnants | Of fool
and feather*.

30 *tennis*: A French game, known in England from the
thirteenth century; it was popular with Henry VIII,
who built the tennis court at Hampton Court, and with
the courtiers of James I.

30-31 *tall stockings, | Short blistered breeches*: Long stockings,
coming high up the thigh, went with the fashion of
short puffed breeches, slashed like blisters to show the
satin lining. In *A Tale of a Tub* (*Works*, edited by
Herford and Simpson, Volume 3) Jonson satirizes 'long
sausage hose' (I.4.11) and 'pinned-up breeches, like
pudding bags' (II.2.125).

31 *types*: Marks, signs.

32 *understand*: (1) Use their minds; (2) use their legs (cf.
Twelfth Night, III.1.77-8, 'My legs do better understand me, sir, than I understand what you mean').

34 *cum privilegio*: By special licence (the phrase applied to
the privilege granted for the publishing of books).

    '*oui*': Talk French. The first Folio reads *wee*; the second
    Folio alters to *wear*, and some editors follow.

35 *lag end*: Latter end.

38 *trim vanities*: Spruce fops.

  marry: By the Virgin Mary (an oath).

40 *speeding*: Successful.

41 *fiddle*: Here, and in some other cases, there may be an
  equivoque; compare Heywood, *The Fair Maid of the
  Exchange* (*Dramatic Works*, edited by R. H. Shepherd,
  1874, II.21), 'Ne'er a wench in all the town but will
  scorn to dance after my fiddle'; and Fletcher, *The Honest
  Man's Fortune*, V.1.37–9:

LAMIRA You two will make a pretty handsome con-
  sort.

MONTAGUE Yes, madam, if my fiddle fail me not.

LAMIRA Your fiddle? Why your fiddle? I warrant
  thou meanest madly.

44–5 *beaten . . . out of play*: Outdone in (amorous) play (cf.
  The Winter's Tale, I.2.187–8, 'thy mother plays, and
  I | Play too').

45 *plainsong*: Simple melody, without frills.

47 *Held current music*: Be accepted as good music.

48 *colt's tooth*: Youthful wildness (especially in older men;
  compare the proverb 'He has a colt's tooth in his head';
  Tilley, C 525).

49 *stump*: Ostensibly 'stump of a tooth', but with a bawdy
  double meaning.

58 *He had a black mouth*: He would have a wicked tongue.

59 *has wherewithal*: He has what he needs to be liberal.

61 *Men of his way should be most liberal*: Probably echoing
  1 Timothy 3.2, 'A bishop . . . must be . . . a lover of
  hospitality'.

63 *stays*: Is waiting.

67 *comptrollers*: Stewards, or masters of ceremonies (comptrollers were the officers regulating expenditure in great
  households; the old spelling still survives).

I.4

0 *Hautboys*: Oboes.

  state: Canopy (with a 'chair of state' below it).

7 *Lord Chamberlain, Lord Sands*: At the actual time of
Wolsey's entertainment (3 January 1527) the Lord
Chamberlain was Lord Sands himself, who succeeded
in 1526. But at the time assumed in the play, before
Buckingham's trial in 1521, the Lord Chamberlain was
the Earl of Worcester.

11 *lay*: Unclerical.

12 *running banquet*: Quick refreshment, appetizer
(implying 'amorous pursuit followed by a feast of love-
making': Eric Partridge, *Shakespeare's Bawdy*). Another
sense, at V.4.64, is a whipping at the cart's tail.

20 *Place you*: Arrange the guests.

30 *kiss you twenty*: Kiss twenty ladies (or, perhaps, kiss
twenty times over). The *you* is virtually superfluous;
this usage, the 'ethic dative', is frequent in Elizabethan
English for a person addressed but only 'indirectly
interested in the fact stated' (*Concise Oxford Dictionary*).
with a breath: In the space of a breath.
Well said: That's right (spoken of something said or
done, in this case probably the seating of the guests).

33 *cure*: (1) Charge, group of parishioners (joking on the
phrase 'cure of souls'; compare the mocking ecclesiastical reference at 32); (2) remedy (for preventing the
ladies' frowns).

41 *beholding*: Indebted.

43–4 *The red wine first must rise | In their fair cheeks*: The
flushing of the skin with drinking was thought to result
from extra blood into which wine was supposed quickly
to transmute itself; compare Marlowe, *Tamburlaine*,
Part 2, III.2.107–8, 'airy wine, | That, being concocted,
turns to crimson blood' (cited by Foakes).

46 *make my play*: Win what I play for (with an equivoque
on 'amorous play'; cf. I.3.45).

49 *Chambers*: Small cannon (for salutes, or theatre use).
The firing at this point set the Globe Theatre on fire
on 29 June 1613.

50 *Look out there*: Cavendish in his *Life of Wolsey* writes
that by Wolsey's order the Lord Chamberlain and Sir
Henry Guilford 'were sent to look': Holinshed,

following Stow, writes that they 'sent to look'. It is
evidently Holinshed who is followed here.

53–86 *A noble troop ... Ye have found him, Cardinal*: This
whole episode follows very closely Holinshed's long
account of the masque, save for two points: Anne Bullen
was not present, and Wolsey failed to identify the King,
selecting instead Sir Edward Neville.

53 *strangers*: Foreigners.

55 *make*: Are coming.

75 *The fairest hand I ever touched*: There is no reference in
any of the chronicles to so early a meeting between
Henry and Anne as the dramatic date of this scene
(1521), though there is some evidence that they met the
next year. According to Holinshed (III.740), Wolsey
learnt of the King's attachment only in 1529, long after
Buckingham's fall in 1521, and at the time of the trial
of Queen Katherine.

84 *take it*: That is, take his place under the 'state'.

89 *unhappily*: Unfavourably.

90 *pleasant*: Merry.

92 *An't*: If it.

93 *Rochford*: Sir Thomas Bullen became Viscount
Rochford in June 1525, later than the dramatic date of
this scene (1521) but earlier than its historical date
(1527).

95 *take you out*: Dance with you.

96 *to kiss you*: As was customary after a dance, the lady
replying with a curtsy; cf. *The Tempest*, I.2.377,
'Curtsied when you have and kissed'.

106 *a measure*: A stately dance.

108 *best in favour*: Best-looking.

      knock it: Strike up.

II.1

0 *several*: Different.

2 *the Hall*: Westminster Hall, the great hall of the royal
palace of Westminster, founded by William Rufus and
reconstructed by Richard II to be the banqueting hall
of the palace; it was the scene of many great state trials
– those of Sir Thomas More and Anne Bullen, as well

as Buckingham, and later of Charles I, Strafford, and
Warren Hastings.

11 *in a little*: In brief.

11–36 *The great Duke ... a most noble patience*: 'The Duke
was brought to the bar, and, upon his arraignment,
pleaded not guilty, and put himself upon his peers. Then
was his indictment read, which the Duke denied to be
true, and (as he was an eloquent man) alleged reasons
to falsify the indictment, pleading the matter for his
own justification very pithily and earnestly. The King's
attorney against the Duke's reasons alleged the examinations, confessions, and proofs of witnesses.

'The Duke desired that the witnesses might be
brought forth. And then came before him Charles
Knevet, Perk, de la Court, and Hopkins the monk of
the priory of the Charterhouse beside Bath, which like
a false hypocrite had induced the Duke to the treason
with his false forged prophecies. Diverse presumptions
and accusations were laid unto him by Charles Knevet,
which he would fain have covered ... Thus was this
prince Duke of Buckingham found guilty of high
treason, by a duke, a marquis, seven earls, and twelve
barons. The Duke was brought to the bar sore chafed,
and sweat marvellously; and after he had made his
reverence he paused a while. The Duke of Norfolk as
judge said, "Sir Edward, you have heard how you be
indicted of high treason ..." The Duke of Buckingham
said, "My lord of Norfolk, you have said as a traitor
should be said unto, but I was never any; but, my lords,
I nothing malign for that you have done to me, but the
eternal God forgive you my death, and I do; I shall
never sue to the King for life, howbeit he is a gracious
prince, and more grace may come from him than I
desire. I desire you, my lords, and all my fellows, to
pray for me' (Holinshed, III.661–2).

13 *allegèd*: Brought forward.

14 *defeat the law*: Refute the case brought against him.

16 *proofs*: Testimonies.

20 *Sir*: A frequent courtesy title for a priest.

29 *Was either pitied in him or forgotten*: Produced merely
   pity for him or had no lasting effect at all.

40 *the end of this*: At the bottom of this.

41–9 *Kildare's attainder . . . from court too*: In order to pros-
   ecute his schemes against Buckingham, Wolsey had to
   remove the Earl of Surrey, Buckingham's son-in-law,
   to a distance. He did so in 1520 by bringing charges
   against Kildare, Lord Deputy of Ireland, and having
   Surrey appointed in his place (Holinshed, III.645).

44 *father*: Father-in-law.

45 *envious*: Malicious.

50 *perniciously*: With deadly loathing.

53 *The mirror of all courtesy*: 'He is termed in the books
   of the law in the said thirteenth year of Henry the
   Eighth (where his arraignment is liberally set down)
   to be the flower and mirror of all courtesy' (Holinshed,
   III.671).

54 *tipstaves*: Officers of the law (charged with taking pris-
   oners into custody; their staves were metal-tipped).
   the axe with the edge towards him: A sign of execution.
   halberds: Long-shafted weapons topped by a spearpoint
   and a blade at right angles.
   Sir Walter Sands: An error for Holinshed's Sir William
   Sands, the Lord Sands of I.3–4, by the date of which
   – 1527 – he had been ennobled.

55 *close*: (1) Out of sight; (2) silent.

57 *lose*: Forget.

60 *sink me*: That is, to hell.

63 *'T has done . . . but justice*: 'Buckingham is made to
   appear sufficiently the innocent victim for Wolsey to
   appear his cruel tormentor, while he is made to appear
   sufficiently guilty to keep the audience from blaming
   the King, or even from regarding him as merely
   Wolsey's dupe' (Paul Bertram, in *In Defense of Reading*,
   edited by R. A. Brower and R. Poirier, 1962, page 161).
   premises: Evidence.

67 *build their evils on the graves*: Forward their crimes by
   destroying the lives. There may be an ambiguity in
   evils, possibly for a building of gross use (jakes?

brothel?'); *Measure for Measure*, II.2.171–2, has a similar
implication of unholy ignominy: 'Shall we desire to
raze the sanctuary | And pitch our evils there?'

74 *only bitter to him, only dying*: The only bitter thing, the
only real sense of death.

77 *Make of your prayers one sweet sacrifice*: An apparent
echo of Psalm 141.2: 'Let my prayer be directed before
thy face as an incense; let the lifting up of mine hands
be an evening sacrifice'.

    sacrifice: Holy offering.

78 *a*: In.

80–81 *If ever any malice . . . forgive me frankly*: See I.2.185–6
for an assertion that Buckingham had threatened
Lovell's death.

82–3 *I as free forgive you | As I would be forgiven*: This echoes
the Lord's Prayer: 'Forgive us our trespasses as we
forgive them that trespass against us'. The falls of
Buckingham, Katherine, and Wolsey alike prompt
speeches of Christian resignation and forgiveness;
cf. III.1.175–81, III.2.440–49, and IV.2 *passim*.

85 *take*: Make.

    envy: Ill-will.

88–90 *My vows and prayers . . . blessings on him*: There are
similar prayers for the King's safety in *Henry V*, II.2,
from the nobles condemned for plotting his death.

89 *forsake*: Leave (my body).

91 *tell*: Count.

94 *monument*: Tomb (with the sense, doubtless, of a memo-
rial to future times).

97 *undertakes*: Takes charge of.

97–103 *Prepare there . . . Edward Bohun*: 'Then was the edge of
the axe turned towards him, and he led into a barge.
Sir Thomas Lovell desired him to sit on the cushions
and carpet ordained for him. He said "Nay, for when
I went to Westminster I was Duke of Buckingham;
now I am but Edward Bohun, the most caitiff of the
world." Thus they landed at the Temple, where
received him Sir Nicholas Vaux and Sir William Sands,
baronets, and led him through the city, who desired

ever the people to pray for him' (Holinshed, III.662).

99 *furniture*: Furnishings.

103 *Bohun*: His family name was Stafford, but he descended
in the female line from the Bohuns, Earls of Hereford,
and held the office of Lord High Constable, which was
hereditary in that family.

105–6 *I now seal it,* | *And with that blood will make 'em one
day groan for't*: 'I now seal my truth and loyalty with
blood, which blood shall one day make them groan'
(Dr Johnson).

107–14 *My noble father ... Restored me to my honours*: 'Henry
Stafford ... was son to Humphrey, Earl Stafford, and
was High Constable of England and Duke of
Buckingham. This man, raising war against Richard
the Third usurping the crown, was in the first year of
the reign of the said Richard ... betrayed by his man
Humphrey Banister (to whom being in distress he fled
for succour) and brought to Richard the Third ...
where the said Duke ... was beheaded without arraignment or judgement ... Edward Stafford, son to Henry,
Duke of Buckingham ... was by Henry the Seventh
restored to his father's inheritance' (Holinshed,
III.671).

108 *raised head*: Raised an armed force.

124 *end*: Purpose.

125 *This from a dying man receive as certain*: The last words
of the dying were proverbially held to be truthful;
compare Tilley, M 514, 'Dying men speak true
(prophesy)'; *Richard II*, II.1.5–6, 'the tongues of dying
men | Enforce attention like deep harmony'; and
Cymbeline, V.5.41–2, 'And but she spoke it dying, I
would not | Believe her lips in opening it.'

127 *loose*: Careless.

129 *rub*: Check.

129–30 *fall away* | *Like water*: An apparent echo of Psalm 58.6,
'Let them fall away like water that runneth apace'.

133 *my long weary life*: Buckingham was in fact only forty-
three.

140–53 *I can give you inkling ... That durst disperse it*: 'This is

the first direct hint at the main action of the play. It is
exceptional for it to be given so late as the second Act'
(D. Nichol Smith, in the Warwick edition, 1899). 'There
rose a secret bruit in London that the King's confessor
Doctor Longland and diverse other great clerks had
told the King that the marriage between him and the
lady Katherine, late wife to his brother Prince Arthur,
was not lawful; whereupon the King should sue a
divorce and marry the Duchess of Alençon, sister to
the French King . . . The King was offended with those
tales, and sent for Sir Thomas Seymour, Mayor of the
city of London, secretly charging him to see that the
people ceased from such talk' (Holinshed, III.719–20).

143 *faith*: Trustworthiness.

146 *confident*: That is, of your discretion.

147 *You shall*: That is, you shall have it.

of late days: Time is much abridged; the events of 1527–8
are made to follow immediately upon those of 1521.
Campeius, reported *lately* arrived (160), landed in 1528.

153–4 *that slander, sir,* | *Is found a truth*: 'It may be a slander
but it is no lie' was proverbial; Tilley, S 520.

156–7 *Either the Cardinal* | *Or some about him*: The first man
Holinshed mentions as instigating the King's scruples
is Doctor Longland, his confessor (see note on 140–53).
Later, Holinshed is uncertain whether Longland or
Wolsey was the initiator (III.736) but attributes to
Wolsey rather than to others the idea that the King
should marry the Duchess of Alençon so as to
strengthen the French alliance (see III.2.85–6).
Divorcing Katherine would conduce to this end and
also shame Charles V, who (Holinshed reports, though
there seems no truth in the allegation) had refused
Wolsey the archbishopric of Toledo; see 162–4 and
Holinshed, III.736. Actually, the Duchess married
Henry of Navarre early in 1527, before any such
scheme, if it ever existed, could have been promoted.

160 *Cardinal Campeius*: Lorenzo Campeggio (Campeius)
reached London in October 1528.

168 *open*: Public.

II.2

1-8 *My lord ... our mouths, sir*: The germ of this letter may
lie in Rowley's *When You See Me You Know Me*, lines
1268-9, where a citizen complains that one of Wolsey's
emissaries 'hath taken up | Commodities valued at a
thousand pound' for Wolsey's advantage.

2 *ridden*: Broken in for riding.

6 *main power*: Sheer force.

14 *sad*: Grave.

17 *'Tis so*: Replying to the Lord Chamberlain, Suffolk's
comment being spoken to himself.

19 *blind*: (1) Blind to the general opinion, or general
welfare; (2) blindfold, like Fortune, arbitrarily controlling men's fates; cf. *Henry V*, III.6.29-34, 'Fortune is
painted blind, with a muffler afore her eyes ... and ...
with a wheel, to signify ... that she is turning, and
inconstant, and mutability, and variation'.
    eldest son: Privileged offspring.

30-31 *like a jewel ... About his neck*: Precious stones were
often worn as pendants around the neck. In *Twelfth
Night*, II.5.59-60, Malvolio will 'wind up my watch, or
play with my – some rich jewel'.

35 *Will bless the King*: As in fact she does, at IV.2.163-4.

37 *These news are*: 'News' was commonly, and ought to
be, plural.

40 *The French King's sister*: as at III.2.85-6.

42 *This bold bad man*: Probably an accepted phrase; it is
found in Spenser, *The Faerie Queene*, I.1.37, Fletcher,
The Loyal Subject, IV.5.91, and Massinger, *A New Way
to Pay Old Debts*, IV.1.160.

46 *From princes into pages*: Holinshed relates that when
saying Mass Wolsey 'made dukes and earls to serve him
of wine ... and to hold to him the basin at the lava-
tory' (III.631).

46-8 *All men's honours ... what pitch he pleases*: This probably alludes to Romans 9.21: 'Hath not the potter power
over the clay, even of the same lump to make one vessel
unto honour, and another unto dishonour?'

48 *pitch*: Height.

60 *The King draws the curtain*: He is disclosed already
   sitting in the curtained recess at the rear of the stage.
68 *business of estate*: State business.
71 *Enter Wolsey and Campeius*: 'But howsoever it came
   about that the King was thus troubled in conscience
   concerning his marriage, this followed that like a wise
   and sage prince, to have the doubt clearly removed, he
   called together the best learned of the realm, which
   were of several opinions. Wherefore he thought to
   know the truth by indifferent judges, lest peradventure
   the Spaniards, and other also in favour of the Queen,
   would say that his own subjects were not indifferent
   judges in this behalf. And therefore he wrote his cause
   to Rome, and also sent to all the universities in Italy
   and France, and to the great clerks of all Christendom,
   to know their opinions, and desired the court of Rome
   to send into his realm a legate, which should be
   indifferent and of a great and profound judgement, to
   hear the cause debated. At whose request the whole
   consistory of the College of Rome sent thither
   Laurence Campeius, a priest cardinal, a man of great
   wit and experience, which was sent thither before in
   the tenth year of this King . . . and with him was joined
   in commission the Cardinal of York and legate of
   England' (Holinshed, III.736).
76–7 *have great care | I be not found a talker*: See to it that
   what I have said is put into effect. 'Talkers are no good
   doers' was proverbial; Tilley, T 64.
81 *so sick though for his place*: So diseased with pride even
   to gain his eminence.
83 *have-at-him*: Thrust. 'Have at you!' signalled an attack;
   see III.2.309 and V.3.113.
87 *envy*: Malice.
90 *clerks*: Scholars.
94 *One general tongue*: One to speak for all.
98 *the holy conclave*: The College of Cardinals.
100 *strangers*: Visiting foreigners.
105 *unpartial*: Impartial.
106 *equal*: Just.

114 *my new secretary*: Gardiner was appointed the King's secretary on 28 July 1529; the time-scale is again abridged. 'About this time the King received into his favour Doctor Stephen Gardiner, whose service he used in matters of great secrecy and weight, admitting him in the room of Doctor Pace [see 120–28], the which being continually abroad in ambassages, and the same not much necessary, by the Cardinal's appointment, at length he took such grief therewith that he fell out of his right wits' (Holinshed, III.737).

120–34 *My lord of York ... meaner persons*: 'Note the strong dramatic effect of this somewhat grim conversation. After loud protestations of justice, Wolsey unblushingly scoffs at virtue, and shows himself indifferent to having caused the death of one who would not be his tool' (D. Nichol Smith, in the Warwick edition, 1899).

120 *Doctor Pace*: Richard Pace (1482?–1536), Dean of St Paul's, Exeter, and Salisbury, was feared by Wolsey as a rival in the King's service. 'He was sent to Switzerland to hire the Swiss against Francis I, to Germany to promote the election of Henry VIII to the empire, and to Italy to secure the Papal chair for Wolsey. When abroad he was subjected to exactions and imprisonment, and his insanity may have been brought on by his sufferings. Wolsey can hardly be held responsible, certainly not for his death, for Wolsey died in 1530 and Pace in 1536' (C. K. Pooler, in the original Arden edition, 1915).

127 *a foreign man still*: Always abroad.

132 *appointment*: Direction.

134 *griped*: Laid hold on, fastened on.

135 *Deliver this with modesty*: Make this known gently.

137 *receipt of learning*: Reception of learned opinion, or learned men.

Blackfriars: This was the Dominican monastery of the Black Friars. 'The place where the Cardinals should sit to hear the cause of matrimony betwixt the King and Queen was ordained to be at the Black Friars in London, where in the great hall was preparation made of seats,

tables, and other furniture, according to such a solemn
session and royal appearance' (Holinshed, III.737).

140 *able*: Vigorous.

II.3

9 *process*: Course of events.

10 *give her the avaunt*: Bid her begone. This is the only
use in Shakespeare of 'avaunt' as a noun, but the *Oxford
English Dictionary* records 'the Devil tempted him, but
he gave him the avaunt with the sword of the spirit',
from William Barlow's *Three Christian Sermons* (1596),
III.132.

13 *temporal*: Merely a thing of this world.

14 *quarrel*: Quarreller. The use of abstract for concrete, or
act for agent, is frequent in Shakespeare, and Johnson's
suggestion that *quarrel* be so taken here is the simplest
of many efforts to explain or emend this line.

15 *sufferance panging*: Anguish as acute. Cf. V.1.68–9, and
the similar idea in *Antony and Cleopatra*, IV.13.5–6, 'The
soul and body rive not more in parting | Than great-
ness going off'. 'Pang' is used verbally in *Cymbeline*,
III.4.93–4, 'how thy memory | Will then be panged
by me', and in a Shakespeare scene of *The Two Noble
Kinsmen*, I.1.167–9, 'when could grief | Call forth, as
unpanged judgement can, fitt'st time | For best solic-
itation?'

17 *a stranger*: An alien.

21 *to be perked up in a glistering grief*: To mourn, decked
out in the shining robes of high station.

23 *our best having*: The best thing we have.

24 *Beshrew me*: May evil befall me.

29 *Affected*: Aspired to.

31 *Saving your mincing*: Despite your affectation.

32 *cheveril*: Elastic, pliant. The phrase 'cheveril conscience'
was quasi-proverbial; Tilley, C 608. 'Cheveril' is kidskin
leather, stretching and flexible; cf. *Twelfth Night*,
III.1.11–12, 'A sentence is but a cheveril glove to a good
wit', and *Romeo and Juliet*, II.4.82–3, 'O, here's a wit
of cheveril, that stretches from an inch narrow to an
ell broad!'

36 *bowed*: Bent.

   hire: Two syllables.

37 *queen it*: Possibly quibbling on 'quean it', play the whore.

40 *Pluck off a little*: Come down a little in rank.

41 *count*: One rank lower than a duke, and equivalent to
   an earl. A bawdy quibble has been suspected in *count*
   – pronounced 'coont', more or less – and would not
   be out of character with the speaker; cf. the quibble on
   'le count' in *Henry V*, III.4.48–50. Anne herself has
   invited ribaldry by her rather unexpected oath at 23,
   By my troth and maidenhead.

   in your way: (1) In your path; (2) (following the possible
   quibble on *count*) in your (virginal) condition.

42 *For more than blushing comes to*: The general drift is
   apparent, though the precise connection of ideas is
   elusive. Anne is blushing at the quibbles; the Old Lady
   says, in effect, 'For all your blushes, and more, and your
   affected modesty, I would not give much for the chances
   of a young count you came across (or for your own
   precarious virginity).'

42–3 *If your back | Cannot vouchsafe this burden*: If your
   strength of body (and sexual power) cannot support
   the weight of a husband.

44 *get*: Conceive.

46 *little England*: (1) England itself (often so called,
   affectionately, in contrast with larger countries); but
   perhaps also, by subconscious anticipation, (2)
   Pembrokeshire (of which Anne is to be Marchioness;
   see 63. It was known as 'little England beyond Wales'
   – 'Concerning Pembrokeshire, the people do speak
   English in it almost generally, and therefore they call
   it little England beyond Wales'; John Taylor the Water
   Poet, *A Short Relation of a Long Journey*, Spenser
   Society reprint, page 19.)

47 *emballing*: Investment with the ball, as emblem of
   royalty. It signified the earth, and sovereignty; cf. *Henry
   V*, IV.1.253, 'the balm, the sceptre, and the ball'. A
   bawdy quibble is implied by the Old Lady's previous
   indelicacies.

48 *Caernarvonshire*: A wild, mountainous Welsh county, and so relatively undesirable.

52 *Not your demand*: It is not worth the trouble of your inquiring.

61 *Commends his good opinion*: Expresses his high regard.

62 *flowing*: Abundant.

63 *Marchioness of Pembroke*: 'On the first of September [1532] being Sunday, the King being come to Windsor created the Lady Anne Bullen Marchioness of Pembroke, and gave to her one thousand pounds land by the year' (Holinshed, III.776).

67–9 *More than my all is nothing … empty vanities*: Could I do more than my utmost it would still be as nothing, my prayers not holy enough, my wishes no more than worthless, ineffectual words.

67–8 *nor … not*: The frequent double negative, for emphasis.

74 *approve the fair conceit*: Confirm the high opinion.

77–9 *and who knows yet … all this isle?*: An anticipation of the accession of Queen Elizabeth in 1558.

78–9 *a gem | To lighten*: Jewels, particularly carbuncles, were supposed to shine with their own light in dark places; compare *Titus Andronicus*, II.3.227, 'A precious ring that lightens all this hole'.

85 *suit of pounds*: Petition for money.

87 *compelled*: Accented on the first syllable.
   compelled fortune: Fortune thrust upon you.

89 *Forty pence*: A proverbial phrase for a small sum or wager.

92 *mud*: The source of Egypt's fertility and wealth.

93 *pleasant*: Merry.

97–8 *honour's train | Is longer than his foreskirt*: What will follow in the way of distinction will outdo these first signs of it.

103 *salute my blood*: Exhilarate me.

II.4

0 *Trumpets … about the stage*: This elaborate stage direction closely follows Holinshed's description of the assembly in Blackfriars together with details from his retrospective account of Wolsey's love of pomp and pageantry (III.762–3).

sennet: Elaborate fanfare.

habit of doctors: Long furred gown and flat cap of Doctors of Law.

purse . . . silver pillars: 'Then had he his two great crosses of silver, the one of his archbishopric, the other of his legacy, borne before him whithersoever he went or rode, by two of the tallest priests that he could get within the realm . . . Before him was borne first the broad seal of England, and his cardinal's hat, by a lord, or some gentleman of worship, right solemnly; and as soon as he was entered into his chamber of presence, his two great crosses were there attending to be borne before him: . . . Thus went he down through the hall with a sergeant of arms before him, bearing a great mace of silver, and two gentlemen carrying two great pillars of silver' (Holinshed, III.760).

Griffith: F does not give his name here, or in the speech heading at 127, but that it was Griffith is clear from the entry direction of IV.2 and from Holinshed, III.738: 'With that, quoth Master Griffith, "Madam, you be called again."'

cloth of state: Canopy.

consistory: Ecclesiastical court.

3 *It hath already publicly been read*: A first session of the court, at which the legates received the papal bull of commission, had been held, according to Hall, three weeks earlier than the main trial, which took place on 21 June 1529. Holinshed does not mention this first session, but says that 'before the King and the judges within the court sat the Archbishop of Canterbury [William] Warham', that when the court had gathered 'the judges commanded silence whilst their commission was read', and that the crier then called the King and the Queen to come into the court (III.737). This might be understood as meaning that the commission was read before the King appeared (and so before this scene begins); or Shakespeare may have decided that the preliminaries to the trial had been long enough already.

13–57 *Sir, I desire you . . . Your pleasure be fulfilled*: This is strikingly close to Holinshed (III.737): '"Sir," quoth she, "I desire you to do me justice and right, and take some pity upon me, for I am a poor woman, and a stranger, born out of your dominion, having here no indifferent counsel, and less assurance of friendship. Alas, sir, what have I offended you, or what occasion of displeasure have I showed you, intending thus to put me from you after this sort? I take God to my judge, I have been to you a true and humble wife, ever conformable to your will and pleasure, that never contraried or gainsaid anything thereof; and being always contented with all things wherein you had any delight, whether little or much, without grudge or displeasure, I loved for your sake all them whom you loved, whether they were my friends or enemies.

'"I have been your wife these twenty years and more, and you have had by me diverse children. If there be any just cause that you can allege against me, either of dishonesty or matter lawful to put me from you, I am content to depart to my shame and rebuke; and if there be none, then I pray you to let me have justice at your hand. The King your father was in his time of excellent wit, and the King of Spain my father Ferdinando was reckoned one of the wisest princes that reigned in Spain many years before. It is not to be doubted but that they had gathered as wise counsellors unto them of every realm as to their wisdoms they thought meet, who deemed the marriage between you and me good and lawful, etc. Wherefore I humbly desire you to spare me, until I may know what counsel my friends in Spain will advertise me to take, and if you will not, then your pleasure be fulfilled."'

15 *stranger*: Foreigner.

17 *indifferent*: Impartial.

32 *to him derived*: Drawn upon himself.

33 *gave notice*: One expects a negative ('did not I give notice?') but this may be implied in *nay*. Or *gave notice … discharged* may be an affirmation, not a question ('I gave him notice …').

36 *Upward of twenty years*: 1509 to 1529.

41 *Against your sacred person*: Owed to, directed towards, your sacred person. Some editors insert a comma after *love and duty*; the phrase would then mean '[*aught*] directed against your sacred person'.

48–9 *one | The wisest*: The very wisest.

58 *of your choice*: Katherine chose the Archbishop of Canterbury and the Bishops of Ely, Rochester, and Saint Asaph 'and many other doctors and well learned men' (Holinshed, III.737).

61 *bootless*: Useless.

62 *That longer you desire the court*: That you urge the court to delay its business.

70–73 *I am about to weep ... sparks of fire*: Hermione speaks comparably in *The Winter's Tale*, II.1.108–12:

> I am not prone to weeping, as our sex
> Commonly are ... but I have
> That honourable grief lodged here which burns
> Worse than tears drown.

74 *before*: Before you are humble (for you will never be so).

77 *challenge*: Objection (a legal term for rejecting a juryman).

79 *blown this coal*: A proverbial phrase; Tilley, C 465.

81 *abhor*: Protest against, reject (a canon law term).

86 *stood to*: Stood up for.

92 *consistory*: College of Cardinals.

96 *gainsay my deed*: Deny something I have in fact done.

98–100 *If he know ... of your wrong*: If he knows me innocent of your charges, he knows too that I am not immune from the wrong of your accusations.

108 *sign*: Display.

in full seeming: With a convincing show.

112 *slightly*: Easily.

113–15 *Where powers are your retainers ... pronounce their office*: Where those in power (or 'the powers you wield') are at your beck and call, and your words, as obedient servants, effect your will in any way you direct them.

116 *tender*: Cherish.

121 *offers*: Shows her intention.

122 *Stubborn*: Resistant.

    apt to accuse it: Prompt to object to it.

127 GRIFFITH: See the fifth note on the opening stage direction of this scene.

138 *government*: Control (of self and others).

139–40 *thy parts | Sovereign and pious else*: Your other excellent and faithful qualities (cf. *Hamlet*, I.4.33, 'His virtues else', that is, his other virtues).

140 *speak thee out*: Describe you fully.

144 *require*: Request.

153 *one the least*: The very least (cf. 48–9 and note).

154–5 *Be to the ... touch of her good person*: Sully her good character.

157 *You are not to be taught*: You need no telling.

159–60 *like to village curs, | Bark when their fellows do*: A form of the proverb 'Like dogs, if one barks all bark'; Tilley, D 539.

161–93 *You're excused ... This world had aired them*: '"My lord Cardinal," quoth the King, "I can well excuse you in this matter ... you have been rather against me in the tempting thereof than a setter forward or mover of the same. The special cause that moved me unto this matter was a certain scrupulosity that pricked my conscience, upon certain words spoken at a time when it was, by the Bishop of Bayonne the French ambassador, who had been hither sent upon the debating of a marriage to be concluded between our daughter the Lady Mary and the Duke of Orleans, second son to the King of France.

    '"Upon the resolution and determination whereof, he desired respite to advertise the King his master thereof, whether our daughter Mary should be legitimate in respect of my marriage with this woman, being sometimes [*sic*] my brother's wife. Which words once conceived within the secret bottom of my conscience engendered such a scrupulous doubt that my conscience was incontinently accumbered, vexed, and disquieted; whereby I thought myself to be greatly in danger of God's indignation. Which appeared to me (as me seemed) the rather for that He sent us no issue male: and all such issues male as my said wife had by me died incontinent after they came into the world, so that I doubted the great displeasure of God in that behalf'" (Holinshed, III.738).

165 *passages*: Proceedings.

166 *speak*: Bear witness for.

167–209 *Now, what moved me to't ... When I first moved you*: Muriel St Clare Byrne, describing Tyrone Guthrie's production at Stratford-upon-Avon in 1949, comments as follows: 'this is the key passage in the play. Anthony Quayle rendered it with sincerity and conviction, beginning slowly as if thinking out this case of conscience, warming up as he went on to speak of the deaths of all his male heirs and of the danger to the Tudor succession and the realm, finally turning with vigorous appeal to the Bishop of Lincoln' (*Shakespeare Survey* 3, 1950, page 125).

178 *advertise*: (Accented on the second syllable) inform.

181 *Sometimes*: (Holinshed's word, too; see note on 161–93) sometime.

183 *spitting*: Piercing.

185 *mazed considerings*: Perplexed broodings.

192 *Or ... or*: Either ... or.

199–200 *Thus hulling in | The wild sea of my conscience*: 'Thus my conscience being tossed in the waves of a scrupulous mind' (Holinshed, III.738).

199 *hulling*: Drifting at the mercy of waves and wind. 'To hull' is to drift with sails furled. A 'hulling' ship cannot be steered; either Shakespeare is writing loosely in 200 – *I did steer* – or his mind has passed from the ship helpless before the storm to its later state when it can be directed towards safety.

204 *yet not well*: Even now not well.

206 *learned*: One syllable; see note on I.2.111.

206–22 *First I began in private ... Under your hands and seals*:

'Wherein ... I moved it in confession to you, my lord
of Lincoln, then ghostly father. And for so much as
then you yourself were in some doubt, you moved me
to ask the counsel of all these my lords: whereupon I
moved you, my lord of Canterbury, first to have your
licence ... to put this matter in question, and so I did
of all you my lords; to which you granted under your
seals' (Holinshed, III.738–9).

208 *reek*: Break into a sweat.

213–14 *Bearing a state of mighty moment in't,* | *And consequence
of dread*: Involving high state importance and consequences to be dreaded.

214–15 *I committed* | *The daring'st counsel ... to doubt*: I hesi-
tated to urge the boldest plan.

217 *moved you*: Opened this matter to you.

225 *allegèd*: Proffered.

229 *primest*: Most excellent.

230 *paragoned*: Held up as a model of perfection.

238 *learned*: One syllable; see note on I.2.111.

III.1

3–14 *Orpheus, with his lute ... or hearing die*: No contemporary musical setting of this lyric survives. The words
find a close parallel, interesting in view of Fletcher's
probable authorship of this scene, in Beaumont and
Fletcher's *The Captain*, III.1.31–8:

> Music,
> Such as old Orpheus made, that gave a soul
> To agèd mountains, and made rugged beasts
> Lay by their rages: and tall trees that knew
> No sound but tempests, to bow down their branches
> And hear, and wonder: and the sea, whose surges
> Shook their white heads in heaven, to be as midnight
> Still, and attentive.

3 *Orpheus*: Son of the muse Calliope; Apollo presented
him with a lyre on which he played so enchantingly
that not living creatures only but rocks and streams
obeyed his music.

lute: This was an Elizabethan, not a Grecian, instrument. In the early performances of the play the song was probably sung by a boy acting as one of the Queen's women, accompanying himself on the lute.

17 *presence*: Presence chamber.

18 *willed*: Bade.

18–19 *Pray their graces | To come near*: According to Holinshed, the Queen rose from her work and went into the 'chamber of presence' to meet the Cardinals formally. In the play she invites them in, and the tone is more personal.

22 *as righteous*: That is, as they themselves should be good.

23 *all hoods make not monks*: Proverbial; Tilley, H 586. Shakespeare quotes it in its Latin form – *'cucullus non facit monachum'* – in *Twelfth Night*, I.5.50–51, and *Measure for Measure*, V.1.261.

24–46 *Your graces find me here ... Pray speak in English*: 'The Cardinals being in the Queen's chamber of presence, the gentleman usher advertised the Queen that the Cardinals were come to speak with her. With that she rose up, and with a skein of white thread about her neck came into her chamber of presence, where the Cardinals were attending. At whose coming, quoth she, "What is your pleasure with me?" "If it please your grace," quoth Cardinal Wolsey, "to go into your privy chamber, we will show you the cause of our coming." "My lord," quoth she, "if ye have anything to say, speak it openly before all these folk, for I fear nothing that ye can say against me, but that I would all the world should hear and see it, and therefore speak your mind." Then began the Cardinal to speak to her in Latin. "Nay, good my lord," quoth she, "speak to me in English"' (Holinshed, III.739).

24 *part of*: In some measure.

31 *corner*: Secrecy. ('Truth seeks no corners' was proverbial; Tilley, T 587.)

38 *that way I am wife in*: How I behave as a wife.

40–41 *Tanta ... serenissima*: So great is the integrity of our purpose towards you, most noble Queen. (The phrase is the dramatist's own; Holinshed merely states 'Then began the Cardinal to speak to her in Latin.')

45 *more strange, suspicious*: More strange, even suspicious.

63 *still bore*: Has always borne.

64 *censure*: Judgement (here in an unfavourable sense; contrast I.1.33).

68–91 *My lords ... In mine own country, lords*: '"My lord," quoth she, "I thank you for your good will, but to make you answer in your request I cannot so suddenly, for I was set among my maids at work, thinking full little of any such matter, wherein there needeth a longer deliberation and a better head than mine to make answer; for I need counsel in this case which toucheth me so near, and for any counsel or friendship that I can find in England, they are not for my profit. What think you, my lords? Will any Englishman counsel me or be friend to me against the King's pleasure that is his subject? Nay, forsooth. And as for my counsel in whom I will put my trust, they be not here; they be in Spain in my own country"' (Holinshed, III.739–40).

70 *suddenly*: Impromptu, extempore.

74 *set*: Seated.

78 *The last fit of my greatness*: 'The last attack which she felt would end the "fitful fever" of her life of greatness' (W. A. Wright, in the Clarendon edition, 1895).

83 *But little for my profit*: Very little help to me.

86 *so desperate to be honest*: So reckless as to stand up for honesty.

87 *live a subject*: Yet be allowed to live in England.

88 *weigh out*: Outweigh, make amends for.

97 *part away*: Depart.

100 *Heaven is above all*: Proverbial; Tilley, H 348.

103 *cardinal virtues*: A punning reference to the schoolmen's list of principal virtues, justice, prudence, temperance, and fortitude, to which faith, hope, and charity – the theological virtues – were added to parallel the seven deadly sins.

104 *cardinal sins*: A punning reference to the seven deadly sins. 'The distress of Katherine might have kept her

from the quibble to which she is irresistibly tempted'
– Dr Johnson; but 'A passion there is that carries off
its own excess by plays on words as naturally, and,
therefore, as appropriately to drama, as by gesticula-
tions, looks, or tones' – Coleridge, on *Richard II*, in
Lectures and Notes on Shakespeare.

110 *at once*: All at once.

112 *mere*: Sheer (cf. *Othello*, II.2.3, 'the mere perdition of
the Turkish fleet').

113 *envy*: Ill-will.

115 *professors*: That is, of Christianity.

119 *'has*: He has.

120 *old*: Actually, about forty.

123–4 *All your studies | Make me a curse like this!*: Let all your
learning conceive me another such affliction, if it can.

124 *worse*: That is, than the reality.

125 *speak*: Describe.

131 *Been ... superstitious to him*: Idolized him.

145 *angels' faces ... hearts*: This is a form of the proverb
'Fair face, foul heart' (Tilley, F 3) and possibly a passing
glance at the familiar story, told in Bede's *History of
the English People*, that Saint Gregory, seeing English
slaves in Rome and being told they were *'Angli'*, replied
'Bene, nam et angelicam habent faciem' ('They have the
faces of angels'); cf. Peele, *The Arraignment of Paris*,
V.1.72–3, 'Her people [Queen Elizabeth's] are y-clepèd
Angeli, | Or, if I miss, a letter is the most'; and Greene,
The Spanish Masquerado (*Works*, edited by Grosart,
V.275), 'England, a little island, where, as Saint
Augustine [really, Gregory] saith, there be people with
angels' faces'.

151–2 *the lily ... flourished*: Similarly Spenser, *The Faerie
Queene*, II.6.16, 'The lily, lady of the flowering field'.

159 *For goodness' sake*: Out of your good nature (not the
modern colloquial sense).

161 *carriage*: Conduct.

174 *utmost studies*: Most diligent endeavours.

176 *used myself*: Conducted myself.

III.2

2 *force*: Urge

8 *the Duke*: Buckingham.

10 *uncontemned*: Unscorned.

or at least: Or have at least not been (the negative may be implied in '*un*contemned').

11 *Strangely neglected*: Treated distantly and neglectfully.

13 *Out of*: Besides.

14 *What he deserves ... I know*: The Lord Chamberlain has changed his view since he defended Wolsey at I.3.57–8, but still remains temperate, and at 332–6 speaks of his fall sympathetically.

16 *way*: Opportunity.

22 *he's settled*: Referring probably to Wolsey, though possibly to the King.

23 *his*: The King's.

26 *contrary proceedings*: (1) Deceptive schemes (as in 30–36); (2) opposition to the King's wishes.

29 *practices*: Intrigues.

30–36 *The Cardinal's letters ... Lady Anne Bullen*: 'Whilst these things were thus in hand [1529], the Cardinal of York was advised that the King had set his affection upon a young gentlewoman named Anne, the daughter of Sir Thomas Bullen, Viscount Rochford, which did wait upon the Queen. This was a great grief unto the Cardinal, as he that perceived aforehand that the King would marry the said gentlewoman, if the divorce took place. Wherefore he began with all diligence to disappoint that match, which, by reason of the misliking that he had to the woman, he judged ought to be avoided more than present death. While the matter stood in this state, and that the cause of the Queen was to be heard and judged at Rome, by reason of the appeal which was by her put in, the Cardinal required the Pope by letters and secret messengers that in any wise he should defer the judgement of the divorce till he might frame the King's mind to his purpose. Howbeit he went about nothing so secretly but that the same came to the King's knowledge, who took so high displeasure with such his cloaked dissimulation that he determined to abase his degree, sith as an unthankful person he forgot himself and his duty towards him that had so highly advanced him to all honour and dignity' (Holinshed, III.740).

36 *creature*: Dependant.

38–9 *coasts | And hedges*: Slinks closely and furtively along.

40–41 *brings his physic | After his patient's death*: Alluding to the proverb 'After death the doctor (physic)'; Tilley, D 133.

45 *Trace the conjunction*: Follow the union.

50–52 *I persuade me . . . In it be memorized*: A further anticipation, like that in II.3.77–9, of the play's happy outcome.

50 *I persuade me*: I am convinced.

52 *memorized*: Made memorable.

53 *Digest*: Stomach.

56–7 *Cardinal Campeius . . . hath ta'en no leave*: In Holinshed, Campeius 'took his leave of the King and nobility' (III.740). Shakespeare's contrary account presumably derives from Foxe (page 906), according to whom Campeius 'craftily shifted himself out of the realm before the day came appointed for determination, leaving his subtle fellow behind him to weigh with the King in the meantime, while the matter might be brought up to the court of Rome'. Foxe later (page 959), in a passage referring also to Anne's Lutheranism (see 98–9), has 'Cardinal Campeius dissembling the matter conveyed himself home to Rome again', with the marginal note 'Cardinal Campeius slippeth from the King'.

59 *Is posted*: Has sped.

64 *returned in his opinions*: Returned in as much as he has sent his opinions in advance, though he has not yet arrived himself. (Another interpretation is that Cranmer has returned, bringing opinions with him; but *in* would be an odd preposition to use for this, and had such been the meaning Suffolk would have answered Norfolk's simple question *When returns Cranmer?* more naturally. The fact that by 400 Cranmer *is returned with*

welcome – the return is news to Wolsey – does not affect the matter here.)

66–7 *all famous colleges | Almost*: Almost all the famous colleges.

68   *published*: Proclaimed.

74   *an archbishop*: Cranmer succeeded when Warham died in 1532 and was consecrated on 30 March 1533.

76   *packet*: Parcel of state dispatches.

78   *Presently*: Immediately.

85–90 *the Duchess of Alençon ... Marchioness of Pembroke*: Chronology is again telescoped: Wolsey's scheme for the Duchess of Alençon is attributed in Holinshed (III.719–20) to 1527 (but for its doubtful authenticity see note on II.1.156–7); Katherine's trial began in 1529 and her divorce was effected in 1533; Wolsey died in 1530; and Anne became Marchioness of Pembroke in 1532. The play necessarily makes events more compact than they really were, and the sources – Holinshed interlaced with Foxe – are themselves far from straightforward in their sense of time.

96–7 *This candle burns not clear; 'tis I must snuff it, | Then out it goes*: This intended marriage has snags which I am expected to remove (to snuff a candle being originally to trim its wick) – but instead I shall quash it.

99   *spleeny*: Hot-headed.
     Lutheran: Anne's Lutheranism seems not to be mentioned in Hall or Holinshed, but Foxe writes 'the Cardinal of York perceived the King to cast favour on the Lady Anne, whom he knew to be a Lutheran' (page 959). In Rowley's *When You See Me You Know Me* Gardiner laments the favour Anne showed to Lutherans (lines 523–32), and Wolsey (quite unhistorically) mentions Katherine Parr as 'the hope of Luther's heresy', under whom 'the Protestants will swell'; he hopes to 'plot the downfall of these Lutherans' (lines 1490–95).

101 *hard-ruled*: Not easily managed.

102–3 *one | Hath*: One who has.

105–6 *fret the string,* | *The master-cord*: Gnaw through the
main sinew. (The heart was thought to be controlled
by vital 'strings' or nerves.)

106 *on's*: Of his.

reading of a schedule: 'When the nobles of the realm
perceived the Cardinal to be in displeasure, they began
to accuse him of such offences as they knew might be
proved against him, and thereof they made a book
containing certain articles, to which diverse of the
King's Council set their hands. The King, understanding more plainly by those articles the great pride,
presumption, and covetousness of the Cardinal, was
sore moved against him; but yet kept his purpose secret
for a while' (Holinshed, III.740).

124 *an inventory*: Shakespeare transfers to Wolsey a misad-
venture suffered by Thomas Ruthall, Bishop of
Durham, who inadvertently delivered into the hands
of Wolsey himself, his enemy, an inventory of his own
excessive wealth (Holinshed, III.540–41).

127–8 *outspeaks* | *Possession of a subject*: Discloses more than
a subject should possess.

134–5 *below the moon, not worth* | *His serious considering*:
Worldly, not the right subjects for his devotion.

140 *spiritual leisure*: The interim of your spiritual concerns.

142 *husband*: Manager.

154 *words are no deeds*: Alluding to the proverb 'It is better
to do well than to say well'; Tilley, D 402.

155–6 *with his deed did crown* | *His word upon you*: Henry VII
appointed Wolsey, his chaplain, Dean of Lincoln and
ambassador to the Emperor Maximilian (Holinshed,
III.757–8).

167–8 *than could* | *My studied purposes requite*: Than my most
attentive efforts could repay.

171 *filed with*: Kept pace with.

172 *so that*: Only in the sense that.

176 *allegiant*: Loyal.

181–3 *The honour of it . . . the punishment*: The honour loyalty
earns is its own reward as, on the contrary, ill repute
is the punishment of disloyalty.

188 *notwithstanding that your bond of duty*: Over and above that general bond of duty you owe to be loyal.

189 *in love's particular*: For the special reason of love.

192–6 *that am, have, and will be ... yet my duty*: The syntax is irregular, conveying Wolsey's passion, but the sense is clear enough.

205–6 *He parted frowning ... from his eyes*: Similarly in Rowley's *When You See Me You Know Me* the fool, Patch, reports 'I thought he would have killed my lord Cardinal, he looked so terribly' (lines 731–2). See note on I.2.186.

207 *galled*: Wounded (and so angered).

208 *makes him nothing*: Annihilates him.

212 *mine own ends*: This shows up the hypocrisy of his professions at 171–4.

to gain the popedom: In 1529 Wolsey heard a false report that Pope Clement VII had died, and ordered Gardiner 'to strike for no cost' to secure his election (Foxe, page 963).

214 *cross*: Perverse.

215 *main*: All-important.

224 *meridian*: Highest altitude. There may be an echo of John Speed's *History of Great Britain* (1611), page 769: 'Cardinal Wolsey fell likewise in great displeasure of the King ... but now his sun having passed the meridian of his greatness began by degrees again to decline, till lastly it set under the cloud of his fatal eclipse' (cited by Foakes, who refers also to the cloud image in Buckingham's fall, I.1.224–6).

226 *exhalation*: Meteor. Meteors, lightning, and other aerial phenomena, whether fiery or cloudy, were thought to result from 'vapours drawn up [that is, exhaled] into the middle region of the air' (Florio, *New World of Words*). Cf. Beaumont and Fletcher, *Thierry and Theodoret*, IV.1.105–6, 'kings, from height of all their painted glories, | Fall like spent exhalations'.

228–50 *Hear the King's pleasure ... who'll take it?*: 'The King sent the two Dukes of Norfolk and Suffolk to the Cardinal's place at Westminster, who went as they were commanded and finding the Cardinal there they

declared that the King's pleasure was that he should
surrender up the great seal into their hands, and to
depart simply unto Asher, which was an house situate
nigh unto Hampton Court, belonging to the bishopric
of Winchester. The Cardinal demanded of them their
commission that gave them such authority, who
answered again that they were sufficient commissioners,
and had authority to do no less by the King's mouth.
Notwithstanding, he would in no wise agree in that
behalf, without further knowledge of their authority,
saying that the great seal was delivered him by the
King's person, to enjoy the ministration thereof, with
the room of the chancellor for the term of his life,
whereof for his surety he had the King's letters patents'
(Holinshed, III.741).

231 *Asher*: Esher, near Hampton Court; *Asher* is an old
form of the name.

my lord of Winchester's: Wolsey was himself Bishop of
Winchester; his successor as such, Stephen Gardiner,
may be the man in the dramatist's mind. Holinshed
says that Esher belonged to the 'bishopric of
Winchester'. In being sent thither, therefore, Wolsey
is being dismissed to one of his own residences.

236-7 *Till I find more than will or words to do it* – | *I mean
your malice*: Till I find more reason for so doing (surren-
dering the great seal) than your mere verbal statement
of the King's will – in fact, more reason than your
malice.

237 *officious*: Interfering. This is only the second instance
of the modern sense recorded in the *Oxford English
Dictionary*; the normal Elizabethan sense is 'zealous in
duty'.

241 *sleek and wanton*: Unctuous and unprincipled.

244 *warrant*: Justification (Wolsey is sarcastic).

250 *Tied it by letters patents*: Ratified it with an open (*patent*)
authorization.

253 *forty*: A conventional, not a precise, number.

255 *Thou scarlet sin*: Alluding to the scarlet of the Cardinal's
robes and the 'scarlet' sins of Isaiah 1:18: 'though your

sins be as red as scarlet, they shall be as white as snow'.

258 *parts*: Qualities.

259 *policy*: (A word then almost always of sinister sense) stratagems.

260 *deputy for Ireland*: See note on II.1.41–9.

Ireland: Three syllables.

262 *gav'st him*: Falsely fixed upon him.

272 *That*: I that.

274 *mate*: Match.

280 *jaded*: Humiliated. The word carries a combined sense of 'cowed', 'treated with contempt', 'fooled', 'dispirited'.

282 *dare us with his cap, like larks*: Daze us, fascinated, with his scarlet cap. (Larks were caught by being 'dared' – dazzled or confused – by pieces of scarlet cloth, or small mirrors, or small hawks, which riveted their attention while the fowling-nets were dropped upon them.)

291 *issues*: Sons.

295 *sacring bell*: Bell rung in the Mass at the elevation of the Host.

brown wench: There seems no specific ground for this jibe, but Wolsey was often accused of immorality; cf. IV.2.43–4, *Of his own body he was ill, and gave | The clergy ill example.*

307 *dare*: Defy.

310–30 *First ... Of all the kingdom*: This is a close rendering of the six main charges against Wolsey as Holinshed records them.

311 *legate*: The Pope's deputy.

314–15 *'Ego et Rex meus' | Was still inscribed*: This charge, so expressed in Hall and Holinshed, has become famous, but it misrepresents the facts, which are that Wolsey was accused not of claiming priority over the King but of treating the King and himself as equals in state correspondence by using the Latin phrase quoted, the English equivalent of which is 'My King and I', not the presumptuous 'I and my King'.

315 *still*: Always.

324 *mere*: Sheer.

326 *innumerable substance*: Incalculable treasure (the words are Holinshed's).

339 *legatine*: As papal legate. F reads *Legatiue*, but Holinshed regularly ends the word in 'ine', and 'iue' is the easiest of misreadings from manuscript.

340 *praemunire*: A writ, beginning *praemunire facias*, which charged a sheriff to summon anyone accused of maintaining papal jurisdiction in England and of appealing from the King's courts to those of the papacy. The penalties were forfeiture of goods, and outlawry; cf. 342–4.

343 *Chattels*: Movables. F reads *Castles*, presumably a transcription error for Holinshed's 'cattels'. 'Chattel' and 'cattle' are forms of the same word, meaning possessions.

353 *blossoms*: Probably a verb.

354 *blushing*: Glowing.

359 *wanton*: Sportive.

359–61 *that swim on bladders ... beyond my depth*: Foakes cites as a possible source John Speed's *History of Great Britain* (1611), page 769, where Wolsey 'being swollen so big by the blasts of promotion as the bladder, not being able to contain more greatness, suddenly burst, and vented forth the wind of all former favours'. But the idea is found elsewhere; for example, in Holinshed, III.613, where Wolsey is 'led with the like spirit of swelling ambition wherewith the rabble of popes have been bladder-like puffed and blown up'; and in Fletcher's *Wit at Several Weapons*, I.1.14–27:

> I rushed into the world, which is indeed
> Much like the art of swimming ...
> For he that lies borne up with patrimonies
> Looks like a long great ass that swims with bladders,
> Come but one prick of adverse fortune to him
> He sinks.

In *A Mirror for Magistrates* (1559) the overweening Wolsey 'did swim, as dainty as a duck, | When water serves, to keep the body brave'.

363 *old*: Wolsey was approaching sixty.

364 *rude stream*: Rough torrent.

365 *Vain pomp and glory of this world*: Echoing the Book of
Common Prayer baptismal service: 'Dost thou forsake
the devil and all his works, the vain pomp and glory
of the world?'

367 *that hangs on princes' favours*: Possibly echoing Psalm
146.2 (3 in the Authorized Version), 'Put not your trust
in princes', and Psalm 118.9, 'It is better to trust in God
than to put any confidence in princes'.

368–70 *There is . . . More pangs and fears*: See note on I.2.20–21.

371 *he falls like Lucifer*: This derives from Isaiah 14.12: 'How
art thou fallen from heaven, O Lucifer'. Compare
440–41, and *Paradise Lost*, I.36–40:

> his pride
> Had cast him out from Heaven, with all his host
> Of rebel Angels; by whose aid, aspiring
> To set himself in glory above his peers,
> He trusted to have equalled the Most High.

For the parallel with *A Mirror for Magistrates*, see the
note on I.1.70–72.

378 *I know myself*: I realize my true nature. The idea of
knowing oneself, and so living in true relationships,
goes back to classical antiquity, and is much repeated
in Elizabethan literature.

378–85 *I feel within me . . . that hopes for heaven*: Holinshed
(III.756) describes Wolsey as 'never happy till this his
overthrow. Wherein he showed such moderation and
ended so perfectly that the hour of his death did him
more honour than all the pomp of his life past'.

393–406 *Sir Thomas More . . . her coronation*: Time is again
abridged. More was chosen Chancellor in November
1529; Wolsey died in 1530; Cranmer was appointed to
the see of Canterbury in 1532 and consecrated in 1533;
Henry and Anne were married secretly in November
1532 or January 1533 and the marriage made public at
Easter 1533; and Anne was crowned in June 1533.

399 *a tomb of orphans' tears*: 'The chancellor is the general
    guardian of orphans [or, rather, of "infants", persons
    under eighteen]. *A tomb of tears* is very harsh' (Dr
    Johnson). William Drummond of Hawthornden has a
    similar conceit in his elegy for Prince Henry, *Tears on
    the Death of Moeliades* (1614): 'The Muses, Phoebus,
    Love, have raisèd of their tears | A crystal tomb to
    him, wherethrough his worth appears' (*Works*, edited
    by Kastner, 1.84).

405 *voice*: Talk.

411 *noble troops*: 'He had also a great number daily attending
    upon him, both of noblemen and worthy gentlemen,
    with no small number of the tallest yeomen that he
    could get in all the realm' (Holinshed, III.760).

420 *make use now*: Take the present opportunity.

442 *The image of his Maker*: Compare Genesis 1.27: 'God
    created man in His own image, in the image of God
    created He him.'

443 *cherish those hearts that hate thee*: Compare Matthew
    5.44: 'Love your enemies: ... do good to them that
    hate you.'

445 *Still*: Always.

448-9 *Then if thou fall'st ... Thou fall'st a blessèd martyr*:
    Thomas Cromwell, Chancellor of the Exchequer in
    1533, Lord Privy Seal in 1536, Lord Chamberlain in
    1539, and Earl of Essex in 1540, was powerful and
    dreaded, but was accused of high treason and executed
    in 1540. The play of *Thomas Lord Cromwell* (1602)
    shows him as an able and generous man, rising high
    from a low estate, and brought to disgrace and execu-
    tion by Gardiner's villainy.

451-2 *an inventory ... 'tis the King's*: 'Then the Cardinal
    called all his officers before him, and took account of
    them for all such stuff whereof they had charge ...
    There was laid on every table books reporting the
    contents of the same, and so was there inventories of
    all things in order against the King's coming ... At
    Asher he and his family continued the space of three
    or four weeks, without either beds, sheets, table cloths,

or dishes to eat their meat in or wherewith to buy any:
the Cardinal was forced to borrow of the Bishop of
Carlisle plate and dishes' (Holinshed, III.741).

452   *robe*: Cardinal's gown.

455–7   *Had I but served . . . mine enemies*: 'If I had served God
as diligently as I have done the King, He would not
have given me over in my grey hairs' (Holinshed,
III.755). Wolsey's famous words were in fact addressed
not to Cromwell but to Sir William Kingston, Constable
of the Tower, whom the King had sent to attend upon
him, and were uttered as he lay dying in Leicester
Abbey. Similar reflections are recorded from a variety
of fallen men; C. K. Pooler (in the original Arden
edition, 1915) gives instances from England, Scotland,
France, Spain, and Persia.

IV.I

1   *once again*: After meeting in II.1.

8   *royal minds*: Good will towards the King.

9   *let 'em have their rights*: To give them their due.
    ever forward: Always eager to do.

10–11   *shows, | Pageants, and sights of honour*: Holinshed's
account of Henry's reign is strikingly rich in accounts
of elaborate spectacles. The narration of Anne's coronation proceedings (III.783–4) is particularly splendid:
'First went gentlemen, then esquires, then knights, then
the aldermen of the city in their cloaks of scarlet; after
them the judges in their mantles of scarlet and coifs.
Then followed the Knights of the Bath being no lords,
every man having a white lace on his left sleeve; then
followed barons and viscounts in their parliament robes
of scarlet. After them came earls, marquises, and dukes
in their robes of estate of crimson velvet furred with
ermine . . . After them came the Lord Chancellor in a
robe of scarlet . . . ; after him came the King's chapel
and the monks solemnly singing with procession, then
came abbots and bishops mitred, then sergeants and
officers of arms, then after them went the Mayor of
London with his mace, and Garter in his coat of arms;
then went the Marquis Dorset in a robe of estate which

bare the sceptre of gold, and the Earl of Arundel
which bare the rod of ivory with the dove both
together.

'Then went alone the Earl of Oxford, High
Chamberlain of England, which bare the crown; after
him went the Duke of Suffolk in his robe of estate also
for that day being High Steward of England, having a
long white rod in his hand, and the Lord William
Howard with the rod of the marshalship, and every
Knight of the Garter had on his collar of the order.
Then proceeded forth the Queen in a circot and robe
of purple velvet furred with ermine, in her hair coif
and circlet as she had the Saturday [that is, the day of
her progress through London, when "her hair hanged
down, but on her head she had a coif with a circlet
about it full of rich stones"], and over her was borne
the canopy by four of the five ports, all crimson with
points of blue and red hanging on their sleeves, and
the Bishops of London and Winchester bare up the
laps of the Queen's robe. The Queen's train, which
was very long, was borne by the old Duchess of
Norfolk; after her followed ladies being lords' wives,
which had circots of scarlet with narrow sleeves ...
Then followed ladies being knights' wives, in gowns
of scarlet, with narrow sleeves ...

'When she was thus brought to the high place made
in the midst of the church, between the choir and the
high altar, she was set in a rich chair. And after that
she had rested a while, she descended down to the high
altar and there prostrate herself while the Archbishop
of Canterbury said certain collects: then she rose, and
the Bishop anointed her on the head and on the breast,
and then she was led up again, where, after diverse
orisons were said, the Archbishop set the crown of Saint
Edward on her head, and then delivered her the sceptre
of gold in her right hand, and the rod of ivory with
the dove in the left hand, and then all the choir sung
Te Deum ... Then went she to Saint Edward's shrine
and there offered, after which offering done she

withdrew her into a little place made for the nonce on
the one side of the choir ... When the Queen had a
little reposed her, the company returned in the same
order that they set forth ... then she was brought to
Westminster Hall.'

21 *beholding*: Indebted.

26 *order*: Rank (presumably the bishops mentioned by
Holinshed as accompanying the Archbishop).

27 *a late court*: A court lately.

28 *Ampthill*: Ampthill Castle in Bedfordshire, forty-five
miles north-west of London, made Crown property
under Henry VII.

31 *main*: Strong.

34 *Kimbolton*: Kimbolton Castle in Huntingdonshire, the
residence of Katherine from her divorce until her death
in 1536. F spells it *Kymmalton*, and presumably accents
the first syllable.

36 *flourish*: Fanfare.

Garter: Garter King-of-Arms (charged with proclaiming the sovereign's accession; see V.5.1–3).

he wore a gilt copper crown: The past tense is curious;
the likeliest explanation is that the writer was so
engrossed by closely following Holinshed's retrospective account as to slip into the past tense for his one
finite verb. The *gilt copper crown* derives from
Holinshed: 'every king-of-arms put on a crown of
copper and gilt' (III.784).

demi-coronal: Narrow circlet or coronet.

Earl of Surrey: In Holinshed Earl of Arundel; probably changed to save a stage part, Surrey having already
appeared.

Collars of Esses: Chains formed of S-shaped links.

robe of estate: State robes.

Duke of Norfolk: In Holinshed Lord William Howard,
Norfolk's half-brother; probably changed to save a
stage part.

four of the Cinque Ports: The barons of the Cinque Ports
(originally Dover, Hastings, Sandwich, Hythe, and
Romney, to which Rye and Winchelsea were later

added) were entitled to carry the canopy over the sovereign at coronations.

in her hair: With her hair hanging loose (the custom for brides; compare *The Two Noble Kinsmen*, IV.1.136, stage direction, '*Enter Emilia in white* [as a bride] *her hair about her shoulders*', and Webster, *The White Devil*, III.2.1–2, 'untie your folded thoughts, | And let them dangle loose as a bride's hair'). Foakes cites interesting parallels to this and other details, from Princess Elizabeth's marriage in February 1613, as described in *The Letters of John Chamberlain* (1939, I.424), 'in her hair that hung down long, with an exceeding rich coronet on her head', and in Henry Peacham's *The Period of Mourning* (1613), 'with a coronet on her head of pearl, and her hair dishevelled, and hanging down over her shoulders'. There is, Foakes observes, no mention of pearl in Holinshed.

45 *all the Indies*: See note on I.1.21–2.

46 *strains*: Embraces.

47 *I cannot blame his conscience*: See note on I.4.75.

54 *Their coronets say so*: 'Every countess a plain circlet of gold without flowers' (Holinshed, III.784); see section 10 of 'The Order of the Coronation'.

55 *falling*: That is, falling from virtue. Foakes cites E.A., *Strange Foot-Post* (1613), B2ʳ: '*Cadentes*, that is, falling stars, whereunto wantons may be compared'.

59 *rankness*: (1) Exuberance; (2) smelliness (cf. *Coriolanus*, III.1.66, 'The mutable, rank-scented meiny').

61 *speak*: Describe.

67 *opposing*: Displaying.

72 *the shrouds*: A ship's standing rigging.

74 *Doublets*: Close jackets (sleeved or sleeveless).

91 *choicest music*: Finest musicians.

94–7 *York Place . . . Whitehall*: York Place, the London residence of the Archbishops of York, was annexed on Wolsey's fall to the King's palace of Westminster and known as Whitehall; Holinshed's marginal note reads 'York Place or White Hall now the palace of Westminster' (III.775).

101–3 *Stokesley and Gardiner . . . London*: Gardiner, appointed
the King's secretary in July 1529 (see note on II.2.114),
became Bishop of Winchester in 1531 but continued as
secretary until 1534. Stokesley was consecrated Bishop
of London in November 1530.

102 *preferred from*: Promoted from being.

110–11 *Master | O'th Jewel House*: In charge of the royal plate
and crown jewels; Cromwell was appointed in April 1532.

112 *one, already, of the Privy Council*: Appointed in 1531.

IV.2

'This scene is above any other part of Shakespeare's
tragedies, and perhaps above any scene of any other
poet, tender and pathetic, without gods, or furies, or
poisons, or precipices, without the help of romantic
circumstances, without improbable sallies of poetical
lamentation, and without any throes of tumultuous
misery' (Dr Johnson); 'the crowning glory of the whole
poem' (Swinburne, in *A Study of Shakespeare*). 'Tender
and pathetic' as it is, and the more moving as it follows
the public splendour of the coronation which ousts
Katherine, it is less interesting in dramatic vitality than
the scene of her trial, her challenge to Wolsey, and
Henry's account of his scruples (II.4). With all its
merits it does not support Swinburne's claim that no
one but Shakespeare could have written it; its main
distinction comes from the sensitive dignity with which
it faithfully versifies Holinshed's own moving account.

6 *child*: Scion (a title tinged by chivalric romance, used
normally for a young hero).

7 *dead*: Wolsey died on 29 November 1530, Katherine on
7 January 1536.

10 *happily*: Fittingly.

11 *voice*: Talk.

12 *stout*: Valiant.

13 *Arrested him at York*: Actually, at Cawood Castle,
Yorkshire, on 4 November 1530; Holinshed, III.752.

14 *tainted*: Disgraced.

17 *roads*: Stages.

19 *covent*: Convent (a common form up to the end of the

seventeenth century – for example, Covent Garden; used for religious companies of either sex).

21 *old man*: See note on III.2.363.

26–7 *the hour of eight, which he himself | Foretold should be his last*: 'Incontinent the clock struck eight, and then he gave up the ghost, and departed this present life: which caused some to call to remembrance how he said the day before that at eight of the clock they should lose their master' (Holinshed, III.755).

33–68 *He was a man . . . he died fearing God*: These contrasting accounts closely follow two assessments in Holinshed, the earlier (III.756, drawn from Edmund Campion) stressing Wolsey's learning, affability, generosity, and final blessedness of spirit (cf. 46–68), the later (III.765) his pride, craft, and vice (cf. 33–44).

34 *stomach*: Arrogance.

35–6 *by suggestion | Tied all the kingdom*: By intrigues brought the whole land into bondage. Holinshed writes that Wolsey 'by crafty suggestion gat into his hands innumerable treasure' (III.765). The play's words are less specific. For F's *Ty'de* the reading 'Tyth'd' (tithed) has been suggested, for Holinshed mentions earlier that Wolsey proposed valuing all men's goods so that a tenth part might be taken for war expenses. Or 'tithed' might more loosely mean 'levied toll'; compare *King John*, III.1.153–4, 'no Italian priest | Shall tithe or toll in our dominions'.

36 *Simony*: Trading in ecclesiastical appointments.

37 *presence*: Royal presence chamber.

38–9 *double | Both in his words and meaning*: Given to false-hood and equivocation

43–4 *Of his own body . . . ill example*: See note on III.2.295.

43 *ill*: Vicious.

45–6 *Men's evil manners live in brass; their virtues | We write in water*: Echoes of proverbial phrases: 'Injuries are writ in brass', 'To write in water'; Tilley, I 71, W 114. For the sentiment compare *Julius Caesar*, III.2.76–7, 'The evil that men do lives after them, | The good is oft interrèd with their bones'.

50 *honour. From his cradle*: Often amended to 'honour from his cradle'. But compare Holinshed's stress on Wolsey's precocity (III.756): 'being but a child, very apt to be learned . . . he was made bachelor of art, when he passed not fifteen years of age, and was called . . . the boy bachelor'.

58 *you*: Apostrophizing Ipswich and Oxford.

59 *Ipswich and Oxford*: The college founded by Wolsey at his birthplace, Ipswich, of which all that remains is a brick gateway, and that at Oxford, Christ Church, originally called Cardinal's College, whose crest, a cardinal's cap, commemorates his munificence.

60 *good that did it*: Goodness that created it.

62 *art*: Learning.

64 *His overthrow heaped happiness upon him*: See note on III.2.378–85.

74 *modesty*: Temperateness.

80 *that celestial harmony I go to*: The soul, freed from the body, was thought to hear the music of the spheres as they circled round the earth; cf. *The Merchant of Venice*, V.1.60–65:

> There's not the smallest orb which thou behold'st
> But in his motion like an angel sings,
> Still quiring to the young-eyed cherubins;
> Such harmony is in immortal souls,
> But whilst this muddy vesture of decay
> Doth grossly close it in, we cannot hear it.

82 *The Vision*: The chronicles provide no source for Katherine's vision, but other plays of the time offer similar supernatural visitations; for example, *Cymbeline*, V.4, *Pericles*, V.1, *The Tempest*, III.3 and IV.1. In *The Winter's Tale* Antigonus reports his vision of Hermione 'In pure white robes, | Like very sanctity' (III.3.21–2). *The Two Noble Kinsmen* has elegant pageant processions and ceremonies in the first and last Acts. The dramatist may have heard (though if so the means are unknown) of the funeral oration in 1550 for Queen

Marguerite of Navarre; this describes her as seeing
before her death 'a very beautiful woman holding in
her hand a crown which she showed her saying that
the Queen would be crowned with it' (see E. E.
Duncan-Jones in *Notes and Queries*, April 1961, pages
142–3). Marguerite was the wife Wolsey intended for
Henry; see II.2.38–40 and III.2.85–6.

bays: Bay-leaves (traditional symbols of joyful triumph).

congee: Curtsy reverently.

changes: Figures in the dance.

94 *Bid the music leave*: Bid the musicians cease.

98 *colour*: F reads *cold*, but Patience throughout is
   describing Katherine's looks, and there seems no reason
   for her to change to coldness, to the detriment of the
   metre. 'Color' might easily be misread as 'cold'.

102 *lose*: Give up. Cf. the similar sense at II.1.57.

105 *staying*: Waiting.

132 *model*: Image.

   his young daughter: Mary Tudor (born in 1516, Queen
   of England from 1553 to 1558).

141 *both my fortunes*: My fortunes good and bad.

143 *now I should not lie*: See note on II.1.125.

145 *honesty and decent carriage*: Womanly honour and
   becoming conduct.

146 *let him be a noble*: Let him be no less indeed than a
   noble.

159 *fashion*: Making.

169 *maiden flowers*: Flowers for chastity (compare Ophelia's
   'maiden strewments'; *Hamlet*, V.1.227).

V.1

2–3 *hours for necessities,* | *Not for delights*: 'Gardiner himself
   is not much delighted. The delights at which he hints
   seem to be the King's diversion, which keeps him in
   attendance' (Dr Johnson).

7 *primero*: A fashionable card game of the sixteenth and
   early seventeenth centuries, introduced from Spain or
   Italy.

13 *touch of your late business*: Hint of what you have just
   been doing, at this late hour.

14 *As they say spirits do*: Spirits were creatures of the dark
hours, like the ghost of Hamlet's father, 'Doomed for
a certain term to walk the night' (I.5.10), and recalled
to the other world at cockcrow.

22 *Good time*: A good delivery. Compare *The Winter's
Tale*, II.1.20, 'Good time encounter her!' (that is,
Hermione, in childbed).

28 *way*: Way of thinking (in religion).

34-6 *Master | O'th'Rolls ... more preferments*: Having been
made Master of the Jewel House (see note on
IV.1.110–11) in 1532, Cromwell became Master of the
Rolls in October 1534 and secretary to the King the
same year; he later became a Knight of the Garter, Earl
of Essex, and Lord High Chamberlain. The Master of
the Rolls was keeper of the rolls, patents, and grants
made under the great seal, and records of the Court of
Chancery.

36 *gap and trade*: Entrance and beaten path.

40-156 *I myself have ventured ... do as I have bid you*: 'Certain
of the Council ... by the enticement and provocation
of his ancient enemy the Bishop of Winchester, and
other of the same sect, attempted the King against him,
declaring plainly that the realm was so infected with
heresies and heretics that it was dangerous for his highness farther to permit it unreformed ... The King
would needs know his accusers. They answered that
for as much as he was a Councillor no man durst take
upon him to accuse him; but if it would please his highness to commit him to the Tower for a time, there
would be accusations and proofs enough against him,
for otherwise just testimony and witness against him
would not appear ...

'The King perceiving their importune suit against
the Archbishop (but yet not meaning to have him
wronged ...) granted to them that they should the next
day commit him to the Tower for his trial. When night
came ... the Archbishop ... coming into the gallery
where the King walked ... his highness said, "Ah, my
lord of Canterbury, I can tell you news. For diverse

weighty considerations it is determined by me and the
Council that you tomorrow at nine of the clock shall
be committed to the Tower, for that you and your chap-
lains (as information is given us) have taught and
preached ... such a number of execrable heresies ...
and therefore the Council have requested me for the
trial of this matter to suffer them to commit you to the
Tower, or else no man dare come forth as witness in
these matters, you being a Councillor."

'When the King had said his mind, the Archbishop
kneeled down and said, "I am content, if it please your
grace, with all my heart to go thither at your highness'
commandment, and I most humbly thank your majesty
that I may come to my trial, for there be that have
many ways slandered me and this way I hope to try
myself not worthy of such a report."

'The King perceiving the man's uprightness joined
with such simplicity said, "O Lord, what manner a man
be you? ... I had thought you would rather have sued
to us to have taken the pains to have heard you and
your accusers together for your trial without any such
indurance. Do not you know what state you be in with
the whole world, and how many great enemies you
have? Do you not consider what an easy thing it is to
procure three or four false knaves to witness against
you? Think you to have better luck that way than your
master, Christ, had? I see by it, you will run headlong
to your undoing, if I would suffer you. Your enemies
shall not so prevail against you, for I have otherwise
devised ... Yet notwithstanding, tomorrow when the
Council shall sit and send for you, resort unto them,
and if ... they do commit you to the Tower, require
of them ... that you may have your accusers brought
before them, and that you may answer their accusations
without any further indurance, and use for yourself as
good persuasions as you may devise, and if no entreaty
or reasonable request will serve, then deliver unto them
this my ring ... and say unto them ... "I ... appeal to
the King's own person."

'The Archbishop ... had much ado to forbear tears. "Well," said the King, "go your ways, my lord, and do as I have bidden you"' (Foxe, pages 1693–4).

43 *Incensed*: Stirred up. Some editors change to 'Insensed', that is, informed, a word found from the fifteenth to the seventeenth centuries. To a listener, either meaning might equally present itself, since the words sound alike. Either meaning would in fact suit here, as also in Rowley's *When You See Me You Know Me* (line 2528), where the Queen's enemies are said to have 'insenst' the King against her.

44 *so I know he is, they know he is*: If the text is correct, the sense is either (1) provided I know he is, they take my word for it; or (2) such I know him to be, and they know him to be too.

47 *broken with*: Broken the information to.

50 *hath*: And has.

52 *convented*: Summoned.

64 *who*: And she (the Queen).

68 *sufferance*: See note on II.3.15.

69 *Almost each pang a death*: In Rowley's *When You See Me You Know Me* the Queen (Jane Seymour) gives birth to Prince Edward but dies in childbed. Holinshed says nothing about Queen Anne's labour.

72 *midnight*: The word could include the small hours; cf. 1, *It's one o'clock.*

74 *estate*: Condition.

75–6 *company | Would not be friendly to*: The presence of others would hinder.

85 *happily*: Opportunely.

86 *Avoid the gallery*: Leave the gallery. The 'gallery' is not the upper stage but the main stage where they all are – 'the gallery where the King walked' (Foxe, page 1694). In Rowley's *When You See Me You Know Me* the King is reported to be 'walking in the gallery | As sad and passionate as e'er he was' (line 550).

106 *You a brother of us*: You being a fellow Councillor.

110–11 *Most throughly ... shall fly asunder*: Cf. *Troilus and Cressida*, I.3.27–30:

Distinction, with a broad and powerful fan,
Puffing at all, winnows the light away;
And what hath mass or matter by itself
Lies rich in virtue and unmingled.

114 *Thy truth and thy integrity is rooted*: See note on
I.2.20–21.

116 *by my holidame*: See note on 153. The sense is, virtually, 'by all that's holy'. 'As help me God and halidom'
originally referred to the 'holiness' of relics on which
oaths were sworn. Condensed to 'by my halidom' it
was also varied to 'by my holidame', by popular association with 'Our Lady', the Virgin Mary.

121 *indurance*: Duress (referring, presumably, to his
proposed confinement in the Tower, 106; Foxe uses the
word twice, though in an unspecific sense: see the notes
on 40–156 and V.3.147–58).

125 *Being of those virtues vacant*: If it is devoid of truth and
honesty.

128–9 *their practices* | *Must bear the same proportion*: Their
plots must be correspondingly many and great.

131 *The due o'th'verdict*: The merited verdict.

135 *Ween you*: Do you reckon on.

138 *naughty*: Wicked (cf. *The Merchant of Venice*, V.1.91,
'So shines a good deed in a naughty world').

139 *precipice*: This was a recent word at the play's date; F's
Precepit may be what Shakespeare wrote, from French
'précépite' (Foakes).

146 *commit you*: Sentence you to confinement.

153 *God's blest mother!*: In Rowley's *When You See Me You
Know Me* such oaths are often in the King's mouth; for
example, 'Mother of God' (lines 148, 754, 798, 1653),
'God-a-mercy' (line 168), 'God's holy mother' (line 262).

165–6 *bless her! 'Tis a girl* | *Promises boys hereafter*: The Old
Lady is temporizing pretty well: *her* and *girl* ostensibly
refer to the Queen, but *her* is ambiguous (the Queen
or the baby) and *Promises boys hereafter* implies that no
boy has yet arrived.

168–70 *as like you ... an hundred marks*: In Rowley's *When You See Me You Know Me* the King says 'Who first brings word that Harry hath a son | Shall be rewarded well', and Will Summers adds 'Ay, I'll be his surety, but do you hear, wenches, she that brings the first tidings, howsoever it fall out, let her be sure to say the child's like the father, or else she shall have nothing' (lines 286–90).

170 *an hundred marks*: Two-thirds of £100, the mark being the value – not a coin – of two-thirds of £1.

V.2

Pursuivants, pages, and others: In F's stage direction Cranmer is solitary; but see 17 and 23–4. Foxe writes that he 'was compelled there to wait among the pages, lackeys, and serving men all alone' (page 1694).

Pursuivants: Junior officers of the heralds.

8 *happily*: Luckily.

9 *presently*: At once.

12 *sound*: (Probably) fathom (with an implication of the physician's 'probe'; the alternative explanation, 'proclaim', 'make known', neglects the fact that the *disgrace* is known to the King already and is not apparently a matter of secrecy).

18 *above*: on the upper stage (the gallery over the rear of the stage).

21 *Body o'me*: An exclamation Henry uses also in Rowley's *When You See Me You Know Me*, lines 2601, 2678, etc.

27 *parted so much honesty*: Shared so much honour.

31 *post with packets*: Courier with letters.

34 *They partly close ... to wait without*: F has no stage direction at all for the King, Butts, or Cranmer, and apparently means the King and Butts to be overlooking the Council's doings, and Cranmer to be waiting at one side while the preparations go ahead for the Council meeting, until he is summoned to the centre of the stage at V.3.7. Such ambivalence of place is not uncommon; for example, in *Julius Caesar*, III.1, the scene changes from the outside to the inside of the Capitol with no pause.

V.3

      Lord Chancellor: Actually Sir Thomas More, as shown at III.2.393–4.

10–15 *we all are men ... Toward the King*: This is from an address made by Bishop Stokesley of London to his clergy in 1531, as given in Hall's *The Union of the Two Noble Families of Lancaster and York* (1809 edition, page 783), and reproduced exactly by Foxe (page 959) though, as Foakes notes, it is separated by more than 700 pages from the other Foxe material used: 'My friends all, you know well that we be men frail of condition and no angels, and by frailty and lack of wisdom we have misdemeaned ourself toward the King our sovereign lord and his laws.'

11–12 *capable | Of our flesh*: Subject to our fleshly weaknesses.

19 *pernicious*: Deadly.

20 *sudden*: Swift.

22 *Pace 'em not in their hands*: Do not put them through their paces while leading them by hand.

23 *stubborn*: Stiff.

24 *manage*: Control (a term for the training of horses).

28 *taint*: Infection.

30 *The upper Germany*: Inland Germany. The allusion is perhaps to the Peasants' Rising under Thomas Münzer in Saxony in 1524, or the Anabaptist rising in Münster in 1535. Foxe refers unspecifically to 'horrible commotions and uproars, like as in some parts of Germany' and 'no small contentions and commotions ... as of late days the like was in diverse parts of Germany' (page 1694). Similarly Rowley's *When You See Me You Know Me* (lines 2201–5):

> Much bloodshed there is now in Germany,
> About this difference in religion,
> With Lutherans, Arians, and Anabaptists,
> As half the province of Helvetia
> Is with their tumults almost quite destroyed.

38 *with a single heart*: A biblical echo, of Genesis 20.5: 'with a single heart, and innocent hands have I done this'.

64 *modesty*: Moderation, temperateness.

66 *Lay all the weight ye can upon my patience*: Oppress my patience as much as you can.

67 *I make as little doubt as you do conscience*: I have no more doubt than you have conscience.

69 *modest*: Cf. 64.

70 *you are a sectary*: You follow a sect (rather than the Church).

71 *Your painted gloss discovers*: Your specious pretence discloses.

72 *words and weakness*: 'Empty talk and false reasoning' (Dr Johnson).

78 *I cry your honour mercy*: Ironical; Gardiner is as much at odds with Cromwell as with Cranmer – see V.1.29–32.

85, 87 LORD CHANCELLOR: *Cham.* (Chamberlain) in F; but the Lord Chancellor is presiding.

94 *strangely*: Uncommonly.

104–5 *we first put this dangerous stone a-rolling, | 'Twould fall upon ourselves*: Cf. Proverbs 26.27: 'he that rolleth up a stone, it will return upon him'. The idea became proverbial; Tilley, S 889.

109 *gave*: Told.

112 *envy at*: Hate.

113 *Ye blew the fire that burns ye*: Proverbial; Tilley, C 465.

114–21 *Dread sovereign ... this great offender*: 'Gardiner's fulsome flattery of the King recalls Wolsey's (III.2.166–79). There is, indeed, a certain similarity between the two ecclesiastics; but Gardiner has nothing of the strength and grandeur of Wolsey' (D. Nichol Smith, in the Warwick edition, 1899).

119 *dear respect*: Heartfelt regard.

122 *sudden*: Extempore.

126 *play the spaniel*: A frequent and proverbial analogy for obsequious flattery; Tilley, S 704. Compare *Julius Caesar*, III.1.43, 'curtsies and base spaniel fawning',

and *Antony and Cleopatra*, IV.12.20–21, 'The hearts |
That spanieled me at heels'.

132 *starve*: Die.

133 *this place*: This seat I appoint you to occupy. F reads
his place, and some editors follow, interpreting as 'a
place like his, as a Councillor'. But this reads awkwardly,
and it is more natural that the King should follow up
his instruction *sit down* (130).

135–46 *I had thought ... had ye mean*: 'His highness with a
severe countenance said unto them, "Ah, my lords, I
thought I had wiser men of my Council than now I
find you. What discretion was this in you, thus to make
the Primate of the realm, and one of you in office, to
wait at the Council chamber door amongst servingmen?
You might have considered that he was a Councillor
as well as you, and you had no such commission of me
so to handle him. I was content that you should try
him as a Councillor, and not as a mean subject. But
now I well perceive that things be done against him
maliciously, and if some of you might have had your
minds you would have tried him to the uttermost"'
(Foxe, page 1694).

146 *mean*: Means.

147–58 *Thus far ... all embrace him*: 'One or two of the chiefest
of the Council, making their excuse, declared that in
requesting his indurance, it was rather meant for his
trial and his purgation against the common fame and
slander of the world than for any malice conceived
against him. "Well, well, my lords," quoth the King,
"take him and well use him, as he is worthy to be, and
make no more ado"' (Foxe, page 1694).

166–7 *spare your spoons*: Save the expense of christening
spoons (the traditional gift from godparents).

167 *partners*: Co-sponsors.

176–7 *Do my lord of Canterbury* | *A shrewd turn and he's your
friend for ever*: 'It came into a common proverb: Do
unto my lord of Canterbury displeasure or a shrewd
turn, and then you may be sure to have him your friend
whiles he liveth' (Foxe, page 1691).

V.4

2 *Parish Garden*: A noisy bear- and bull-baiting resort on the south bank of the Thames, near the Globe Theatre. The name probably meant what it said, but the place was often called Paris Garden, supposedly 'from Robert de Paris, who had a house there in Richard II's time' (Thomas Blount, *Glossographia*, fourth edition, 1674) or, by popular mythology, from the Homeric hero (John Taylor, *The Carrier's Cosmography*, 1637).

3 *gaping*: Bawling.

4–5 *belong to th'larder*: Work in the pantry.

7 *crab-tree*: Crab-apple (a very hard wood).

8 *switches*: Twigs.

10 *ale and cakes*: Traditionally served at christenings, festivals, and so on; cf. *Twelfth Night*, II.3.111–12, 'Dost thou think, because thou art virtuous, there shall be no more cakes and ale?'

15 *May-day morning*: A holiday, begun before dawn, when May-day dew was gathered for the complexion.

16 *Paul's*: St Paul's Cathedral.

22 *Samson ... Sir Guy ... Colbrand*: Heroes famed for superhuman strength; Sir Guy of Warwick was renowned in medieval romance for slaying the Danish giant Colbrand in a duel at Winchester before Athelstan.

26 *see a chine*: Look on meat (a chine is a backbone or a joint of meat from an animal's back).

27 *not for a cow, God save her*: This is a phrase of uncertain and perhaps garbled sense, meaning, more or less, 'not for anything at all, God bless it!' The phrase 'I would not do that for a cow, save her tail' was recorded from Devon in 1862. Foakes also quotes the anonymous play *The Tell-Tale* (Malone Society Reprint, from line 1052):

VICTORIA ... rather than my beauty
    Should play the villain ...
    Thus would I mangle it.
JULIO Not for a cow, God save her.

Hilda M. Hulme, in *Explorations in Shakespeare's Language* (1962), discusses *chine* and *not for a cow* in detail but provides no assured explanation.

33 *Moorfields*: The district outside Moorgate in London, made into a park in 1606 and frequented by holiday crowds.

34 *some strange Indian*: Indians from America were shown as curiosities; compare *The Tempest*, II.2.29–32, 'There [in England] would this monster make a man . . . When they will not give a doit to relieve a lame beggar, they will lay out ten to see a dead Indian.' The condition and inhabitants of Virginia (founded in 1608) were matters of particular interest.

tool: Penis.

35–6 *fry of fornication*: (1) Offspring of fornication; (2) swarm of fornicators.

39 *spoons*: Christening spoons (cf. note on V.3.166–7).

40 *brazier*: Brass-worker.

41 *dog-days*: Hottest days of the year, supposedly from early July to mid-August, when the Dog-star, Sirius, rises at about the same time as the sun.

42–3 *under the line*: On the equator.

43 *fire-drake*: Fiery phenomenon (compare *meteor* in line 49).

46 *mortar-piece*: A short piece of ordnance with large bore; that is, 'gaping upwards' (Foakes).

blow us: Blow us up.

48 *pinked porringer*: Bowl-shaped cap, pierced or scalloped for ornament; cf. *The Taming of the Shrew*, IV.3.64–5, 'Why, this was moulded on a porringer – | A velvet dish'.

50 *Clubs*: The cry summoning London apprentices to intervene in a fight.

51 *truncheoners*: (A nonce word) cudgel bearers.

52 *the hope o'th' Strand*: Likely lads of the Strand (a street of fashionable merchants' shop-dwellings, with apprentices living on the premises).

54 *to th'broomstaff*: To close quarters.

55–6 *loose shot*: Unattached marksmen.

57 *work*: Fort.

61 *tribulation*: Troublemakers, pests.

   Tower Hill: A rough London district; the most famous
   scaffold in England was a permanent feature, and execu-
   tions attracted crowds of brutal spectators.

63 *in Limbo Patrum*: In durance vile, gaol. (*Limbus Patrum*
   was a place of departed spirits in medieval theology,
   the abode between Heaven and Hell of the just who
   died before Christ's coming, and of unbaptized infants.)

64 *running banquet*: Light refreshment (cf. note on I.4.12;
   here, in fact, a whipping through the streets).

65 *beadles*: Minor officers of the law, who administered
   whippings, took offenders into custody, and so on.

69 *made a fine hand*: Made a good job of it (ironical).

71 *suburbs*: Rowdy districts outside the City's jurisdiction.

79 *round*: Heavy.

80 *baiting of bombards*: Refreshing yourselves with drink.
   To 'bait' is to take refreshment; 'bombards' were leather
   jugs for liquor, so-called because in shape and colour
   they resembled cannon. Falstaff is 'that huge bombard
   of sack' in *Henry IV Part I*, II.4.439.

85 *Marshalsea*: The famous prison, near Saint George's,
   Southwark.

88 *camlet*: Fine cloth (of silk or Angora goat's hair).

   get up o'th'rail: This may be a contraction of 'on the
   rail' or 'off the rail' and may refer to the rail that, in
   some illustrations, can be seen at the edge of the stage.
   The Porter may be addressing the audience. The matter
   is discussed by J. W. Saunders in 'Vaulting the Rails'
   (*Shakespeare Survey* 7, 1954, pages 69–81).

89 *peck you o'er the pales*: Pitch you over the railings. Which
   pales are intended is as uncertain as which *rail* in the
   previous line.

V.5

0 *Garter*: See note on IV.1.36.

   standing bowls: Bowls with legs.

1–3 *Heaven . . . Elizabeth*: This closely follows the formula
     as pronounced by the Garter King-of-Arms in
     Holinshed (III.787): 'God of His infinite goodness send

prosperous life and long to the high and mighty Princess of England, Elizabeth'. It would probably connect in spectators' minds with the marriage ceremonies of Princess Elizabeth and Prince Frederick in 1613, when the Garter King-of-Arms 'published the style of the Prince and Princess to this effect: "All health, happiness, and honour be to the high and mighty Princes, Frederick . . . and Elizabeth"' (quoted by Foakes from Henry Peacham's *The Period of Mourning*, 1613, H2ᵛ).

5 *partners*: Co-sponsors.

12 *gossips*: Godparents (from 'God-sib', related in God).
prodigal: 'The Archbishop of Canterbury gave to the Princess a standing cup of gold, the Duchess of Norfolk gave to her a standing cup of gold, fretted with pearl; the Marchioness of Dorset gave three standing bowls pounced [embossed], with a cover; and the Marchioness of Exeter gave three standing bowls graven, all gilt with a cover' (Holinshed, III.787).

17 *still*: Ever.

23 *Saba*: The Queen of Sheba, who, as related in 1 Kings 10, visited Solomon to prove him with hard questions and found that his wisdom and prosperity 'exceedeth the fame which I heard'. The spelling is that of bibles preceding the Authorized Version of 1611, save that the Geneva Bible (1560) has 'Sheba' in the text, though 'Saba' in chapter headings.

26 *piece*: Person (probably in the sense of 'example'; compare *Pericles*, IV.6.110, 'Thou art a piece of virtue'; *The Winter's Tale*, IV.4.419–20, 'thou, fresh piece | Of excellent witchcraft'; and *The Tempest*, I.2.56, 'Thy mother was a piece of virtue').

33–5 *In her days . . . all his neighbours*: Biblical echoes: 1 Kings 4.20, 'And Juda and Israel were many, even as the sand of the sea in number, eating, drinking, and making merry', and 4.25, 'And Juda and Israel dwelt without fear, every man under his vine, and under his fig-tree . . . all the days of Solomon'; similarly 2 Kings 18.31, Isaiah 36.16, and Micah 4.4. Foakes points to frequent references to these visions of peace in sermons and other literature praising James I's reign.

36 *God shall be truly known*: True religion shall prevail.

40 *maiden phoenix*: The fabulous Arabian bird, living
unmated, and dying to give rise to a successor, a symbol
often used for monarchs in respect both of their unique-
ness and of their linking together precursors and successors; it was applied to Queen Elizabeth and to Princess
Elizabeth (Foakes). In Rowley's *When You See Me You
Know Me* Henry marks the death of Queen Jane, giving
birth to Prince Edward, with a Latin proverb translated as 'One phoenix dying gives another life' (line
491). In Dekker's *The Whore of Babylon*, III.3.235, King
James is 'A second phoenix', arising after the death of
Queen Elizabeth.

42 *admiration*: Cause of wonder.

43 *one*: James I.

44 *this cloud of darkness*: This world where we live darkly.

47 *fixed*: As a fixed star.

50–54 *Wherever the bright sun ... plains about him*: An echo,
as Foakes observes, of God's promises to Abraham in
Genesis 17.5–6: 'a father of many nations have I made
thee. I will make thee exceeding fruitful, and will make
nations of thee; yea, and kings shall spring out of thee'.
The words were frequently alluded to in discourses on
Princess Elizabeth's marriage to the Elector Palatine.

52 *new nations*: Probably alluding to the settlement of
Virginia, which started in 1608.

53 *cedar*: Echoing Psalm 92.12, 'The righteous shall
flourish like a palm tree and shall spread abroad like a
cedar in Libanus', and Ezekiel 17.22–3, 'Thus saith the
Lord God, I will also take off the top of this high cedar
... and will plant it upon an high hill ... that it may
bring forth boughs ... and be an excellent cedar; and
under it shall remain all birds, and every fowl shall
remain under the shadow of the branches thereof'.

57 *An agèd princess*: Queen Elizabeth died in 1603, aged
sixty-nine, having reigned since 1558.

65 *get*: 'Achieve, quibbling on "beget"' (Foakes).

74 *sick*: Unhappy.

75 *'Has*: He has.
76 *holiday*: *Holy-day* in F, a reminder of religious significance.

Epilogue

The Epilogue, in its commonplace banter and careless
colloquialism, is very like that, by Fletcher, to *The Two
Noble Kinsmen*.

5–6 *to hear the city* | *Abused*: Citizen life was often satirized
in the drama as mercenary and illiberal.

9–10 *only in* | ... *women*: For the 'rhyme', see note on
Prologue, 25–6.

10 *construction*: Interpretation.

PENGUIN SHAKESPEARE

HENRY IV, PART I
WILLIAM SHAKESPEARE

WWW.PENGUINSHAKESPEARE.COM

Prince Hal, the son of King Henry IV, spends his time in idle pleasure with dissolute friends, among them the roguish Sir John Falstaff. But when the kingdom is threatened by rebellious forces, the prince must abandon his reckless ways. Taking arms against a heroic enemy, he begins a great and compelling transformation – from irresponsible reprobate to noble ruler of men.

This book includes a general introduction to Shakespeare's life and the Elizabethan theatre, a separate introduction to *Henry IV, Part I*, a chronology of his works, suggestions for further reading, an essay discussing performance options on both stage and screen, and a commentary.

Edited by: Peter Davison

With an introduction by Charles Edelman

General Editor: Stanley Wells

PENGUIN SHAKESPEARE

HENRY IV, PART II
WILLIAM SHAKESPEARE

WWW.PENGUINSHAKESPEARE.COM

Angered by the loss of his son in battle, the Earl of Northumberland
supports another rebellion against King Henry IV, bringing the country
to the brink of civil war. Sick and weary, the old King sends out his
forces, including the unruly Sir John Falstaff, to meet the rebels. But as
the conflict grows, he must also confront a more personal problem –
how to make his reprobate son Prince Hal aware of the duties he must
bear, as heir to the throne.

This book includes a general introduction to Shakespeare's life and the
Elizabethan theatre, a separate introduction to *Henry IV, Part II*, a
chronology of his works, suggestions for further reading, an essay
discussing performance options on both stage and screen, and a
commentary.

Edited by Peter Davison

With an introduction by Adrian Poole

General Editor: Stanley Wells

PENGUIN SHAKESPEARE

HENRY VI, PART II
WILLIAM SHAKESPEARE

WWW.PENGUINSHAKESPEARE.COM

Henry VI is tricked into marrying Margaret – lover of the Earl of Suffolk, who hopes to rule the kingdom through her influence. There is one great obstacle in Suffolk's path, however – the noble Lord Protector, whom he slyly orders to be murdered. Discovering this betrayal, Henry banishes Suffolk, but with his Lord Protector gone the unworldly young King must face his greatest challenge: impending civil war and the rising threat of the House of York.

This book includes a general introduction to Shakespeare's life and the Elizabethan theatre, a separate introduction to *Henry VI, Part II*, a chronology of his works, suggestions for further reading, an essay discussing performance options on both stage and screen by Rebecca Brown, and a commentary.

Edited by Norman Sanders

With an introduction by Michael Taylor

General Editor: Stanley Wells

PENGUIN SHAKESPEARE

JULIUS CAESAR
WILLIAM SHAKESPEARE

WWW.PENGUINSHAKESPEARE.COM

When it seems that Julius Caesar may assume supreme power, a plot to
destroy him is hatched by those determined to preserve the threatened
republic. But the different motives of the conspirators soon become
apparent when high principles clash with malice and political realism.
As the nation plunges into bloody civil war, this taut drama explores
the violent consequences of betrayal and murder.

This book includes a general introduction to Shakespeare's life and the
Elizabethan theatre, a separate introduction to *Julius Caesar*, a
chronology of his works, suggestions for further reading, an essay
discussing performance options on both stage and screen, and a
commentary.

Edited by Norman Sanders

With an introduction by Martin Wiggins

General editor: Stanley Wells

PENGUIN SHAKESPEARE

KING JOHN
WILLIAM SHAKESPEARE

WWW.PENGUINSHAKESPEARE.COM

Under the rule of King John, England is forced into war when the
French challenge the legitimacy of John's claim to the throne and
determine to install his nephew Arthur in his place. But political
principles, hypocritically flaunted, are soon forgotten, as the French
and English kings form an alliance based on cynical self-interest. And
as the desire to cling to power dominates England's paranoid and
weak-willed king, his country is threatened with disaster.

This book includes a general introduction to Shakespeare's life and the
Elizabethan theatre, a separate introduction to *King John*, a chronology
of his works, suggestions for further reading, an essay discussing
performance options on both stage and screen, and a commentary.

Edited by R. L. Smallwood

With an introduction by Eugene Giddens

General Editor: Stanley Wells

PENGUIN SHAKESPEARE

KING LEAR
WILLIAM SHAKESPEARE

WWW.PENGUINSHAKESPEARE.COM

An ageing king makes a capricious decision to divide his realm among his three daughters according to the love they express for him. When the youngest daughter refuses to take part in this charade, she is banished, leaving the king dependent on her manipulative and untrustworthy sisters. In the scheming and recriminations that follow, not only does the king's own sanity crumble, but the stability of the realm itself is also threatened.

This book includes a general introduction to Shakespeare's life and the Elizabethan theatre, a separate introduction to *King Lear*, a chronology of his works, suggestions for further reading, an essay discussing performance options on both stage and screen, and a commentary.

Edited by George Hunter

With an introduction by Kiernan Ryan

General Editor: Stanley Wells

PENGUIN SHAKESPEARE

OTHELLO
WILLIAM SHAKESPEARE

WWW.PENGUINSHAKESPEARE.COM

A popular soldier and newly married man, Othello seems to be in an enviable position. And yet, when his supposed friend sows doubts in his mind about his wife's fidelity, he is gradually consumed by suspicion. In this powerful tragedy, innocence is corrupted and trust is eroded as every relationship is drawn into a tangled web of jealousies.

This book includes a general introduction to Shakespeare's life and the Elizabethan theatre, a separate introduction to *Othello*, a chronology of his works, suggestions for further reading, an essay discussing performance options on both stage and screen, and a commentary.

Edited by Kenneth Muir

With an introduction by Tom McAlindon

General Editor: Stanley Wells

PENGUIN SHAKESPEARE

RICHARD III
WILLIAM SHAKESPEARE

WWW.PENGUINSHAKESPEARE.COM

The bitter, deformed brother of the King is secretly plotting to seize the throne of England. Charming and duplicitous, powerfully eloquent and viciously cruel, he is prepared to go to any lengths to achieve his goal – and, in his skilful manipulation of events and people, Richard is a chilling incarnation of the lure of evil and the temptation of power.

This book includes a general introduction to Shakespeare's life and the Elizabethan theatre, a separate introduction to *Richard III*, a chronology of his works, suggestions for further reading, an essay discussing performance options on both stage and screen by Gillian Day, and a commentary.

Edited by E. A. J. Honigmann

With an introduction by Michael Taylor

General Editor: Stanley Wells

Read more in Penguin

PENGUIN SHAKESPEARE

He just wanted a decent book to read ...

Not too much to ask, is it? It was in 1935 when Allen Lane, Managing Director of Bodley Head Publishers, stood on a platform at Exeter railway station looking for something good to read on his journey back to London. His choice was limited to popular magazines and poor-quality paperbacks – the same choice faced every day by the vast majority of readers, few of whom could afford hardbacks. Lane's disappointment and subsequent anger at the range of books generally available led him to found a company – and change the world.

'We believed in the existence in this country of a vast reading public for intelligent books at a low price, and staked everything on it'
Sir Allen Lane, 1902–1970, founder of Penguin Books

The quality paperback had arrived – and not just in bookshops. Lane was adamant that his Penguins should appear in chain stores and tobacconists, and should cost no more than a packet of cigarettes.

Reading habits (and cigarette prices) have changed since 1935, but Penguin still believes in publishing the best books for everybody to enjoy. We still believe that good design costs no more than bad design, and we still believe that quality books published passionately and responsibly make the world a better place.

So wherever you see the little bird – whether it's on a piece of prize-winning literary fiction or a celebrity autobiography, political tour de force or historical masterpiece, a serial-killer thriller, reference book, world classic or a piece of pure escapism – you can bet that it represents the very best that the genre has to offer.

Whatever you like to read – trust Penguin.